THE SINGLE

FAMILY OFFICE

Creating, Operating & Managing Investments of a Single Family Office

By Richard C. Wilson

Single Family Office Management | Family Office Club

This book is dedicated to my amazing daughters

Bella & Maya Wilson.

Table of Contents

Chapter	Page
Preface	5
Part 1: Single Family Office Fundamentals	7
Chapter 1: Introduction to Single Family Offices	9
Chapter 2: Single Family Office Talent & Teams	17
Chapter 3: Single Family Office Operations	35
Chapter 4: Single Family Office Governance	47
Part 2: Starting a Single Family Office	59
Chapter 5: Creating Your Family Compass	61
Chapter 6: Starting a Single Family Office	69
Chapter 7: Partners, Vendors, & Service Providers	87
Chapter 8: Investment Committees & Advisory Boards	93
Part 3: Single Family Office Investment Portfolios	109
Chapter 9: Family Office Investment Management	111
Chapter 10: Investment Fund Manager Selection & Monitoring	113
Chapter 11: Direct Investing & Operating Businesses	131
Chapter 12: Co-Investing & Club Deals	171
Chapter 13: Real Estate Investments and Hard Assets	191
Part 4: Single Family Office Best Practices & Models to Emulate	205
Chapter 14: $1 Billion+ Single Family Offices	207
Chapter 15: Intergenerational Money Management	227
Chapter 16: Converting from a Single Family Office into a Multi-Family Office	233
Chapter 17: Outsourced Chief Investment Officers	243
Chapter 18: Virtual Family Offices	247
Chapter 19: The Future of the Single Family Office Industry	261

Acknowledgements

The Single Family Office book would not have been possible to write without the help of many smart and dedicated professionals. While I cannot thank everyone who played a part in this book's creation, I want to especially acknowledge the contributions of all those who invested their time and energy in editing, contributing insights, and sharing resources, including:

Theodore O'Brien, Tyler McNicholas, Douglas Scott, Rafael Tassini, Rahul Koshal Dubey, Michael Oliver Weinberg, Richard Ross, John Bishop, Abe Tatar, Bret Magpoing, Andrew Hector, Chris Allen, Geoffroy Dedieu, Ira Perlmuter, Harris Fried, David Fisher, John Jonson, Christian Zabbal, Shiraz Poonevala, Michael Connor, Brendan Holt Dunn, Tony Kypreos, Ingemar Hulthage, Steven Goakes, Frank Casey, John Grzymala, Matthew Andrade, and Elizabeth Hammock.

Disclosure

Free Family Office Podcast

We have recently launched the first podcast on the family office industry. This podcast covers family office investing, ultra-wealthy family challenges, how to start a family office, how to acquire operating businesses, and global trends in the family office industry.

This is a variety show podcast with short two to three-minute episodes, mid-length client case studies and insights, and longer industry interviews and recordings of speeches given at family office conferences.

To subscribe today, please visit http://FamilyOffices.com/Podcast

If you would like to appear as a guest on the Family Office Podcast under a short 15-20 minute interview format, please reach out to our team at (305) 333-1155 or Podcast@SingleFamilyOffices.com

4 Free Webinars ($396 Value)

The following webinars are sold on our website for $99, and contain over six hours of conference presentation quality information on family office investments. Our hope is that by providing these to you for free, we can help some of you take action and make tangible progress on improving your single family  office team, investment portfolio, and investment goals overall.

The following webinars are available:

Single Family Office Investing: This 90-minute webinar reviews what the members of our family office association, and Billionaire Family Office are investing in and why they consistently do so. It discusses the maturity of the investment portfolios between single family offices in Asia, Europe, and the United States and also suggests some best practices for single family office investment management.

Creating a Single Family Office: As the title suggests, this 90-minute webinar discusses the steps required to launch a single family office. Similar to the content provided in our chapter on this topic, this presentation reviews the Family Office Compass concept, why it is so critical, and walks listeners through the importance of following proven single family office startup steps. All family offices are unique, but so are all businesses, and there is no sense trying to start a single family office without collecting best practices on the process first.

Direct Investing, Co-Investing, & Club Deals: This webinar dives into direct investing, co-investment, and club deals. After listening to this recording, you will know the difference between these types of investing, why they are growing in popularity, and get an introduction as to how to navigate deals. This is perhaps our most technical and valuable webinar completed to date for those who have been in the industry for some time already.

Family Office Investment Priorities: This 90-minutes webinar reviews what most families are investing in, why they invest in those areas, and discusses their investment priorities. Similar to the Single Family Office Investing webinar above, this recording reviews where the industry is headed and why our association believes that is so. This webinar is most appropriate for advisors such as attorneys or CPAs that have started to work with a few single family offices and are trying to get a better understanding of the industry.

As a thank you for purchasing this book, please download these webinars; please visit http://SingleFamilyOffices.com/Webinars

Preface

This the content of this book draws from experiences working with our clients, as well as case studies and interviews gathered from operating Billionaire Family Office, or Wilson Conference series events on family offices, and our Family Office Club, the #1 largest family office association.

We are committed to helping formalize the single family office niche as part of the greater wealth management industry. As you will see from our benchmark study, families report that sharing best practices is the largest source of value for them and particularly helpful as they seek to connect and network with each other.

This text reflects that desire by single family offices; we have integrated concise interviews with real single family offices, in a transparent fashion which shares the real family's name, stories, and lessons learned. We have also embedded several templates, working documents to adapt for your family, as well as more than forty video modules, essentially providing you with a Single Family Office 101 multimedia training program for under $10.

A statement that I hear time and time again at industry events is, "If you have gotten to know one family office, you know one family office." The point is that every family office is different and it is impossible to understand and learn about the industry in the same way one would for any other investor group or type of business. I find this comment not only to be an unproductive assessment, but also one that is false. Certainly, no one family is alike in all respects, but among single family offices there are similarities, models that single family offices can emulate and adopt from each other, and best practices that we will share within this book. We have met with 1,000 family offices face-to-face in 22 countries, and while, like this industry, we feel that we are just getting started, we have identified some models, best practices, and insights that almost every single family office could benefit from.

As you have likely experienced before, many industry conferences have stages crowded with service providers, software vendors, and consultants. At our conferences, we try to pack the schedule with family office speakers—for example, our Family Office Super Summit this year has 59 speakers over 3 days, and 50+ of these speakers are family office executives. We have taken that same approach with this book. I have read almost every book written on the industry and I often grow frustrated by how often the authors quote dozens of service providers, vendors, consultants, etc. to the point where at the end it feels like I have read an anthology of sales brochures. For this book, we stick to interviewing the source of the real experience and knowledge: the single family office executives and ultra-wealthy families. Also, to hold ourselves accountable to only reporting on what is true, rather than presenting case studies which leave the reader uncertain as to whether the examples are authentic or invented. We transparently publish the family or family office's name in many of the case studies, and interviews provided in this book.

The Single Family Office is organized so that we first cover the fundamentals in Part 1, how to start a family office in Part 2, followed by investments in Part 3, and best practices and trends in the final Part 4.

We invite your comments, feedback, participation in the Family Office Club (association) and single family office services and deal flow assistance through the Billionaire Family Office. Feel free to connect at Richard@SingleFamilyOffices.com or by calling (305) 333-1155.

Part 1:

Single Family Office

Fundamentals

 Counterintuitive Family Office Lesson: This video explains what we have found to be the most counterintuitive lesson about family office investing: http://SingleFamilyOffices.com/Overview

The Single Family Office by Richard C. Wilson

Chapter 1: Introduction to Single Family Offices

Single Family Office Definition: A single family office is a holistic, full-balance-sheet wealth management solution for an affluent individual or family.

Free Video: While recently meeting with a single family office in Prague, I recorded this short video defining the term:

http://SingleFamilyOffices.com/SFO-Explained

According to the 2013 World Wealth Report by Capgemini, there are 111,000 ultra-high net worth individuals (those with $30M or more in net worth) around the word. Our experience suggests there are between 7,000 to 10,000 formalized single family offices globally. Our research and surveys also indicate that there are over 20,000 families with $100M in wealth or greater. If you look at global wealth trends, you can see that there is an astounding increase in new wealth being created, and not only in traditional wealth hubs like North America and Europe, but we are already seeing a shift in affluence to emerging markets such as China, India and fast-growing economies in the South Pacific.

With so much new wealth creation, single and multi-family offices have emerged as a preferred structure to handle the needs of high net worth individuals and ultra-high net worth individuals. The family office model provides a much-needed structure for managing wealth and all of the important services that are used by exceptionally affluent families.

Single family offices have the ability to best serve ultra-wealthy families, in the most focused, holistic, and aligned way possible. The amount of alignment is high with most multi-family offices, but as the diagram below depicts, you move further out of alignment with different types of service organizations which serve varying types of families and non-family clients, each of which have very distinct needs and place unique demands on the core service and investment team.

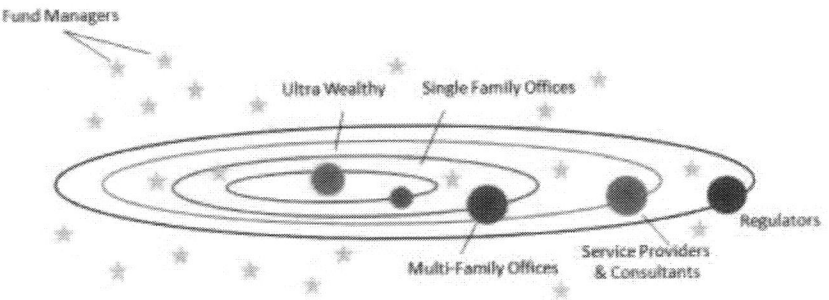

Single family offices are not well understood, and yet they are all around us and actively engaged in business, the community, and any number of different activities that affect us. Single family offices are often behind venture capital firms, operating private businesses, backing the powerful politicians that we love (and those that we don't), and owning the sports teams that we enjoy watching. Ultra-high net worth individuals control more than one-third of the total high net worth individual wealth in the world and represent less than one percent of the global high net worth individual population. These individuals possess extraordinary assets and represent some of the greatest success stories in modern history, from Wal-Mart's Sam Walton to the Wizard of Omaha himself, Warren Buffett. With these families' major impact on society and business, it is no wonder that so many people are interested in learning more about how these affluent families protect their assets and manage their resources.

As I noted in the preface, one of my least favorite statements I hear in the family office industry is, "If you have seen one family office, you have seen one family office." This is a common excuse employed by people who are asked directly about industry best practices and commonalities. The comment often has the effect of skirting a direct question and avoiding analysis of the single family office industry. There are certainly many variations on single family offices, but I believe it is disingenuous to brush off someone's sincere pursuit of guidance in this industry by simply stating that every family is unique. In fact, our team has found many best practices, areas of common ground among family offices, and strategies that apply to many different single family offices. Instead of saying, "if you have seen one single family office, you have seen one single family office," we prefer to think about the persistent patterns and themes that we have discovered in our relationships with more than 1,000 single family offices and how we can solve common problems and deliver solutions to these families.

Family businesses dominate the corporate world globally, and entire industries, such as beer, cable TV, and newspapers, are run by just a small handful of powerful families. Many family-owned businesses have a competitive advantage because of their long-term view and investment periods (Eisenmann 2000). At the same time, multi-generational struggles, governance issues, and what is best for the family vs. best for shareholders of one specific business entity the family owns are not always aligned (Minichilli 2010).

The concept of a single family office has roots back in the 6th century, when stewards would be appointed to manage the assets of kings. Wealthy European banking families formalized this practice for industry titans over several centuries, and the modern-day family office structure took shape when J.P. Morgan founded the House of Morgan to manage his family's assets. In the 1880s, the Rockefellers founded their own family office, and since then, thousands of additional single family offices have been organized.

Free Video: If you would like to learn more about the history of the family office industry, please see this short video recorded at 10,000 feet in the Swiss Alps:

http://SingleFamilyOffices.com/History

As I alluded to above, single family offices are thriving globally, with a new organization being launched every day. Our team estimates that there are nearly 5,000 single family offices globally, a good portion of which have no website, no business cards, and only a select few people who are informed regarding their actual legal structure or holdings.

I have found that it is helpful to segment the family office industry by size and number of clients. In the image below, you can see the Family Office Sandbox, with single family offices and multi-family offices divided and then each half divided by size.

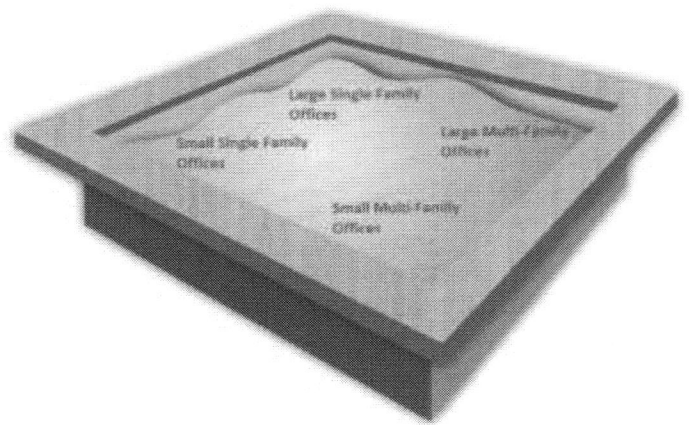

This rudimentary representation is helpful when you are thinking about how the family office industry is composed and where your family office might fit in. It has become common to use the term "family office" to describe the entire industry without consideration of the different challenges, values, objectives, structure, and composition of a small multi-family office, a global multi-family office with thousands of clients, a $2 billion single family office, and a $100 million single family office. In this book, we focus on the single family office side of the sandbox and how families can form, manage, and preserve their own single family office.

Free Video: While in Liechtenstein for a family office conference, I recorded a video on the state of the single family office industry:

http://SingleFamilyOffices.com/Industry

Some commentators in the press have claimed that the family office industry is not an industry; but family offices, and particularly single family offices, have unique needs, challenges, resource demands, and aspirations. The single family office segment alone controls over $1 trillion, and several forces are speeding up the formalization of this space. If you have attended one of our family office conferences or met with a group of family offices, you will have seen first-hand the common interests, characteristics, and organizational structure that set family offices apart from other firms and defines this industry.

The Family Office Club is an association that I founded in 2007 has more than 80,000 global members, making it by far the largest association in the industry. Our mission at the Family Office Club is to make the family office industry more efficient as a marketplace, help ultra-wealthy families learn the fundamentals of family offices, and to grow the industry on a global basis.

Free Video: Here is a short video overview recorded in Prague to explain the single family office industry.
http://SingleFamilyOffices.com/SFO

At the Family Office Club Association we believe that it benefits all parties when we connect ultra-wealthy families and family offices of all types to each other and to the fundamentals, common pitfalls, and best practices of the industry. The educational aspect of this mission is an area that we have made great progress on to-date, but there still is much work left to be done. In 2010, I appeared on *The Brian Tracy TV Show* which aired on affiliates of NBC, FOX, ABC, etc. Another guest of the show was a wealth manager from New Jersey who had never heard the words "family office." If a New Jersey-based wealth manager with $500M in assets under management can operate without hearing the term "family office," we have to assume that there are scores of ultra-wealthy individuals who became wealthy from owning mineral rights in Texas, a manufacturing plant in Penang Malaysia or real estate holdings in Sao Paulo Brazil may not have heard of the term "family office" either in the course of their work.

We recently conducted a global family office benchmarking study and found that above and beyond anything else, families want to connect with other families to share best practices. We also found that while finding new talent is sometimes the most important component, the referral of service providers and fund managers was often highly valued as well.

Here is the data on that survey data point:

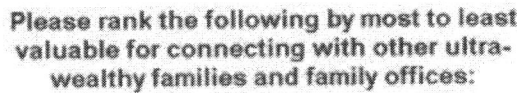

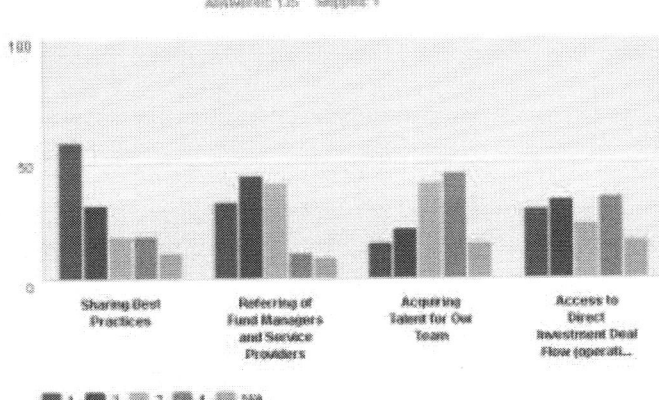

	1	2	3	4	N/A	Total	Average Ranking
Sharing Best Practices	42.22% 57	22.96% 31	13.33% 18	13.33% 18	8.15% 11	135	3.02
Referring of Fund Managers and Service Providers	23.70% 32	31.85% 43	29.63% 40	8.15% 11	6.67% 9	135	2.78
Acquiring Talent for Our Team	11.11% 15	15.56% 21	29.63% 40	32.59% 44	11.11% 15	135	2.66
Access to Direct Investment Deal Flow (operating business investments)	21.48% 29	24.44% 33	17.04% 23	25.19% 34	11.85% 16	135	2.48

A large part of our education at the Family Office Club is tailored to single family offices, and that has resulted in meeting 61 billion-dollar families and hundreds of families with $100 million or more in assets over the past several years. These families' stories, questions, challenges, and requests have fueled requests to publish this book.

The Single Family Office by Richard C. Wilson

Free Video: To learn more about why the family office industry is thriving and why it will continue to do so, please see this video:

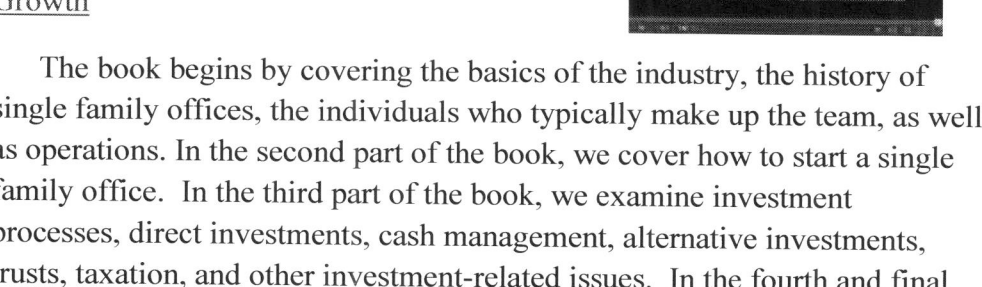

http://SingleFamilyOffices.com/Industry-Growth

The book begins by covering the basics of the industry, the history of single family offices, the individuals who typically make up the team, as well as operations. In the second part of the book, we cover how to start a single family office. In the third part of the book, we examine investment processes, direct investments, cash management, alternative investments, trusts, taxation, and other investment-related issues. In the fourth and final part of the book, we explore softer issues on the psychology of money, bringing up children in an ultra-wealthy family, virtual family offices and the future of the single family office industry.

Free Resources: Throughout the book, you will find links to templates, video modules, expert audio interviews, etc. In spite of the private nature of this industry, we have made these resources 100% free to access, with no registration, email opt-in, or cost associated with it. We have found that the more value we give away openly the more powerful ultra-wealthy and $1B+ families approach us regarding working together.

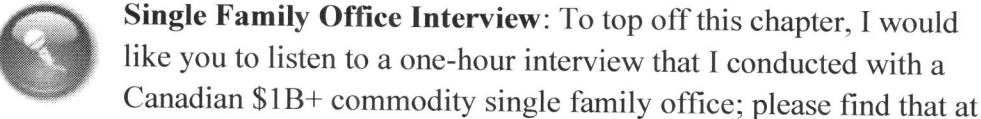 **Single Family Office Interview**: To top off this chapter, I would like you to listen to a one-hour interview that I conducted with a Canadian $1B+ commodity single family office; please find that at:
http://SingleFamilyOffices.com/Audio3

References:

Villalonga, B. and C. Hartman, 2007, "The New York Times Co.," in Harvard Business School Case 207-113, Boston, MA, Harvard Business School Publishing.

Eisenmann, T., 2000, "The U.S. Cable Television Industry, 1948-1995: Managerial Capitalism in Eclipse," *Business History Review* 74, 1-40.

Minichilli, A., 2010, "Top Management Teams in Family-Controlled Companies: Fairness, Fault lines, and their impact on Financial Performance." *Journal of Management Studies* 47, 205-222.

The Single Family Office by Richard C. Wilson

Chapter 2: Single Family Office Talent & Teams

"The secret of success is not in doing your own work, but in recognizing the right man to do it." - Andrew Carnegie

To run a successful single family office, you need a diverse team to handle the many types of investments in the context of taxation and legal issues. Both long-standing single family offices and seasoned single family office executives find frustration in the inefficiency of finding professionals with single family office talent.

While some claim that every single family office structures their team differently, I have not found that to be the case. There are certainly a number of variations in team structure at the 5,000+ single family offices globally, but there are more commonalities than differences.

The most dominant things affecting a team structure include the level of net worth of the family, whether they actively run operating businesses, the number of unique family generations and family groups being served, the level of direct investment or co-investment activity being pursued, and whether the family is engaging many outside investment consultants, due diligence consultants, etc., or attempting to conduct most of that work in-house.

Video: Top Single Family Offices: To watch a short video on best practices used by top family offices, please watch this short four-minute video from Prague in the Czech Republic: http://SingleFamilyOffices.com/Top-SFO

Many times, the patriarch, matriarch, or individual who created the wealth makes the hiring decisions inside of the single family office, and that person's ability to trust the expertise and experience of the employee is a chief concern. Many families hire professionals they have known for several years already, instead of someone else who may be technically better qualified, because the family needs to be able to work with someone who will exercise discretion, balance competing priorities, and not violate family values and norms.

At the same time, many single family office executives are slow to move jobs because they don't know where to look for their next position. Many large single family offices don't speak with each other often, and if they were seen shopping their résumé around, then they may be let go without another job lined up. More than a dozen $500M+ single family office CEOs and CIOs have approached our firm for help in finding their next family office position, because of the aforementioned issues.

For example, while writing this chapter of the book I was recently approached by a Chief Investment Officer of a $3B+ single family office who explained that he felt underpaid and undervalued at his current employer and he didn't foresee the situation changing anytime soon. The patriarch in this case created their wealth by being thrifty and they aren't intending on changing that attitude now that they are protecting their wealth via a single family office.

Most single family offices that I have worked with employ 4-7 full-time professionals. The team will typically include two to three of those professionals who have 15+ years of experience, often in a specific niche or area of expertise. The five most valued types of expertise:

1. Family Office CEO Chief Investment Officer (CIO) level investment expertise

2. Private Equity or Direct Investments

3. CFO/Accounting Expertise from other family offices, trusts, private banks, or wealth management firms

4. Taxation and Trust & Estate Law

The Single Family Office by Richard C. Wilson

5. Risk Management / Insurance

The most common error committed by aspiring family office professionals is approaching would-be family office employers without a clear focus or expertise. If you do not have one of the above types of expertise, you will have a tougher time convincing a single family office to enlist your services. At our Single Family Office Summit I met a professional who wanted to work for a family office. I inquired into his background and learned it was fairly diverse (a few years of real estate management, a short stint at a technology startup, sales and marketing jobs, etc.). When I asked if he had a specific area of expertise or focus that he felt would be especially valuable to a family office, he shrugged and said that he was more of a general management type who could help with whatever the family needed. I understand that job-seekers don't want to close the door on any opportunities and appear too narrowly focused on a single area of business, but this can make the decision difficult for a single family office. You are essentially asking a single family office to bring you into the fold and provide compensation commensurate with what you could command in the private sector, but you aren't clearly explaining why that money would help the family and why you are more deserving of a position than other potential employees. In short a balance must be struck between a macro understanding of various functions but a clear ROI on investing in you is needed.

For example, our team is trying to attract a new executive to Wilson Holding Company right now, we know that he can wear many hats and probably indirectly boost our revenues enough to pay for his salary, but we are hesitant to pull the trigger until we find a division in our business to run. We haven't been able to find one so we are conducting due diligence on a distressed 17 year old data services business and will hopefully acquire that for ourselves so this professional can ramp up the revenues of this company, pay for himself in very direct fashion, while also leveraging his legal counsel and operational execution skills across our entire portfolio of businesses. While writing this chapter I introduced a $1B+ single family office CIO to a $600M mini corporate conglomerate owned by two families and they have a similar type of negotiation starting now, how to form a new business or expand a division to create a clear ROI on the new executive being hired.

Top family office executives are often compensated with a $200,000-$400,000 base salary along with some performance-based bonus or performance pay. Most professionals who are capable and experienced enough to serve as a family office CEO or CIO can easily command at least $300,000 a year in the marketplace; this is why most single family offices have $100M or more in capital—otherwise, a relatively high percentage of the overall capital will be spent each year on human capital overhead each year. In other words if you have under $100M in net worth and are not careful your overhead could effectively create a high management fee if you try to match the brain trust of a $1B+ single family office. Since many single family offices are set up to primarily defend the portfolio and preserve capital, there is not typically a strong incentive to aim for 30-50% returns per year, but rather to diversify, protect the capital, and produce 6-15% type returns over a whole portfolio.

 **Single Family Office Audio Interview**: To add some color to this chapter, we have interviewed a single family office CFO who talks about their acquisitions in 20 different companies with a two-person team, and how much acquiring new talent costs for a single family office. To stream or download this audio interview for free, please see http://SingleFamilyOffices.com/Audio4

Chief Executive Officer (CEO) Responsibilities: The CEO role typically includes selecting the systems, consultants, software programs, overseeing the CIO, CFO, and other staff to make sure they are performing as expected, and helping make hiring decisions for the core team and advisory board. Many times, the CEO is a family member or someone such as a CPA or investment consultant that has worked for the family for some time. Other times, they are hired away from other single family offices, or taken out of roles where they were expected to wear many different hats at once while serving ultra-wealthy families in a private bank or asset management firm.

One of the biggest mistakes consistently made by single family offices is placing a CEO in operational control of the total organization, overseeing the entire team including the CIO, yet financially rewarding them as if they were not leading an investment organization. In other words, if the CIO of your family office is being offered upside on producing positive performance for

The Single Family Office by Richard C. Wilson

the family, the CEO should as well.

Many CIOs and CEOs leave their current positions or constantly have one foot out the door due to not being able to participate in upside performance of a portfolio, and even if a CEO seems to be one-step removed from day-to-day CIO responsibilities, they are responsible for the total team and results at the end of the day, and that should always be reflected in their level of compensation. Out of the 55 families we know with $1B or more in capital, 10% of the executives from those families came to us because of frustration with their current compensation level.

Chief Financial Officer (CFO) Responsibilities: CFO responsibilities include working on tax returns, finance procedures, financial reporting, accounting, partnerships, financial models, lending, family bank responsibilities and oversight, cash flow management, bill paying/bookkeeping, direct investment ROI and acquisition/sell responsibilities, lines of credit, loans, etc.

Not all family offices have a formal CFO; many times, the CEO or CIO is also playing the CFO role. But many families with over $500M in assets, or more complex smaller size portfolios, do have a formal CFO separated from other roles.

Chief Investment Officer (CIO) Responsibilities: The CIO of a single family office helps form and direct the implementation of the investment portfolio of the family. Their responsibilities can include investment policy management, tactical and strategic investment decision making, portfolio risk management, and oversight or hands-on due diligence of potential investment fund managers and direct investment opportunities. Many CIOs of family offices are hired away from private equity funds, banks, wealth management firms, or investment consulting firms, as most families would like to employ someone with 10+ years of experience with the ability to understand broader global trends, while paying great attention to detail to help protect the family from making bad investments.

The work required of a CIO will vary based on the size of the portfolios, areas of investment being considered, and whether the family office employs an active CFO or CEO at the time. In many single family offices, the CEO is a family member who may be too busy to work 40-50 hours/week on family office matters.

Chief Direct Investments Officer (CDIO) Responsibilities: Many family offices do not have this position formalized yet, but some family offices have hired someone to do nothing but look after their operating businesses and help acquire new ones. This role may involve some raising of capital for the businesses, or buying and selling an operating business from time-to-time as well. One family office I have worked with has 20 operating businesses. So they have hired someone to watch over just this part of their portfolio from a high-level, to make sure the businesses are sharing resources, being optimized, and helped when needed. Another single family office from Asia I have had speak at my Singapore family office workshop owns 60 operating businesses and they have multiple dedicated professionals to helping manage those organizations at a very high-level.

The rest of the team is typically made up of analysts, portfolio managers, accountants, or professionals who support the various operating businesses that the family office may own. Many single family offices operate so many direct ongoing business enterprises that the single family office headquarters serve as a backbone for those operations in terms of IT support, access to financing and capital, or introductions to new business partners. Many junior to mid-level professionals inside a single family office are paid $50,000 to $125,000 in annual salary. This is consistent with the compensation that skilled financial professionals command from banks, corporations, and other potential employers vying for talent.

Lean family office angle: A growing trend for many family offices is to outsource almost everything so that there are only 2-4 members of the family office who work full-time. By outsourcing the accounting, reporting, administration, IT, and even investment roles, the core in-house members are able to focus on adding value within one or two focused strategic areas, such as direct investments or venture capital investments. This model is becoming more popular, but there are drawbacks. For one, the cost savings comes with less privacy, which is incredibly important for wealthy families. Another consideration is that the outsourcing model may sometimes slow down the ability of the family office to quickly adapt to rapidly changing financial environments.

Globally team make up differs, single family offices in Latin America and Asia for example, on average, tend to be smaller than western counterparts, often with only 1-2 investment professionals working on a team. In Asia particularly, a family member is often the head of the single family office and acts as the CEO and CIO of the organization. A slightly lower percentage of Asian family offices will be managed by family members in the near future, but I don't predict that we will see their typical size increase by much.

It should go without saying that anyone you interview for a family office position should have to go through a background check and have references checked from each previous employer, whether they provide that firm as a reference or not. Many single family offices refuse to hire anyone that they have not had a professional or personal relationship with for several years, even if that means hiring someone more expensive or less experienced than necessary. The level of trust needed to help operate a $100M or $1B+ portfolio is high enough that it often trumps other factors.

Family Office Executive Directors: Here is a short video on family office executive directors that I recently recorded in the Swiss Alps when I was in Zurich:

http://SingleFamilyOffices.com/Executive-Directors

Attracting Talent

Many single family offices struggle with finding highly qualified professionals to help run their operations and investments. That is because there are only so many single family offices in the world, many of them are very private, and most single family offices don't actively speak with others in the industry.

We have identified seven proven ways to attract talent to your single family office. If you are looking to hire, these tips should directly help you:

- **LinkedIn**: While I write off most of social media as a waste of time for business use, LinkedIn has brought us many key institutional and large single family office relationships. On way to leverage the platform is by searching for "family office" on LinkedIn and select the geographical region corresponding to your city or those nearby, you may find some qualified professionals you could reach out to. You could also try joining the 80,000+ member Family Office Club Association as a base or charter member on FamilyOffices.com.

- **Conferences & Workshops**: Many single family office executives who are unhappy with their positions may be more likely to attend industry events, conferences, and training workshops. By attending these, you will slowly build a network of expert professionals in the field from which you can hire in the future.

- **Unique Compensation Packages**: If you can offer the right type of compensation package, you may be able to steal someone away from a great position somewhere else. This unique package could include a share of the carry or portion of the proceeds on deals that the professional helps close. Another attractive option is to include performance bonuses calculated as a percentage of the gains in a portfolio, or some other means of additional upside for someone who is ambitious and wants a chance to prove what they can do. One company that we have a equity stake in provides 10% gross revenue shares with new divisions and acquisitions lead by a single senior executive. Not all unique compensation packages need to be strictly about cash however, at this same company we are putting together a new level of senior partner in the firm which provides access to luxury villas and sports cars at the company's expense to keep top talent loyal long-term.

- **Qualified Family Office Professional (QFOP)**: Hundreds of global professionals have enrolled in this family office training and certificate program. You can join other family offices in using this self-paced audio and video training program to train new hires or access a specialized talent pool of professionals who hold this designation. This is a great tool for identifying talent with family office industry focus and it costs next to nothing compared to employing a traditional family office executive search service. Those family offices with 60% or more of their senior staff enrolled or who

The Single Family Office by Richard C. Wilson

have completed the program may refer to themselves as a Qualified Family Office (QFO).

- **Cherry Picking**: One method for acquiring talent with the skills you need is targeting professionals at institutional firms such as multi-family offices, CPA and tax advisory firms, private equity funds, and investment banks. Many single family office executives made the transition after working for years with a single family office and eventually the family asked the professional to join full-time. Top 100 endowment funds are excellent fertile grounds for finding slightly under-paid but bright and well groomed talent for managing a family office portfolio.

- **Grow your single family office brand**: A few single family offices have discovered the benefits of being highly visible. These offices access greater deal flow, attract better talent applying for jobs, and connect with more families wanting to work together on co-investments or requesting help in managing their assets, compared to those families that shy from the limelight and insist on a high degree of privacy.

- **Family Office Executive Search**: While I have found most family offices are not willing to pay executive search fees using a family office executive search firm is another option for finding talent. Few firms focus just on the family office industry, but many are happy to jump in and help in this high-end space if you want the professional assistance.

Three Questions to Ask *Yourself* When Hiring a New Family Office Professional

Single family offices making a new hire should ask themselves three questions. The first question the employer should ask is whether this person is going to return a multiple of his or her salary. Any new employee should produce revenue for the SFO that far exceeds the annual salary investment. The only exception should be made if the hire will significantly ease the family's stress or peace of mind. For example, an in-house financial advisor may not produce exceptional gains beyond the salary the advisor receives, but it could be a worthwhile hire still if it removes the family's concerns over managing money through a private bank or unfamiliar investment house.

The second important question to ask when hiring is if this person will provide real benefit in at least one area of the family office. As stated above, family office employees should have at least one area of real expertise that they bring to the table. A specialization is important, whether the professional is a seasoned investment banker who can help with direct investments and deals, or the hire has a legal background that will limit the family's liabilities and assist in navigating different laws and regulations. Single family offices should think carefully before hiring anyone claiming to be a generalist. In my experience, it is better to hire a specialist and gradually expand that person's role to take on more general responsibilities.

The third question that I suggest asking yourself before you hire a new single family office professional is: how will this individual fit in with my team and objectives? Single family office executives and principals have a number of exceptionally talented friends, connections, and former colleagues. As your network of single family office professionals grows, it can be hard to avoid hiring opportunistically, based solely on a connection's intelligence and experience. But single family offices should be careful to avoid the trap of taking on too much overhead paying talented professionals that do not fill a specific need or may bring a skillset that is redundant with another member of the team. It is tough to turn down talent, but you will be better off in the long-run if the person is not a necessary fit with your team or your objectives.

Compensation Strategies

If you want to hire someone with deep single family office experience or more readily available chief investment officer experience, you will need to think about how to retain those professionals long-term.

Working at a single family office can be somewhat isolating for someone accustomed to working at a 100 or 1,000+ person organization. Also, dealing with the family politics and nepotism that often occurs within single family offices can be a deterrent to quality professionals. Some of the best compensation agreements I have seen have clauses that align the long-term incentives of the CIO with that of the family. One example includes a provision that every year during which the portfolio produces a positive return and outpaces inflation, the executive receives a bonus of let's say $250,000, but that bonus may be paid out over a five-year period at a rate of

$50,000 per year. If the portfolio loses money within any of those subsequent years, the executive loses the percentage lost in the single family office's portfolio by a factor of seven. So if the investment portfolio is down 10%, the professional loses 70% of the anticipated bonuses for that year. This payout over time allows the executive to earn a sizable bonus, discourages the professional from leaving, and severely cuts back compensation if the portfolio loses value.

Some family offices are more aggressive and willing to share a 5-20% performance fee with the chief investment officer for positive returns in the portfolio, although these families are still the exception. A high-water-mark provision is often adopted in these cases, so that when losses do occur, the portfolio value must be recovered before awarding any additional performance fees.

It can often take 12-18 months to get a new chief investment officer 100% familiar with the family's portfolio and priorities. It is important to get to know the professional you decide to hire and ensuring that he/she is making a long-term employment commitment. Although not legally enforceable, getting verbal agreement to a five to seven year commitment expectation at the onset of the hiring can set the tone for what you expect.

Interview with Michael Oliver Weinberg

 To provide some advice to those reading this book who are looking to the join the team of a single family office, I thought it would be helpful to interview someone who not only acts as CIO of a single family office, but who also has worked for Soros Fund Management (George Soros) in the past. Michael is an Adjunct Professor of Finance & Economics at Columbia Business School and you can meet him in person at some of our single family office conferences or at our annual Family Office Super Summit in Miami.

Richard C. Wilson: For those looking to move from working for a hedge fund or private equity fund into the single family office industry, what words of direction, caution, or advice could you provide that may help them more easily make that transition?

Michael Oliver Weinberg: Though in our experience it is more common for family office investors to want to move into hedge funds, we have also seen hedge fund and private equity analysts look to move into the SFO industry. We believe the former desired transition is more common than the later desired transition. This is due to the greater perceived excitement, glamour and potential monetary rewards. That said, to quote one of the hedge fund legends, Michael Steinhardt, we have a variant perception on each of these three points that we will delineate.

However before we do this, we would like to highlight relevant experience that we believe validates our opining on the subject. Having been very fortunate to have been a portfolio manager at Soros, not only one of the world's best and most successful hedge funds for multiple decades, but also a family office, gives us a unique perspective on the issue. Having also been an allocator at Financial Risk Management, FRM, a world-class fund-of-funds for the past nine years, where my global research team and I did hundreds of meetings per year with hedge funds, ranging from the largest to the smallest, and the best to the worst, also gives us a unique perspective.

Our first variant perception is that the hedge fund world, which we enjoyed and think very highly of for many reasons, is NOT as glamorous as it is perceived. Rather, it is an extraordinarily competitive industry that rewards hard and tedious work. The most successful analysts and portfolio managers we know are hardworking investors who spend their days, and often nights and weekends, poring over company, industry and economic data, research reports, other security-related information and public filings. Though we enjoyed doing that very much, we would hardly say it is glamorous.

Our second variant perception that we have relates to the perceived excitement of hedge funds. Yes, there are some very trading-oriented hedge funds that hold position for minutes, hours, intraday or for days; however, those are the minority. It is far more likely that the holding period of securities is weeks, months, and in some instances years. Though we are indifferent to holding periods in terms of manager selection, we would hardly say such long-term investing is "exciting" in the commonly perceived way, though often a great way to compound capital at high rates of return, and therefore something we are a proponent of.

Our third variant perception regards the potential monetary rewards. As far back as the early '90's, we recall a certain industry publication highlighting the most profitable hedge funds, and both then and in today's dollars, the numbers were and are astronomical. This is still the case for the top earning hedge funds. However, what is underappreciated is that these are 10, 20, 50 or 100 of what is now a universe of roughly 10,000 hedge funds. In percentage terms, that equates to 0.1%, 0.2%, 0.5% and 1% of the industry.

What is also underappreciated is how many sub-$10, $25, $50 or $100Mn funds there are and how difficult it is to raise capital for smaller managers. Today, with the greater compliance and regulatory requirements post the global financial crisis, as well as institutional investors' (and some more sophisticated family offices') greater infrastructure requirements and substantial fee pressure on smaller managers, it is very difficult to run such sub-scale funds at all, let alone at a profit, or to compete with larger, more well-resourced funds.

We believe anyone in a family office looking to move to or launch a hedge fund should be cognizant of these facts before they endeavor upon such a transition. That said, or those disclaimers aside, we are very much believers in the hedge fund model, and have written articles published by Institutional Investor's *Hedge Fund Intelligence* that espouse hedge fund investing versus more traditional long-only investing.

Next let us look at the other side of the trade—the move from working for a hedge fund into the single family office industry. One of our most striking observations contrasting the two fields is the average quality of the respective investment staffs.

Nearly a decade ago, when we personally transitioned from hedge fund portfolio management and analysis to fund-of-fund portfolio management and analysis, we observed that the average hedge fund analyst and portfolio manager was far smarter, hungrier, aggressive, and impressive than the average fund-of-fund analyst or portfolio manager. In fact, the reason we joined Financial Risk Management, FRM, was because they were one of the few of dozens of fund-of-funds that we met with that actually appreciated the value of hiring former "risk-takers," i.e. hedge fund portfolio managers, analysts, and similar market professionals, as opposed to hiring former fund-of-funds professionals without such relevant and high quality experience, and who often comparatively were "B" players. We can think of countless examples where we met with managers, and our own experiences having done the same thing were integral in achieving superior manager selection in terms of who to invest with and as importantly who to avoid.

Why is this bit of ancient history relevant to the hedge fund to single family office transition question? Because we believe the analog of going from a hedge fund to a single family office is nearly identical. Based on our extensive experience in both spaces, we believe that the average hedge fund analyst and portfolio manager is far smarter, hungrier, more aggressive, and impressive than the average family office analyst or portfolio manager. Considering the large balances of capital at stake, we have often pondered how this is possibly the case.

Our best explanation is the following. A handful of the smartest and most financially sophisticated families, such as the one we worked for, Soros, appreciate how valuable capital allocation is and view it as a profit center. However, sadly most of the rest of the family offices view capital allocation as a cost center. The family often earned the capital in a non-financial business, such as an operating business or real estate, and unlike those that are in the financial services industry or the minority of families that earned their capital in that industry, there is an under-appreciation of the value and returns that "A" talent can achieve. Family offices often view these employees no differently than other employees, who have far less of an ability to have such a meaningful impact on a family's finances or well-being.

Similarly, as these investment professionals are not deemed to be terribly important by families, they are generally not terribly well-compensated either, at least compared to hedge fund portfolio managers and analysts. As we formerly worked at Soros, we are well versed in and enjoy applying George Soros's theories, such as feedback loops, to our analyses. We believe this subpar compensation in turn attracts mediocre or lower quality investment talent, which in turn results in subpar returns, which reinforces the notion of lower compensation.

Moreover, based on compensation surveys we have seen on the family office, the vast majority of remuneration schemes are not performance based. This further diminishes the incentive to achieve superior performance, or for the best and brightest to be incented to work at family offices. Even worse, it potentially results in a similar phenomenon to that which occurs in the long-only active management world. In this world, managers are incented to perform in-line with their benchmarks and not take risk that would result in material deviation above the benchmark, as material deviation below the benchmark would result in redemptions. As we believe Soros would conclude, the confluence of all of these factors results in a fairly typical negative feedback loop.

The bad news for those that are looking to make this transition from hedge funds to single family offices is that sadly, more often than not, their value will be underappreciated and underpriced in all but a handful of the best single family offices. The good news is that if they are able to make the transition into the space, they are then likely in the minority of "A" players competing mostly against "B" players, or worse.

For the few that are successfully able to make this transition, it is very possible that they are able to achieve outsized returns and "pick" alpha up from their inferior competitors. Then of course the question is whether this is adequately appreciated by the family and they are similarly remunerated. If not, the alternative is of course to move on to greener pastures, defined as a family that is appreciative of this alpha and more generous in remuneration. In actuality, that is easier said than done, as those families are more difficult to find.

Family office roles are often less stressful due to a diminished focus on performance. There is also less sophistication, which affords lower quality and quantity of work, which results in less hours and a higher quality lifestyle compared with hedge funds. To quote economics 101, this often results in a "sticky" labor-force, where those in the roles hold on to them for very long periods with little movement. Schumpeter's creative destruction often bypasses family offices, all of which perpetuates the aforementioned negative feedback loop.

Interview with Richard Ross

Below are a few thoughts from the interview that I conducted with Richard Ross who has worked for Summer Road, LLC, a New York based family office.

Richard C. Wilson: Do you think that $500M or $1B families should be employing large 30, 50, or even 100+ person teams, or do you believe the norm of having a small team that wears many hats is actually a healthy, positive thing?

Richard Ross: Richard, as you know, I did startups in California for 25 years, so I believe a small, dedicated team (say three to six people) can solve most problems. A family office, either large or small, might need an operations guy, a "data wrangler," some technology expertise, an understanding of economics, an appreciation of modern finance (including its limitations), and knowledge of financial opportunities (including, but not limited to, various hedge funds, hedge fund strategies, and ETFs). I believe back-office functions (record-keeping or taxes, for example) are not a competitive advantage, and may be outsourced.

One individual can indeed wear many hats, as you propose, so all this expertise could be embodied in, say, four people. As in a startup, I think it's optimal for each person to be an expert in more than one area, so, for example, your "quant" can handle operations if need be.

Richard C. Wilson: What unique challenges and opportunities do large $1B+ family offices face which you just don't see at a typical $100M-$200M family office?

Richard Ross: Larger offices obviously have more opportunities, but I think it's not a categorical difference: whether you make 40 investments averaging $25M each, or 20 investments of $10M each, you still have to do your homework. A large office may have the opportunity to be more fee-efficient, by negotiating better terms with a new hedge fund, or setting up a '40 Act fund. Also, a larger office may have access to more investment opportunities, such as PE or VC, but these tend to be riskier assets, so I would suggest that a long-term, conservative investor should be minimizing investments in these entities in any case, independent of investor size.

Conclusion

To wrap up this chapter: single family offices often require one to three senior executives who can wear many hats. The talent marketplace is so small and trust is so important that it can often take years for a single family office to find the right professional to hire. This will slowly change as the industry matures, but it will take a decade or more before a broad pool of talent can be readily identified by employers.

Chapter 3: Single Family Office Operations

The goal of this chapter is to focus on how single family offices operate so you can check these best practices against how your family office is managed and what to expect once you have a single family office in place. If you have established a virtual family office, then your experience may be different; fortunately, we have a whole chapter dedicated to virtual family offices in this book, so we will cover that in detail there.

Family Office Operations: Here is a video I recorded in Liechtenstein in which I highlight the three operating models that are most common in the family offices that I work with: http://SingleFamilyOffices.com/Operations

One thing to keep in mind is that when you operate a single family office, you are doing more than just investing capital; you are running a business. You need to worry about payroll, legal formation rules, taxation, liability, human resource issues, and the unpredictable challenges that come along with managing all of the above. That is why this book does not just talk about portfolio management and investing, and why, if possible, it is important to have at least a part-time CEO quarterbacking your team, and not just a sharp CIO running everything.

An average-sized family office team consists of a CEO (often a family member), a CIO, and one to two analysts or associate level team members. In this case, the day-to-day activities include:

1. Ensuring that the business of the single family office is being taken care of, employee issues are resolved, the business is stable, cash on hand is adequate for payroll, etc. These are small issues, but they can

chew up a lot of time as the investments grow more complex and the team expands.

2. Looking at incoming deal flow, fund manager pitches, direct deals, etc. At well-known single family offices, staff must coordinate and prioritize relationships amid a constant flow of in-person meetings, a bloated email inbox, and a seemingly endless barrage of phone calls. To manage the chaos, you will have to implement processes to quickly evaluate the opportunity, deflect those deemed to be wastes of time, and have junior analysts screen the promising deals.

3. Conducting in-depth due diligence. This means following a due diligence process aimed at ensuring that any fund manager selected or investment made fits within the family mandate and meets the family and CIO's criteria. This is critical to avoid frauds, underperforming fund managers, and wild goose chases running after poorly structured investment banking deals.

4. Monitoring the markets and portfolio. The degree of work here will vary based on how closely the family is involved in directly investing in the public markets or other liquid securities. Monitoring direct investments, real estate, and private equity funds is also a component of the total portfolio monitoring activity. However, direct investments rarely require daily attention, unless the family office has employed a Chief Direct Investment Officer (CDIO) to cover that area.

5. Speaking with other family offices and investors with similar investment portfolios and challenges, and sharing best practices with others. If this activity is ignored, then the team will grow stale and they will be slow to respond and take tactical moves to defend the portfolio.

6. Creating documentation and reports needed for accounting and taxation purposes. Additionally, single family offices prepare a weekly, monthly, or quarterly report to send to the family. Often times, this reporting process is complex and requires expensive or custom-built software solutions to capture an accurate picture of where the money is invested right now and what those investments are worth.

7. Coordinating with outside tax, insurance, risk management, or investment consultants on specific transactions on the horizon, pending legal agreements, or private placement opportunities being considered.

8. Creating reports and working with reporting systems to communicate investment returns to stakeholders in the single family office.

Video: Family Office Services: In this video recorded in Prague, I discuss the different range of services offered by virtual family offices, single family offices, and multi-family offices. http://SingleFamilyOffices.com/Services

Keeping Expenses in Check

A single family office is effectively a business. Until you are earning consistent revenue from operating businesses or returns on your investment portfolio, you need to keep a tight grip on your finances. I recommend running a very lean operation and not investing in all of the various services that will be pitched to you. As head of your family office, you will no doubt encounter an endless tide of marketers pushing expensive products and services that are "essential" to the success of your single family office. Keep in mind that these professionals are typically paid commissions and have an interest in making the sale, not making sure that the product or service is a fit for your developing single family office. Once you are an established single family office and comfortable with your consistent profits generated by your investments, then you should consider those luxuries that will truly improve your single family office. In the early stages though, it's important to guard against blowing up the balance sheet with annual subscriptions to investor research products, buying expensive office space, and other nice-to-have's that aren't critical for the immediate success of your firm. This is why most family offices like to seek out expertise, identify resources, and work based on just-in-time referrals from their peers rather than be cold called and spam emailed to buy a service or invest in something. This is exactly how we stumbled into our first family office relationships 10 years ago, by providing value first and working via referrals and sharing of best practices.

Another expense that needs to be tightly managed is the compensation awarded to your employees. As I explain in other chapters, compensation is important and leading single family offices routinely pay employees mid six-figure salaries and lucrative success bonuses. In the early stages, however, it's important to express the need to keep your expenses in check to all of your employees so that they don't have unreasonable expectations in the first few years. Too often, businesses that have early successes then give in to employee demands for higher salaries based on that success. But a base salary increase is incredibly difficult to reduce and contracts are often multi-year agreements. So, when the next year sees sales drop or losses in the investment portfolio, the business suffers doubly because the company committed to paying high salaries negotiated at a time when profits were higher. The worst-case scenario is marrying your single family office to a high salary negotiated at a time when profits were exceptionally high. If the year is an anomaly, then you've committed the firm to paying that salary at a high-water mark that may never be reached again or at least not for several years. Then, you will likely resent the employee (or at least her compensation agreement) and the employee will eventually feel unappreciated when you are unwilling to increase her salary or add bonuses in the future.

I've found that successful investment firms (and many small businesses) have managed compensation agreements by offering a reasonable starting salary and driving most increases in compensation through performance-based bonuses. Under this model, if you encounter an exceptional year, you can reward your employees with bonuses based on pre-determined performance measures or at your personal discretion. The bonuses are one-off expenses and you can adjust or maintain the bonuses in the future. This is the best way to avoid committing yourself to expensive compensation agreements that can be largely uncorrelated to the success of the firm. If you find yourself in the unenviable position of already having committed to these types of agreements with your family office employees, then the best path forward is to address the problem with the individual(s) and explain that changing the compensation structure will enable you to reward their successes more and ultimately earn more if the firm does better. In my experience working with family offices and running my own businesses, it's often better for both parties to have compensation designed to reward consistent long-term excellent performance, not just "good" performance and to do so in a way that is aligned with the family offices investment objectives and values.

Keeping a tight grip on expenses—from employee compensation to the rent you pay for your office space—is an important aspect of operating a family office. If you do not have the experience or interest to manage a business and keep a close eye on the financials, then it's best to hand off the number-crunching duties to a trusted employee or advisor who can help you stay informed on the day-to-day operations of the business and your financial situation. No matter how involved you are in managing the firm's balance sheet, it is critical that the key personnel at your single family office have a regular meeting that includes a candid look at the financial figures and an assessment of how your SFO is doing.

Selecting an Office Space

The geographical location of your office space is discussed elsewhere in this book, so in addition to that decision the size and functionality of your office space will depend entirely upon its function. One $1B+ family I work with purchased a large 10,000+ square foot church, while another operates from their ranch, and many have traditional office space to house their staff members. The only important considerations I have seen on this front is proximity to operating businesses that the family owns, ease of access to the airport, and to potential co-investment partners and investment targets if that is going to make up a large part of the family's investment activities. I would also note that the quality of your team and office do make up part of your reputation and how serious others take you, from vendors and potential new hires to other families looking to potentially co-invest with you.

For-Profit or For-Later?

While operating a single family office, you will need to decide on whether growing the investment portfolio or preserving it is the chief goal. This will change who you hire, how operations are run, and how much money should be spent on office space and overhead overall. This is a question we will explore in the section of this book on creating a single family office, and again near the end of the book when we discuss converting a single family office into a multi-family office.

Recommended Reading

The purpose of this book and my other resources that I have shared with families is to educate families on managing a family office, an area that I feel is sorely lacking in thought leadership and training. Until there is an adequately large library of family office-specific books, you will have to learn the majority of your family office management strategy by reading available general management books, ignoring the irrelevant sections, and focusing on those lessons that do apply to managing a family office. I recommend setting aside a few hours each week to read through these books below, all of which have ample content relevant to running a family office. At all of my companies, these books are required reading for the executive team.

From Good to Great: Why Some Companies Make the Leap . . . And Others Don't (2001)

Author: Jim Collins

ISBN-13: 978-0066620992

Quick Take: Jim Collins is an exceptional management consultant and thought leader who has written a number of best-selling business management books, including *Great by Choice*, *Built to Last*, and *How the Mighty Fall*. Collins and his research team review hundreds of companies and evaluate the lessons, strengths, and failures of a select few companies. The author extracts telling insights from the decisions made by these companies' executives and shares his thoughts on how your business can avoid a costly mistake or learn from a savvy move. Collins' books are full of valuable research and delivered in an easy-to-consume format that is full of interviews, anecdotes, and tips.

Mastering the Rockefeller Habits: What You Must Do to Increase the Value of Your Growing Firm (2002)

Author: Verne Harnish

ISBN-13: 978-0978774943

Quick Take: For those of you looking for a biography of John D. Rockefeller, the famous industrialist and one of the wealthiest men to ever live, this book won't quite deliver on that front (*Titan: The Life of John D. Rockefeller*, Sr. is better for a purely biographical read). However, if you are searching for a great management guide with fascinating tales of success and failure culled from not only Rockefeller, but also clients of Harnish's consulting business, then you should order this book. I've used this book as management training for all of my employees and it is a great resource for specific guidance and tools for managing your business. Similar to Collins' *Good to Great*, this book is written by a well-informed consultant and observer of management strategies. Harnish writes with the expertise of someone who has managed both small and medium-sized fast growing businesses, and has experienced not only the successes but also the failures. I recommend revisiting this book with your team once you've structured your family office and managed it for at least a year; then, you can use this book to put into place key performance indicators, your strategic one pager, and to help you identify choke points in your operating businesses.

Work the System: The Simple Mechanics of Making More and Working Less (2009)

Author: Sam Carpenter

ISBN-13: 978-1608322534

Quick Take and Bonus: One of my other favorite books that related to running a family office efficiently and a business in general is *Work the System*. Sam Carpenter is an expert on implementing practical systems, procedures, and checklists within a fast-growing small- to medium-sized business such as a single family office. This book is a valuable guide to business professionals who want to perform better and manage their company more effectively; it's been very helpful to me as a business owner running several different companies.

In fact, I enjoyed this book so much that I asked the author to join me for an interview on the book and his business management philosophy. Sam agreed and we had an hour-long discussion about running businesses and improving your performance. If you would like to listen to this author interview with Sam Carpenter of *Work the System*, you can do so by visiting: http://SingleFamilyOffices.com/Sam-Carpenter

The Single Family Office Essentials Checklist

There are many critical things that you must have in place to operate a single family office. The following is a checklist of items which you will want to at least consider:

- ✓ Software: You will need to look at what trading, payroll, reporting, market research, accounting, and basic office functionality software that you may require. Note: your trading and reporting software will typically be the most expensive software.

- ✓ Payroll & HR: You will want to create an employee handbook, get proper insurance, and make sure that you have your payroll and employee management systems and ethical policies in place. You may also want to have team members sign an NDA or confidentiality agreement.

- ✓ Office Space: Early on, as noted previously in this book, making sure you have proper office space set up is obvious. Many families find it beneficial to have the office space adjacent to operating businesses or at least close geographically as wealthy families are always very busy with constant demands on their time.

- ✓ Contractors: In addition to your core team members, you may want to leverage talent networks, or specialized consultants, to help with financial modeling, due diligence, on-site visits, co-investment work, or investment banking.

- ✓ Compliance & Legal Representation: Large family offices typically have an internal Chief Compliance Officer, but many use an outside counsel or attorney to supplement someone internally who has some level of regulatory knowledge.

- ✓ Legal Structure: Upfront, you will want to make sure that your legal structure is set up correctly, and make sure that your DBAs and current structures are still appropriate on an annual or quarterly basis depending on how quickly acquisitions are

The Single Family Office by Richard C. Wilson

being made. My advice would be to never work with an attorney that hasn't worked with at least 20 families that are worth over $50M, I'm not compensated for doing so but am happy to help steer families clear of attorneys who claim to work in the space but only do so once a year or once every few years. Setting up the wrong legal structure can expose you to liabilities, higher taxation rates, limited investment directives, and extra challenges when it comes to philanthropy and multi-generational planning.

A final note on this section—most single family offices have operating businesses and there may be ways to leverage your family office resources and expenses to benefit those holdings. For example, a $1.2B client of ours is a single family office that is acquiring several additional operating businesses and then streamlining their back office, operations, marketing/advertising, and distribution. This should not be confused with melding together your operating business completely with your family office so the two cannot be distinguished, but looking at where assets can be leveraged and used in creative ways.

Lessons learned from operating businesses can be applied to running a single family office as well, as it really is running a small business team that is focused on investing. Management, incentives and processes are just as important here in a single family office as they are in a traditional for-profit operating business.

Family Offices Operating in Tax Havens:
We are helping create $100M, $200M, and $850M family offices right now, and helping formalize a $10B+ single family office. In each case, the topic of jurisdiction and geographical  office vs. investment vehicle discussion arises. Many family offices ask me about how many families are set up in tax haven type locations, so here is a short video recorded in the Cayman Islands on this topic: http://SingleFamilyOffices.com/Tax-Havens

Interview with John Bishop

 In the following chapter on governance, we quote John Bishop regarding how his firm's governance processes have evolved. I had the opportunity to interview John on the topic of family office operations and governance and that conversation is shared below.

Richard C. Wilson: All single family offices are resource constrained; how has your thinking evolved on doing more things yourself or in-house vs. outsourcing and hiring consultants, service providers, and fund managers, etc.

John Bishop: Every SFO is resource constrained. Perhaps the most disappointing experience has been the lack of professionally qualified service providers to the SFO. We have dealt with numerous individuals, some part of reputable brand names, that do not understand the basics. I mean the basics of investing, wealth creation, management and preservation; these folks are trying their best, but are ignorant in the pure meaning of the word. We now require service providers/potential service providers to provide us with a resume before we discuss any matters. The gene pool can be limited in some organizations, and we are not entertained by spin. A growing requirement is for service providers to have a fiduciary responsibility to the SFO. As time evolves, the requirement to put the interest of the SFO ahead of the external organization becomes more significant. It's an interesting evolution.

Richard C. Wilson: Do you have any suggestions for someone setting up a new single family office in terms of operational best practices? What has your family learned about operating in a way that is efficient yet robust and thorough?

John Bishop: My advice to a family setting up an SFO is to map out a solid business plan. What is the purpose of the wealth? What are the needs of the family? What infrastructure is required? Surround yourself with professionally qualified individuals. Mapping out who is required to do what in the business plan reduces the divergent points of view.

Conclusion

The operations of your family office will vary based on your level of outsourcing, areas of investment, and how dynamically you are re-adjusting your portfolio. I hope the video content, interviews, and insights shared in this chapter were helpful in seeing a few different flavors of what that can look like in real life. The next chapter will discuss governance followed by Part 2 of the book on how to start a family office.

Chapter 4: Single Family Office Governance

"It takes 20 years to build a reputation and only five minutes to ruin it. If you think about that, you will do things differently."
- Warren Buffett

It is important for every single family office to have a governance structure that matches their size, complexity, and inter-generational needs and critical for almost every single family office to have some basic governance processes and procedures in place. Governance simply means that there are rules by which the family office operates, hires and fires, invests and donates money, disburses cash, etc. These rules guide decisions, processes, allocations of capital, and protect the family from internal family members or outside advisors from making decisions that could put the family's capital, interpersonal relationships or sustainability as an organization at risk.

Governance procedures are put in place to ensure long-term stability, accountability, transparency, and fairness among family members. Many families get torn apart from favoritism, mismanaged expectations, and inconsistent application of family rules that are not always followed by later generations.

I am sure a number of first generation family offices will see this entire chapter as simply extra paperwork and a thought exercise, but as other family members get involved, and a 2nd generation or later gets involved, governance becomes a critical asset by which hiring, firing, expansion, investment, and operational decisions are made. If you feel somewhat lost by the mention of governance, just think of it as management policies and rules for working together as a family—along with your family office team. These rules govern and enforce the operations discussed in the previous chapter.

Most single family offices that I work with have a top-down management system in place, with the patriarch or matriarch who created the wealth making the rules, as well as hiring, investing, and spending decisions. Some of these families have family councils and town hall-style meetings to seek input and votes from the entire family. Not many, but a few of the largest $1B+ families have more corporate-like boards of trustees, audit committees, and non-executive board members in place.

Free Single Family Office Interview: In a 40-minute-long recorded audio interview with a $1B+ single family office from California, we discuss governance and the value of developing an ethics policy. To listen to this audio interview, please see http://SingleFamilyOffices.com/Audio2

The following is a quote from John Bishop again, he recently converted his single family office into a multi-family office and he provided the following overview of his due diligence process and his governance structure:

> "Our due diligence process is thorough, and ever evolving. We have uncovered less than reputable individuals associated with investment opportunities, and walked away. In a previous life, when I was a financial statement auditor, I uncovered frauds. Appreciating the reality of disingenuous investment types, we have developed a 'checklist' to apply to anyone with whom we contemplate business transactions of a material amount. The first screen on the checklist is to make the counter-party/service provider aware of the fact that we examine their present and past representations. It has been interesting to witness some folks evaporate themselves during the due diligence process.
>
> We only work with people whom we get to know over a reasonable period of time and have a deep understanding of what they are offering. We start with a review of the resume to determine if the individual actually has the required skills and experience. The in-person meeting fills in the material not captured on the resume. Discussion with past and existing investors is mandatory. Everything has a beginning, middle, and end. If the beginning, middle, and end

are not clearly set in the investment proposal, we move on. It is not our responsibility to educate investment promoters to the basics; a clearly defined exit is a basic requirement of any investment proposal.

John Bishop Presents to a Group of Executives at One of Our

Recent Family Office Workshops

The investment fact pattern determines how we move forward with those whom we invest alongside; each opportunity is slightly different. Setting expectations early in the process saves both sides significant time. Walking through the details of the transaction sometimes uncovers 'blind spots' that need to be addressed. A thorough due diligence checklist that is applied to the revenue stream and expenditure flow is a solid starting point. Experience and professional judgment are the 'glue' that hold the due diligence process together, and 'hopefully' minimize the risk of nefarious activity arising.

The tone is set at the board level. We started with a 'standard' best practices framework and built in the specifics as time and experience have required. As an SFO moves from a 'monarchy' to a 'democracy' and multiple families, the requirement for a strong leader in corporate governance is required. For some people, governance is irrelevant, and for others it provides the backbone for responsible decision making. Those that do not view governance as paramount are educated during the governance setting process, or as they assume responsibilities in the organization.

It does not take much movement for the 'double-edged sword' of governance to become a priority to those that initially question its relevance. Our governance, policies, and procedures revolve around the line items on the financial statements as a starting point. By making the governance process relevant, adherence and acceptance of the requirements are easier."

The Cost of Poor Governance

To drive this point home, here are four examples of how things can go wrong without proper governance procedures in place:

1. One family worth over $500M has seen multiple children end up in jail, have problems with drugs, and end up completely broke by the third generation. The biggest loss in net worth for several family members was when a family friend attorney allowed for the almost complete dilution of the family's shares in their $1B+ a year company. After five years of failed lawsuits, the family is trying their best to move on. Governance policies on how advisors are selected, and how their objective or independent advice is confirmed, may have prevented this from happening.

2. A second generation daughter of a $100M+ family took $200,000 out of the family business, without permission and without anyone knowing for four years, to pay for her husband's medical bills. When confronted, she reasoned that it was not a lot of money and it may have saved his life. Governance steps such as an annual audit, checks on monthly expenditures, or dual approval for check writing and wire transfers could have caught this early on or prevented it from happening in the first place as this money could have been used to feed a drug habit or overly lavish lifestyle without anyone knowing.

3. A family I know in Singapore just gave their 29-year-old son a $2M downtown condo. His career as a 30 some year old include hobbyist photography and volunteering 10-15 hours a week at a few non-

profits. He is producing less than $10,000 a year in income and he spends about that much each month on average. I'm not sure if this was an intended outcome, but many families I speak with want to avoid this very situation. Governance rules over when family members get access to money, and how they earn that access or can spend the money, can go a long way in this area. Some families will match what someone earns, so if they want more money, they must go out and earn more—if they make $100,000 a year, then the family will match that sum with another $100,000 a year. If they don't care about money and choose a $20,000 a year job, that is their choice. Other families create a family bank, and only provide money for a single mortgage of up to $1M, approved types of education, and for approved entrepreneurial ventures to encourage family members to start businesses, and help create the next generation of wealth. Warren Buffett put it nicely when he said, "I want to give my kids enough money to do anything, but not so much money that they can do nothing."

4. Countless families dissolve a central family office and move to just individually managing money between the second and third generations because without communication among the family and governance in place, jealousy, favoritism, suspicions of hiring friends as advisors, etc. are rampant. One $3B+ family I met with in Europe recently has decided to split up their family's wealth into three buckets, and these different divisions of the family rarely invest or meet with each other.

As part of your Family Compass documentation, you should create a governance plan for your family office which includes the following details:

1. **Employee Handbook**: This is standard for any business, and there are countless templates out there which can be used. If it helps you get one in place, you can use our generic template as a starting point. Please note that you will need to customize this for your country, state, jurisdiction and check with a labor attorney or advisor to make sure you are not breaking any laws or creating some liability for yourself by not adjusting this for your own use in your legal jurisdiction: http://SingleFamilyOfficeAdvisors.com/Employee-Handbook

TABLE OF CONTENTS

Section Name	Section Number	Last Revised			
		Date	Date	Date	Date
Table of Contents	—		—	—	—
Welcome Message	1.0	1.1.10			
Company Operations	2.0	1.1.10	5.10.10		
Equal Opportunity, Immigration Law	3.0	1.1.10			
Equal Opportunity Statement	3.1	1.1.10			
Immigration Law Compliance	3.2	1.1.10			
Americans with Disabilities Act	3.3	1.1.10			
Policies and Rules	4.0	1.1.10			
Employment Classifications	4.1	1.1.10	5.10.10		
Confidentiality	4.2	1.1.10	5.10.10		
Personal Information	4.3	1.1.10			
Attendance and Punctuality	4.4	1.1.10	5.10.10		
Dress Code	4.5	1.1.10			
Work Hours and Overtime Pay	4.6	1.1.10	5.10.10		
Time Clock and Time Cards	4.7	1.1.10	5.10.10		
Lunch Periods	4.8	1.1.10			
Safety and Accident Rules	4.9	1.1.10			
Smoking	4.10	1.1.10			
Use of Company Property	4.11	1.1.10	5.10.10		
Use of Company Computers, E-mail, and Internet	4.12	1.1.10			
Substance Abuse	4.13	1.1.10			
Harassment and Discrimination Policy	4.14	1.1.10			
Performance & Salary Reviews, Provisional Period	4.15	1.1.10			
Payroll	4.16	1.1.10			
Reported Absences	4.17	1.1.10			
Benefits and Services	5.0	1.1.10			
Holidays	5.1	1.1.10			
Vacation	5.2	1.1.10	5.10.10		
Sick Leave	5.3	1.1.10	5.10.10		
Maternity Leave	5.4	1.1.10			
Funeral Leave	5.5	1.1.10			

Initials _____ G.T.C. Institute, LLC 3300 NW 185th Ave. Suite #108 Portland, OR 97229   2

Here is the table of contents for a past Employee Handbook used by one of my operating businesses. I have included this so you can see some of the common topics covered by the employee handbook

2. **Employee Hiring Criteria and Process**: This document is typically just one to two pages long, but details the important process of deciding who you will hire as long-term members to your team. Areas to consider include:

   a. Whether family members, friends of the family, stepchildren, or spouses are considered for positions and how they may be treated differently in this process.

   b. How compensation levels, benefits, and bonuses are calculated and adjusted for all employee levels.

The Single Family Office by Richard C. Wilson

c. Number of references required for each applicant. The best rule of thumb I have found is to call and email at least four, and try to meet in person with at least one of these references. At the very least, I try to conduct a video conference call with one or more reference.

d. Some families conduct required drug testing and criminal background checks on each applicant, no matter who they are.

3. **Business Partner & Service Provider Selection Criteria**: Many times, family offices hire employees, business partners, or service providers based on referrals and long-term relationships. So how do you avoid hiring someone just because they are a good friend of the family? And how do you avoid the fact that one person may trust this advisor, but their level of expertise for the cost of their services is subpar? While writing up your governance documentation, you will need to decide how you will balance these issues, and how strict you are with the hiring of advisors for critical functions, such as accounting and reporting, software solutions, investment consulting, legal advice, etc.

4. **Ethics Policy**: It is important that you have a formal ethics policy, separate from the employee handbook mentioned above, that sets the tone for how your family office operates and does business. If there are no set rules on what is acceptable and what isn't, then it will be hard to hold people accountable down the road.

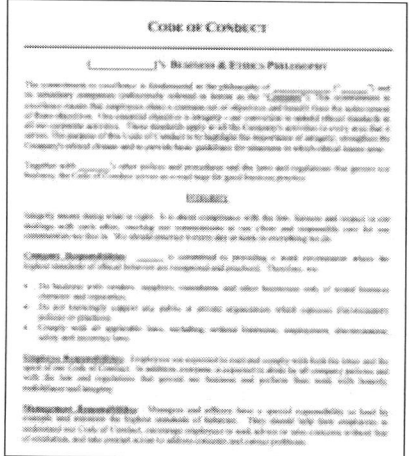

Free Ethics Policy Template: If you don't already have it from my last book on family offices, here is where you can download a template document for creating your own code of ethics. Again please note the following Ethics Policy Template should serve only as a starting point for creating your own, which you should do under the advisement of qualified counsel and advisors: http://SingleFamilyOffices.com/Ethics/

5. **Audit Process**: Who will be auditing the family office financials, or at least checking them for unusual activity? At the very least, an independent CPA who is not a family member should be doing a reasonability check. Still, most families who have $300M or more in assets have a formal audit done every year.

6. **Board Members & Independent Directors**: In addition to an advisory board, those families with over $500M or $1B may want to seriously consider creating a formal board which can help review compensation policies, corporate strategy, managing conflicts of interest, and ensuring the accuracy of the family's financial and accounting systems.

   Independent directors are non-family members who have an understanding of the single family office industry and can provide perspective, connections, advice, and guidance from a more objective standpoint. Many families bring in one or two independent directors to their board of directors, advisory board, or team.

7. **Family Meetings:** Most families who have moved past the first generation, the wealth creators, try to hold annual or quarterly meetings where as many family members as possible get together to discuss the family business, family investments, priorities, and the latest challenges. While many large families bring in family business consultants or facilitators, sometimes this is best done internally, as it can be a good opportunity to get the next generation engaged in the family business. Through these meetings, the next generation becomes aware of the responsibilities and hard work that are required of families maintaining significant wealth.

8. **Segregated Duties Regarding Money**: This is perhaps the most important governance area as a family grows larger through the second and third generations. Typically no single employee—whether they are a family member or not—should have the ability to withdraw large sums of money from the business and if someone is allowed that privilege, it should only be after receiving approval for that movement of funds. Areas to review include wire transfers, expense accounts, bonuses paid out, payments to contractors, and dual-signature wire transfer and check writing processes for anything over a set of amount, such as $5,000, or $10,000.

9. **Giving Plan & Approval Process**: Related to the area above, decisions on where family money is donated, in what amounts, and to what types of charities should be decided as a family and documented. Tax authorities are cracking down on the ultra-wealthy and a misinformed family member could cause criminal or expensive financial difficulties if rules are not followed while operating a foundation or giving money away to charity.

10. **Family Bank Policies**: Many wealthy families have capital available to help family members launch new business divisions or entirely new businesses. Some restrict these to a specific industry, require approval of older generations, or require the plans to be signed-off by at least three senior family members to ensure that advice is being sought and careful planning has been made before investing the capital in the new venture.

11. **Family Member Lines**: Who will be considered part of the family and who is able to receive the benefits of association in the form of educational support, access to credit from the Family Office Bank, etc.? If there is a divorce, does the non-bloodline ex-spouse still continue to get support? Do their children? What if someone is separated, but not divorced? These are things which many times can be handled as they come up, but as a family expands from second to third, fourth generations, and so on. The sprawling family will often face these complex and emotionally charged decisions. It is important to have objective rules setup upfront as early as possible to prevent bitterness from perceived favoritism real or not that can leave scars for a lifetime between family members.

12. **Investment & Portfolio Management Policies**: While your investment goals, strategy, and policies may be documented elsewhere, it is important in your governance documentation to talk about how you manage changes to your investment policy. What is the approval process before an investment is made? What controls can you put in place to make sure proper due diligence has been conducted? How should conflicts of interest be disclosed and what actions need to be taken to work through those? Who gets to decide what percentage of the portfolio will be invested in real estate, hedge funds, private equity or commodities?

13. **Key Performance Indicators (KPIs)**: Everyone from the CEO and CIO down to the analyst and associate should be judged by objective Key Performance Indicators. Ideally these KPIs should be monitored daily or weekly. KPIs help management and team members who want to self-manage, valuate their ability to meet goals, uphold standards, and allow for objective comparison of team members which can be helpful when some happen to be family members while others working in the family office are not.

14. **Secure Storage of Records**: As the regulatory burdens of family offices increase, it is important that everyone in your family office knows how records are kept, and who has access to them. For a variety reasons, full access to past and current records should be strictly limited, and those restrictions should be documented in your governance documentation.

Family Office Governance Video: To review a short video on family office governance, please visit:

http://SingleFamilyOffices.com/Governance

The Cost of Governance

It can take time to gain buy-in from an entire family on new governance measures for a family, and there are real costs associated, as well. Family meetings require travel, audits are expensive, boards can cost money to maintain, and financial reporting software costs more than one might expect. While it is nice to think families can try to act like big corporations in terms of governance, my experience has led me to believe otherwise. Many families that we work with do not have formal office space; they have family members scattered across the world who rarely get together even once a year, due to business demands, personal commitments, and global residencies.

Creating a governance process and system that works specifically for your family is what is most important and that includes considerations of time requirements, costs, buy-in from multiple generations, and practical implementation that matches the current state of your single family office. In the end, there should be confidence that investing in governance is going to provide more stability, predictability, fairness among family members and hired professionals, and long-term a more well-connected family with a sustainable management process of their capital.

 **Family Office Governance Worksheet:** It is important to us that families get real benefit, that their family offices, and that their conversations change upon reading this book. To help with that, and before ending this chapter, we would like to leave you with one additional tool—a family office governance worksheet. This can be viewed, printed, and easily shared in PDF or Word document formats, both of which are shared directly below:

 Governance Worksheet PDF:
http://SingleFamilyOffices.com/Family-Office-Governance.pdf

 Governance Worksheet DOC:

http://SingleFamilyOffices.com/Family-Office-Governance.doc

Conclusion

Governance best practices for single family offices are important, but often times are not seen as a critical activity until a horror story unfolds or is told by another wealthy family. These are the types of stories that are often made more real when shared at our live events, at times bringing speakers to tears on stage, and I would encourage any family skipping over this chapter without noting action items to think again about how to review and strengthen their family's governance policies.

Not making the rules of the game clear from the start can be destructive to both personal family relationships and the investment portfolio of the family. At the very least every single family office should have 1 pager of governance rules in place that is at least a start and there is no excuse not to have that very minimal level of rules in place before Day 1 of operating.

Part 2:
Starting a Single
Family Office

RES NON VERBA

wilson

Chapter 5: Creating Your Family Compass

"According to an old French motto, noblesse oblige—one must live up to one's name. The Rothschilds' condition of life has imposed on them a second motto: richesse oblige—one must live up to one's fortune."
- Guy de Rothschild

This chapter is the first of several in this part of the book on how to start a single family office. We have helped dozen of families put together their unique single family office structures and teams, and while some consultants charge $400 an hour to provide such advice we share here openly what we have learned as part of our mission to help this industry formalize, grow, and mature. Affluence affords families of considerable means the lifestyle, pleasures, and stability that solve many of life's otherwise daily problems. Still, money can also be a source of discord, especially when a family's money is shared between different family members, with different objectives, values, and processes.

It is important to establish a framework by which you can guide your family office through any issues. Your Family Compass is the set of documents and policies that will help you navigate your way through uncertainty and ensure that you never stray too far from the ideals, objectives, and policies that you value.

It is important to create a set of policies, guiding documents, and rules by which a family office will operate. Many single family offices talk about these issues in their motivation to start their organization, but never take the time to formalize these so that everyone is aware of them and invests and operates based on them.

Many families talk about all of the issues below, but never document them or put them into writing and this leads to misunderstanding. Something which was critical in building the family wealth, or is a top-three issue for parents or grandparents in a family, may be lost in translation as the next generation inherits wealth or control of the family business unless it is written out and communicated over and over again in many ways. The most successful process I have seen for transferring ideas from one generation to the next is using stories, having just a few core principles, and repeating these values often.

"Vision is perhaps our greatest strength... it has kept us alive to the power and continuity of thought through the centuries, it makes us peer into the future and lends shape to the unknown."

- Li Ka-shing, estimated to be the wealthiest man in Asia

The following are the core documents and policies needed to create your Family Compass:

1. Mission, Values, & Goals

You cannot hold a team accountable if you don't have a clear mission statement and know what objectives you would like them to accomplish. The mission of a single family office can look very different than that of an endowment, pension fund, or even traditional wealth management firm, so it is important to document these principles and objectives.

This is the first, fundamental task for creating your Family Compass. Writing down your family office mission will force you to settle on the exact objectives of your family office. Are you looking to grow your wealth with the goal of giving the majority of it to charities and worthy causes? Are you concerned with protecting your fortune for future generations? How will you use your means to support your family? The goals of your family office are important and you will need to have your objectives set before you start structuring the family office to meet those goals.

As you bring in advisors and structure your family office, you should think about the culture and values that you want to instill in your family and those that work on its behalf. When I meet successful single family office executives, I am often struck by how ingrained the values of the founder are in the executives, even if they are not related to the family. By defining your values, you will be able to more easily determine whether a new hire is a good fit or whether a business venture fits with your family's ideals.

Your goals, values, and vision should all be reflected in your mission. This document will lay the groundwork for the rest of your Family Compass.

Governance Policies: In case you skipped over part of the last chapter, each family office should have a thorough governance policy document to help communicate how decisions are made. This document should outline who has the power to make hiring decisions, investment portfolio allocation changes, compensation adjustments, profit distributions from the family office to family members, and when the next generation of the family is to receive capital and the process for those distributions. This document can help guide the family when there is a sudden death in the family, losses in the investment portfolio overall, or a dispute of some type. It also helps ensure that no single family member gains more control over the family wealth than was intended.

1. **Ethics Policy Document**: An ethics policy should explain what is acceptable behavior as a family member or employee of the family office. It may include elements such as personal use of family business assets, standards in dealing with third-party vendors, reporting of issues to a compliance officer or board member, insider trading concerns, conflicts of interest, anti-bribery policies, employment policies, privacy expectations, gift policies, press and media relations, and other areas unique to each family's operations and investments. To download an example ethics policy template, please visit http://SingleFamilyOffices.com/Ethics

2. **Core Values:** If you don't know what the top five values your team holds, it will be more challenging to hire, fire, and invest with conviction. Our team worked for seven years without values defined. To connect our team further, we defined our seven core values and within two weeks of defining them clearly, we fired two of our team members and "gracefully exited" a family office who had us on a $7k/month advisory retainer because all of those professionals were clearly at odds with what we stood for and the goals that we were trying to accomplish. These values can be especially valuable when

deciding which family members to include in the family office or core operating business operations, and which may not be a great fit for such a full-time position. We post our core values on the walls of our office, and on our board room table and talk about them during our weekly strategy meetings, to see an example of what we post to get an idea of how these help make decisions day-to-day please see http://SingleFamilyOffices.com/Values

3. **Investment Mandate**: This document helps guide where the capital should be invested, and exactly how it should be deployed, diversified, and protected. It should detail priorities in terms of capital preservation, taxation, growth, income, etc. It should also balance income and risk management needs with the liquidity and cost concerns in the space where investments are being made. For example, one family I know invests exclusively in real estate and the commodities industry and their investment mandate would involve many details around illiquidity of investments, cash and liquidity needs of the family, and how various investments should be ranked or evaluated amongst themselves. Many times, this document is created by the Chief Investment Officer upon their arrival, or is discussed weekly with the investment team. The document may need to be formally revised monthly or bi-monthly, and will most likely need input from several members of the family, as well as the Chief Investment Officer and Chief Executive Officer of the family office. It is important to not let your highly paid CIO, influential board member, or other family offices dictate your investment mandate, those individuals can help provide input and a roadmap on how to get from A to B, but your objectives, mission, and values should tell you where "B" is for you and your family, or the family you are serving.

4. **Key Performance Indicators:** As noted in the previous chapter when talking about Verne Harnish's book, a Key Performance Indicator (KPI) is an objective measure of performance of a task, investment, or completion of a regular critical action within the family office. It is helpful to implement KPIs for each member on the team in order to manage and evaluate their performance and that of the family office overall. If you have a team of five professionals running your single family office, it can be useful to create a total of 15 KPIs and three "smart numbers" which combine various KPIs to

give you an overall picture of the effectiveness of the team and health of the portfolio.

5. **Systems & Processes**: Within a year of starting a single family office, standard processes should be developed so that each team member could be replaced by another professional, and quickly that new person should be able to understand what is going on and how the work was being carried out. Most professionals carry out 5 to 15 processes that directly correlate with the value they add to the organization. Make it a requirement for everyone on your team to know what these processes are, what steps are taken to get them done every week or month, and document them within an overall operations binder for the family office. Each individual then can have their own mini-process book for how their job gets done, and key executives should be able to see how the whole family office is operating.

I have met face-to-face with over 1,000 family offices globally, and I can count on one hand how many have all 5 of these points in place and updated. Doing so will give your team less turnover, more accountability, and allow important decisions to be made with more clarity than otherwise possible.

Radio Show Interview: I was recently interviewed for a national radio show called *Money In Your Life* on the importance of a family charter, values, and objectives when it comes to setting up a family office and protecting your capital: You can download this radio show or stream it online here: http://SingleFamilyOffices.com/Radio

Richard was interviewed for Money In Your Life and discussed some of the values and goals that are common amongst single family offices.

Your family compass does not need to be a professionally-bound, 200-page manifesto. Whether it takes your family two long weekends to come up with 10 pages documenting beliefs, priorities, and objectives, or whether it takes you three years to put this together, the process of doing this is part of the benefit. Many times, these topics get very little, if any, table time at family gatherings and meetings.

The cost of not creating a compass for your family is incredibly high; it can lead to additional family disputes and mismanaged expectations, loss of capital due to misaligned priorities within the family, slow decision making among voting family members, and even lawsuits. In some cases, ignoring this area could make the difference between a family sustaining wealth through the second, third, and fourth generation. It is also very hard to articulate exactly what you are looking for to your advisors, service providers who call on you, or own team members if you have not thought it through and explicitly written it out as a family or single family office team.

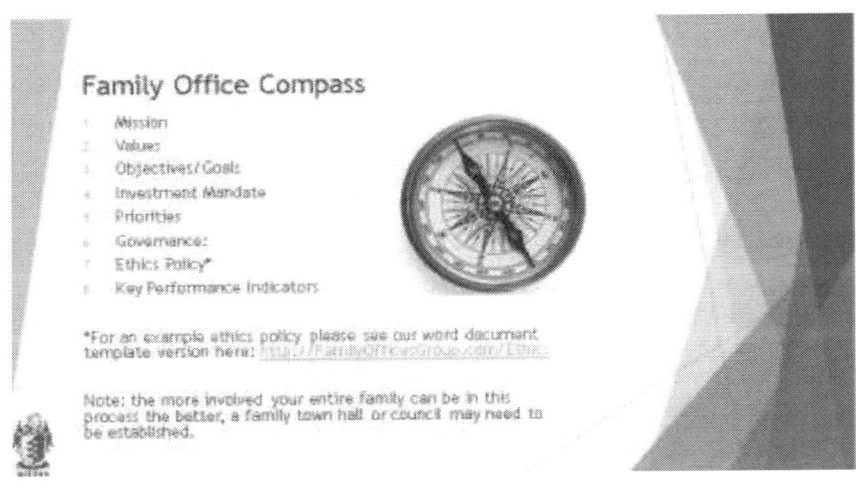

If you need assistance in setting up these documents, please let our team know; we can make this process straightforward and effective.

Compare Your Family Office to Others

We recently conducted a survey covering over 100 family offices globally, and the following responses show the level of organizational sophistication among the family offices within our association that completed the survey. You can see from this chart that less than half of all family

The Single Family Office by Richard C. Wilson

offices surveyed have fully formalized family office operations.

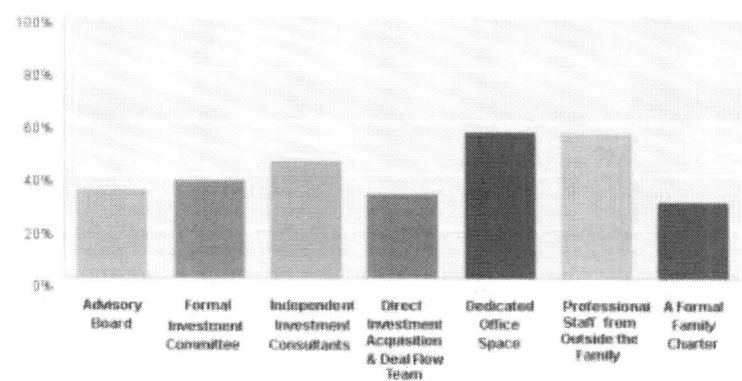

Answer Choices	Responses	
Advisory Board	34.07%	46
Formal Investment Committee	37.78%	51
Independent Investment Consultants	45.19%	61
Direct Investment Acquisition & Deal Flow Team	32.59%	44
Dedicated Office Space	56.30%	76
Professional Staff from Outside the Family	55.56%	75
A Formal Family Charter (Goals, Mission, Objectives, Values, etc.)	29.63%	40

In a few chapters, you will have a chance to read my interview with Geoffroy Dedieu, CEO of the TY Danjuma single family office. Here is an excerpt from that interview that is especially relevant to this chapter:

Richard C. Wilson: If you were to advise someone on creating a family office, what do you think the first step should be, and out of all of the steps, what are two to three critical things to get right, and focus the most energy on?

Geoffroy Dedieu: Step number one is, just like for any business decision the family took in the business area, have a well-structured, detailed plan. Write it down: what are your objectives, what do you need, what are the Key

Success Factors (KSFs), what will it cost? There is no reason to be less structured when it comes to creating an SFO than the family was when it created its business.

Step number two is to hire a veteran of the industry with a proven track record. Step number three is to let him/her gather enough information to map the current situation, prepare a total wealth report, inclusive of a risk register and a 90-day action plan. Depending on the complexity of the family and the political or relational landscape in an emerging market situation, this could take three to six months.

Conclusion

While the next few chapters dive deeper into the process of creating your family office, it all is based on reading your Family Office Compass first and knowing where you want to go. I have had dozens of conversations with journalists, radio hosts, and ultra-wealthy families who ask me about my recommendations and guidance on what to do first while creating a single family office. I always have the same initial reaction to the question: Nothing. Do nothing, until you know exactly what you want and don't want, and what your priorities, objectives, mission, and values are from the very start. Everything else is constructed based on what the compass has told you.

Chapter 6: Starting a Single Family Office

While this entire book is instructional for anyone looking to start a family office, this chapter will address this topic directly. The guidance here is taken from my work with families, including my most recent work with a $150M and $1B family in 2014.

Creating a Single Family Office Video: This video from Prague is on creating a single family office and provides details on what your family should expect and some of the costs and hurdles to launching.

http://SingleFamilyOffices.com/Creating

This chapter will share many of the important aspects that you should consider as you start your single family office.

Timeline: Many single family offices take three to eight months to establish, while more deliberate families may take up to three years to fully establish and begin operating full-force. Often, the most time-consuming components of launching a single family office are the acquisition of talent, and balancing of diverse family member needs and requests. For some, the experience of attempting to start a family office is enough to convince them that they want nothing to do with the investment decisions of the rest of their family.

Family Tree: It is helpful to start the process by drawing out the family tree, starting with the original wealth-creating individual, and maintaining a current version of this with G1, G2, and G3 individuals labeled as such. This will ensure that all of the advisors to the family office remember exactly how many generations are involved, and the full size of the family while offering their input on strategies to implement. It is helpful to do this visually, not in a two to three page typed-out document.

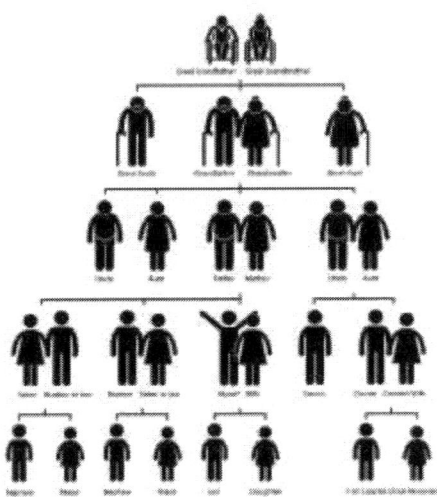

Family Tree Example for Depicting Relationships

Mind Mapping: Another visual tool you should create when you start a family office is a "mind map" or hierarchy of the advisors you are using and the team you have built. Many will find that before starting their own single family office, you simply had the wealth creator at the middle, with direct lines out to five to seven advisors who don't speak with each other more than once a year.

After your family office is created, you should at least have appointed a CEO, COO, or Chairman of the Board who coordinates between all of the experts on the family's behalf. If you launch a formal family office with several full-time staff, then your organization may take on a traditional hierarchical format. You can create your own Mind Map with free software like Bubbl.us or simply using PowerPoint.

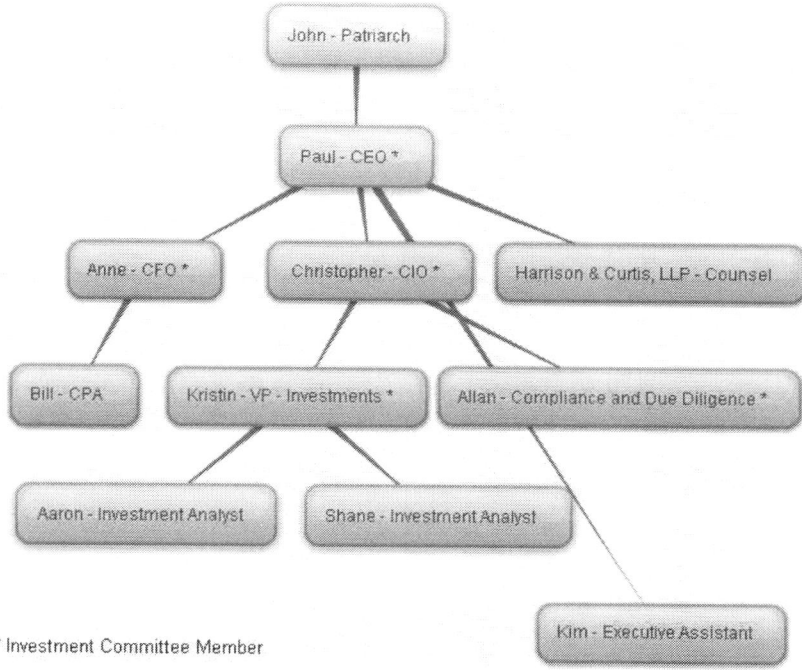

The Mind Map Above Shows an Example Family Office Structure

Creating a Family Office—Pantheon Process: One of the core values in our office at Billionaire Family Office and other related Wilson Holding Company operating businesses is "Pantheon Thinking" which to us means thinking long-term over a generation of time about what we are building, what value we are providing, and why we are investing energy into a project. Below is the five-part process that we are using right now to help one of our family clients create their single family office:

1. **Listening & Needs Assessment** (Estimated Time Needed—Two Weeks): Identify what is known, expected, review past troubles, stories of others to emulate. Follow on active dialogue to dig into issues deeper, explore and define priorities.

2. **Family Office Compass Construction** (Estimated Time Needed— One to Three Months): Values, Mission, Objectives, Constraints, Governance, Ethics, Confidentiality, Public Image, Life management, etc. (Active dialogue).

3. **Resource & Talent Assessment** (Estimated Time Needed—Two Weeks): Family Office Construction Plan, Timeline & Budget, Advisory Board Construction & Missing Professional Roles.

4. **Implementation Phase** (Estimated Time Needed—Two to Six Months).

5. **Ongoing Operations, Processes, and Investment Decision Making Policies** (Estimated Time Needed—Ongoing).

Video: Here is one of the more popular videos that I recorded on starting a family office:

http://SingleFamilyOffices.com/Startup

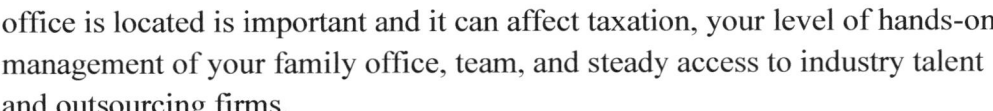

Family Office Location: Where your family office is located is important and it can affect taxation, your level of hands-on management of your family office, team, and steady access to industry talent and outsourcing firms.

While many families simply set up their single family office in the location where their wealth was created, but some states are less tax friendly to millionaires and billionaires. For this reason, many single family offices are based or structured in places that have lower taxes, such as Texas, Florida, and Nevada in the United States. Abroad, favored destinations are London, Bahamas, Puerto Rico, Monaco, Singapore, Switzerland, and the Cayman Islands.

We have identified Florida as an especially attractive location for many family offices, particularly Miami. The state has established a pro-business climate and receptiveness to affluent individuals, unlike some other states or locales that tax businesses, investments, and wealth excessively. There are a growing number of family offices establishing offices in Miami and many large single and multi-family offices at least have one team member in Florida. In addition to our New York City office, I personally have moved to Key Biscayne, an island community just a few minutes from Miami.

In some places, such as the Cayman Islands, legal structures and representatives are all that is tied to the location. But with most of the family living nearby, they may have changed their place of residence to establish their single family office. In some cases, changing the location of the family office could save enough money annually to operate the entire single family office.

Video: If you haven't considered starting a virtual family office, you may want to look into this. Here is a short video I recorded in Berlin on Virtual Family Offices: http://SingleFamilyOffices.com/Virtual

Accounting & Administration: While the CFO or CIO of most single family offices has some form of accounting background, the accounting and administration work at many small to mid-sized family offices is outsourced. The administration in a family office involves formal reporting, value calculations, and distribution calculations for various members of the family. Traditional accounting is more challenging for a family office than a typical business because of illiquid assets such as: real estate, operating businesses, large public stock market investments, hedge fund allocations, and venture capital or private equity commitments. Any of these illiquid investments may pose valuation challenges and potential tax liabilities. Creating systems and processes to accomplish this requires some powerful technology solutions.

Technology Solutions: Many family offices face significant IT expenses to cover accounting, fund administration, reporting, aggregation of trading, overall portfolio risk vs returns tracking, data room services, risk management, and inter-family or team communication. Aggregating accounts and building custom reporting or accounting systems can become very costly. Many family offices spend $20,000-$100,000 on technology and software each year, but larger ones often spend over $200,000 annually.

Direct Investing & Operating Businesses: Our research indicates that more than 85% of single family offices own operating businesses, and typically these holdings make up 40-75% of the family's net worth. One 6th generation family that I know has diversified their investments across a dozen different industries, while others that I know only invest in certain industries like commodity businesses, for example, because that is where they made their wealth initially. While direct investing has always been a top priority for Asian and Middle Eastern families, it is just now thriving as a core component of single family offices in the United States which in the past had done direct investing, but also had trusted more in traditional private equity funds and the public markets. We have included this area in a few chapters in this book because it is critical that families who are newly ultra-wealthy or operating a single family office know how other families manage their direct investments, operate these holdings, co-invest with other families, and participate in club deals.

Investment Management: Traditional investment management covers a family's investing activities in publicly traded equities, cash equivalents, real estate, commodities, hard assets, bonds, money market funds, REITS, mutual funds or ETFs, MLPs, and alternative investment funds, such as private equity or hedge funds. Part Three of this book touches on these areas of investment management in detail.

Risk Management: Every area of investment brings with it different types of risks. For each type of investment (real estate, operating business, alternative investment fund, etc.), your risk should be analyzed separately or classified so that the unique risks to that area can be assessed by a professional who is familiar with the area. Families can manage risk by using seasoned investment professionals, risk consultants, independent insurance advisors, and, to some degree, their internal systems and real-time investment reporting. While forming your family office, you will need to assess which types of risk are most prevalent given the investments you are making, and what processes, professionals, and systems are in place to mitigate those risks. Managing risk and protecting capital are the chief reasons why most family offices are established.

Insurance: By the time someone becomes ultra-wealthy, they typically have multiple types of insurance in place. The goal of the single family office is to assess the technical coverage of the insurance against the real risks that the individual or family faces. Many policies may have overlapping coverage, exclusions, or technicalities that could be devastating for the client. The types of insurance often used for families of exceptional wealth include personal and business property, excess liability or umbrella policies, general liability, and life insurance. This list is not comprehensive and an insurance professional with extensive experience in the field should be consulted or hired in-house before making changes to coverage. The level of insurance will depend on the operations, direct investments, liquidity of the family's wealth, and intergenerational considerations.

Philanthropy and Charitable Giving: Philanthropy can be a way to unite multiple generations of a family, create good press for a business, and add meaning to an ultra-wealthy family's work. One client of mine explained to me that he didn't need any more money for himself; he wouldn't even know what to do with it really. He simply works now to give more away every year to children in need and that is what motivates him to make sure his businesses perform well now.

There is a lot of confusion and even conflict around the idea of giving away money that the family has worked so hard to earn. The issues you may face include:

1. A lack of understanding by second and third generation family members, which may lead to frustration, arguments within the family, and disappointment if someone feels like they are not getting their expected "fair share." Establishing your family's core values, objectives, and mission first will help avoid this type of trouble.

2. Being aware of the taxation rules and documentation procedures that apply to writing off monetary donations to a non-profit or foundation administered by a family member.

3. Ensuring that there is some governance and process around how and when the money is given away. Once these are set in place, you need to resolve how you deal with giving opportunities which don't fit within those procedures. A governance process should be followed even when exceptions arise.

I grew up around my father advising ultra-wealthy individuals and non-profit hospitals and universities on philanthropy. My father has raised over $1B for these groups through this philanthropy advisory work and this led to an early appreciation for what goes into ensuring donors are getting a positive ROI as well as transparency on their donated money.

Privacy & Control: While setting up a family office, the level of public exposure needs to be decided early on in the process. Will the family have a public-facing website or will everything be hidden behind a password-protected area online? Will staff have business cards, encouraged to write books, allowed to attend conferences and speak at seminars, or will they even be allowed to speak on the record in any way? If so, is there a process that they must follow regarding certain non-disclosure rules? Many $1B+ single family offices have been quoted in this book, speak at our events, and otherwise provide value publicly; but most of these executives have little direct motivation to do so, as they can't accept new clients even if they are approached by them. Privacy policies regarding family matters should be set up from the beginning and violations of these policies should be met with swift repercussions in order to set an example to other team members. As I mentioned in my last book on family offices, many people in this space like to operate on the theory that "a submerged whale does not get harpooned." As a number of families have learned, once a thread is revealed, a media professional will keep pulling until he or she unravels a story. This might mean that the original story is blown out of proportion or exaggerated in subsequent reports. Privacy controls and media relations processes help to guard against these issues. One simple compromise is to create a holding company which operates under The XYZ Single Family Office name instead of the family's name to keep the press and general public at arm's length away from the actual family.

Security: Even families who primarily reside in the United States have a wide variety of security measures in place, ranging from identify theft prevention, background checks, ex-military drivers, random insurance, and bulletproof cars and bodyguards while traveling abroad. Defining what these risks are, how much it would take to mitigate them, and how far the family wants to go to improve their safety is something that should be discussed upfront. Often, this important issue is glossed over by traditional wealth management firms and private banks.

Press & Public Relations: From the beginning, it should be decided what public relations and press goals exist. As we discussed in the previous

The Single Family Office by Richard C. Wilson

chapter, a family's PR needs depend greatly on their investing and personal activities. Does the family want to stay 100% below-the-radar, or use their foundation and philanthropic activities to shed a positive light on the family and connect commercial enterprises?

Some families may want to capture their legacy within a book and video format to help carry on their message to future generations or the general public. Many families shy away from attention, but don't often have an open discussion of the trade-offs involved in adopting a public vs. private strategy.

Concierge Services & Lifestyle Management: Many single family offices

have the side benefit of helping leverage the patriarch or entire family with lifestyle and concierge services. These services can include assistance with purchasing concert tickets, chartering a helicopter or private plane, ordering a wedding dress, renting a car, or simply planning a trip.

These services could also involve interviewing potential nannies for a child, visiting prospective private schools and evaluating them, or helping manage the family's calendar and activities. Most multi-family offices shy away from offering any concierge services because they are afraid of losing a $100 million account over ordering the wrong wedding dress, but this is a significant benefit of having a single family office.

Strategic Partners & Outsourcing Solutions: Many entrepreneurs are thrifty at heart; they don't want to spend too much money on an area like an accounting department if they don't feel that is their strength. This thriftiness and the hope that a lean single family office can be created drive many organizations to refer their investment work to an outsourced chief investment officer service or investment consultant. This allows the family office to focus their energy exclusively on those few industries that they feel like they have a strategic advantage in, such as real estate, commodity investments, or industry-specific operating businesses.

The desire for an internal focus on core competencies has led to a major trend of outsourcing many areas of a single family office and dozens of options exist for those who wish to do so. The number one strategic priority in this first phase of setting up a single family office should be in creating the strongest brain trust possible for the family.

Scenario Planning: While deciding what expertise you need on your board and core team, think through the top five to seven most likely and extreme scenarios and how you would react to each of them. These scenarios could include another Great Recession, death of the patriarch or matriarch, a lawsuit, a change in industry norms, and other undesirable events. If you agree on what these scenarios are, write out a series of step-by-step instructions and assign the power for someone to carry those out in case the situation ever arises. You will then be able to identify which experts are still missing from the advisory board or core team. This type of scenario planning activity can create an improved sense of comfort for the wealth creator.

Critical Questions: Anyone that recommends a type of family office that you should create before at least asking many of the questions provided to you below as a minimum starting point may not understand your personal goals, values, and objectives. The following should serve as a starting point for getting down to the core needs of your single family office:

Information Gathering:

1. How did you first hear about family offices, single family offices, and what is your understanding of what a single family office is and isn't?

2. What form of a single family office or wealth management solution do you have in place right now?

3. What has been your experience with this current solution and past ones that were in place before it?

4. Why do you want to form a single family office?

5. Are there a few single family offices or ultra-wealthy individuals that you have heard of or would like to emulate in the creation of your family office?

The Single Family Office by Richard C. Wilson

6. What are your top two fears in setting up a single family office; what do you want to avoid at all costs?

7. What is more important to you, capital preservation, growth of wealth, taxation, or income?

8. Which of these items is most important to you in managing your non-operating-business investible assets: peace of mind with light oversight, active involvement, extreme diversification, or focused industry investments in areas that you understand?

9. Can you provide us access to your balance sheet, financial reports, estate plans, and other financial details so that we can put together a high-level view of your finances?

10. Who are your most trusted advisors?

11. If not already mentioned, who do you trust most in the areas of wealth management, taxation, real estate, direct investments, and trust & estate planning?

12. Which of your advisors do you need to replace, and which are good but not great?

13. Is there an advisor or two so excellent that a second opinion to make sure everything is set up right legally, operating effectively, and insured to the right levels would not be needed?

14. What pieces of wealth management and asset protection do you have in place that you would want to keep going forward?

15. What insurance policies do you current have, and what assets are these protecting?

16. What is your total liquid and illiquid net worth and where is that money invested right now?

17. What types of legal structures do you have set up around your assets, real estate, public market, land, business, joint venture, co-investment, and other types?

18. What level of retirement planning and asset protection strategies do you have in place now or would like to have in place?

19. What is your investment risk appetite?

20. What are your income needs annually for you and your extended family?

Digging in with Deeper Questions

1. Is it most important to be quick, or lean, or have ultimate control and transparency on decisions and the investment portfolio? This mindset going into these deeper questions is important, as every option has a trade-off.

2. Do you want to keep a low profile or be a high profile single family office that attracts attention and as a result, deal flow as well? How will you "fly under the radar" and keep a low profile if that is what you want to achieve?

3. What type of day-to-day control, management, and decision-making responsibilities do you want for yourself?

4. To what degree do you want to rely on family members for core family office positions such as CEO, CIO, Portfolio Manager, etc.?

5. What is your annual budget for operating the single family office operations?

6. How are investments being structured?

7. How will you set up legal structures and investments so that multi-generations are being considered or planned for in each case? Or is that even important to you and your family right now?

8. How will you insert the perspective and opinion of your tax advisor into every investment move you make, so mistakes aren't made on investments, purchases, location decisions, etc.?

9. Where are your personal and business assets located now, and what possible locations would you want to have an office or team in, vs. your personal residence?

10. How will complex assets be managed, such as sports teams, commercial real estate, boats, vacation houses, bullion, etc.?

11. Have you spoken to an attorney on where to domicile your assets, and have you considered that being different from where your team is based?

The Single Family Office by Richard C. Wilson

12. Who is going to be on your advisory board and investment committee and how often do you plan on having those two groups meet?

13. How will charitable giving decisions be made?

14. Will someone be in charge of family concierge services, such as family trip planning, car rentals & purchases, etc.?

15. Are you going to set up a family bank of some type, and are intra-family loans provided if certain terms are agreed to?

16. What powers and real decision-making authority will the CEO or President of the single family office have, particularly if that person is not going to be you?

17. What will be the scope of investments for the organization—will you only invest in one industry, diversify into all types of hedge funds, CTA funds, private equity funds, real estate, etc.?

18. How strategic vs. tactical do you want to be with your investments? Do you want to have two investment committees—one that is strategic and meets monthly and one that is tactical and meets weekly and can meet on-demand intra-day as needed?

19. What is the investment mandate and priorities, how much income is needed to be produced monthly, how important is holding cash, preserving capital, investing globally, etc.?

20. How will you set up governance for the single family office? Who will be able to hire service providers, fund managers, etc. in a way that ensures favors aren't being done for college friends, or family members of employees or your own family, to the detriment of the investment portfolio.

21. What types of insurance, security, and risk mitigation solutions do you need in place for your organization and family overall?

22. How will you define success for your single family office?

Implementation Questions

1. By what date would you like the single family office to launch and be baseline operational?

2. Who is going to be the project manager in charge of this single family office launch to make sure that bottlenecks are taken care of, and details are managed along the way?

3. What do you foresee as the top three challenges in getting launched? Here is a hint, identifying and recruiting talent, and deciding on legal domicile/residence location can both slow things down by an entire year or more in some cases.

4. What is needed to get operational vs. fully launched and operating in a more robust long-term established manner?

5. What daily, week, and monthly things need to happen like clockwork in the single family office to operate at full steam? Who needs to create what report, what systems are needed, what daily meetings, payroll processing, portfolio reviews, etc.? Create an operational binder for the single family office which answers this question.

Family Office Startup Checklist: The following is a high-level list of things which you should consider having in place while forming a single family office. This list is not exhaustive, and would need some customization for each family's unique needs and goals, but it should help guide the process.

✓ A Family Compass document has been created to ensure that from the beginning, the vision, objectives, goals, values, mission, and history of the family has been documented and incorporated into the investing and operating plans of the single family office.

✓ An operating plan on how day-to-day activities are carried out within the single family office has been established. A binder has been created which documents each of the Key Performance Indicators and critical processes to ensure the family office is operating as it should.

✓ Financial controls are in place to prevent embezzlement, unauthorized investments, and style drift within an investment portfolio.

✓ A core team has been identified and one individual has been appointed as the single family office CEO and/or CIO to act as the key executive making operational and/or investment decisions.

✓ Ethics and governance policies have been established to set out expectations for how personnel decisions are made, who can use family assets for personal benefit, how conflicts of interest should be managed, and what ethical obligations each family member is under.

- ✓ Legal structures set up properly for real estate holdings, operating businesses, investments, etc. Legal counsel has reviewed the entities to ensure that if one goes bankrupt or gets sued that it would not take down the entire family empire.

- ✓ Independent insurance professionals have been consulted who are not on commission to sell you more insurance to ensure proper coverage.

- ✓ Contingency plans for death, disasters, divorces, etc. how adaptations to breaking up the larger family office or changing family goals/values will be dealt with, etc.

- ✓ A diverse advisory board and investment committee have been established with policies on how they operate and help oversee governance issues within the single family office.

Interview with Abe Tatar of the Hysek Group:

 To help provide some insight on one family's single family office, we interviewed Abe Tatar from the Hysek Group, a single family office based in London and New York. Abe offers great insights on the differences between European and American family offices and how his family office operates globally:

Richard C. Wilson: Do you see a big difference in European-based single family offices vs. single family offices in America?

Abe Tatar: Definitely there is a difference, mainly the culture. The culture in our office, whether in NY or London is the same where we are structured like a private equity firm. Quite a few European and even Middle Eastern SFOs are typically run by a trusted friend or advisor of a principal family member and all professionals who work there are close friends and relatives of the principal. U.S. SFOs tend to hire professionals based on professional skills and experience. At Hysek, we prefer to hire candidates with backgrounds in investment banking or private equity, with an extensive network of contacts, sector knowledge, transaction structuring experience, and business development and deal originations skills.

Richard C. Wilson: Do you see different types of deal flow reach each office?

Abe Tatar: In the U.S., we see some very high quality and off-the-radar deals which we like to refer to as Off-Market Transactions. Such deals are generated by our own network of contacts who prefer to keep such deals within a closed ecosystem of trusted investors, as opposed to over-shopped and over-marketed deals. Out of London, we tend to see good quality deals that have been marketed for quite a bit. An advantage of a London presence is that it provides us access to some proprietary deal flow from frontier markets that offer significant returns.

Richard C. Wilson: What made your family want to start a single family office in the first place, and what resources did you leverage while doing so?

Abe Tatar: Rather than outsourcing the wealth management and preservation to third parties such as private client groups, MFOs, or even private equity firms, an SFO provides a better platform for managing a family's wealth and multi-generational transfer of wealth. The main benefits are governance, privacy, alignment of interests, control, and potential higher returns.

Richard C. Wilson: How important is governance to your family office, do you have formalized governance procedures in place and if so, what led you to create those procedures?

Abe Tatar: Governance is extremely vital to our operation. With the family's investment objectives in mind, the team provides strong governance and oversight to handle the complexities of the family's wealth and to avoid future conflicts. Strict oversight over operational risks, performance, and management reporting enables our advisory team and principals to make effective decisions that meet our investment objectives.

Video: In this video from Berlin, Richard offers the Top 5 Mistakes in Starting a Single Family Office:

http://SingleFamilyOffices.com/Mistakes

Conclusion

The process of creating a single family office is complex, but it is a process that can be adjusted and implemented for families ranging from $30 million to $30 billion in net worth. Asking the right questions can sometimes be more powerful than any piece of advice a consultant or advisor could provide to a family looking to start a single family office. If you have comments based on the creation of your single family office, or areas you think we should expand upon please let us know.

Chapter 7: Partners, Vendors, & Service Providers

One of the benefits of the family office industry's recent maturation is that there are more options for business partners and service providers than ever before. Many single family offices like to run very lean and have most of their activities outsourced, with just a few key in-house activities that the team feels they have a competitive edge in delivering.

The following are the types of services and partners you can engage with while running your single family office:

Outsourced Chief Investment Officer or Investment Consulting Firms: One of the most popular options for single family offices is hiring an investment consulting firm or outsourced chief investment officer to help them make investment decisions. Many times, a family is comfortable investing on their own in real estate or bonds, for example, but they lack confidence investing in many other asset classes.

I am working with one family with a $1 billion family office and there is only one full-time professional managing the investments, the family patriarch's son. As you can imagine, with $1 billion under management and only one full-time individual manning the helm, the son's time is stretched pretty thin. The family has deep expertise in direct investments, so the area they need help with is the more liquid investments and hedge funds. To compensate for their weaknesses outside of direct investments, they are in the process of hiring an outsourced investment consulting firm which focuses primarily on ultra-wealthy families and single family offices. Chapter 18 of this book is dedicated to discussing the trend of using outsourced CIOs because it is so important for single family offices to understand.

Fund-of-Funds or Alternative Investment Advisory Firms: While the fund-of-funds name has seen better days, many family offices I know do still invest in a few fund-of-funds because they don't have the resources in-house to hire and fire 10-15 hedge fund managers. Also, once you get above a $20M or $30M+ size of investment, you can negotiate more on fees, get customized fund-of-fund portfolios, and advisory services included, which make the deal even better for those families willing to commit those levels of assets to a fund.

Just as some wealth management firms are incorporating the words "multi-family office" into their wealth management firm names, many fund-of-funds are finding that their conversations go better if they instead refer to themselves as alternative investment advisory firms or hedge fund advisory firms. These firms still offer a fund-of-funds structure, but the rebranding removes some of the unwanted baggage associated with the fund-of-funds model.

Family Office Accounting, Reporting, and Back Office Solutions: Many single family offices look to hire professionals who can wear many hats and thus your CFO, CEO, or analyst will typically already possess enough accounting expertise to complete all reporting in-house.

If this doesn't happen while building your core team, then I would strongly encourage that you outsource this activity and not hire someone full-time just to focus on this aspect. The only exceptions are if you manage well over $1B in assets under management or feel like reporting is a particular blind spot that has hurt your performance in the past.

Fund Administration & Trust Administration Work: Fund administration work is different from simple family office accounting and reporting solutions. This area is most relevant for those family offices that have complex trust or fund structures in place. For example, if you run a fund of hedge funds for your family or a few other families, then you may be well served having a third-party group assist with valuation, reporting, and administration. This will lead to more trust, reduce your chances of fraud, limit your error-related litigation exposure, and it will free up your team to focus on other activities.

Direct Investments, Co-Investing, & Investment Banking: Many family offices are pitched by investment bankers on deals, such as buying a $20M retail business or a $10M piece of real estate. What is less common is for a single family office to have an investment banker working on mandates exclusively for them. It can be very advantageous if you can identify an investment banker who is experienced, well-connected, and available to work on sourcing very specific types of acquisition opportunities. My family, for example, hired someone earlier this year full-time and he investigates acquisition targets, and potential new business launches for Wilson Holding Company. We have this role in-house, but it might be less expensive for you to partner with someone outside of the core team.

Information Technology (IT) Solutions: As mentioned earlier some large single family offices spend $20,000 to $200,000 every year on information technology solutions. These expenses typically have to do with accounting, reporting, trading execution, and investment management needs which are customized for that family. Still, these costs are not necessary for every family office and many family offices could reduce their overhead in this area if they carefully evaluated their IT needs and expenses. Additionally, technology is becoming increasingly web- and cloud-based, which simplifies the very basic IT needs at most businesses. If you do foresee complex IT needs, however, there are dozens of firms that will work under retainer, on one-off projects, or hourly for your family office. If you can contract this work to an IT firm, you may be able to avoid hiring someone full-time, providing space for that person in your office, and hoping that they will be able to meet a high percentage of your IT needs and challenges as those arise.

Virtual Family Office Solutions: We have a whole chapter on virtual family offices, but it is important to note that a virtual family office essentially outsources everything to business partners and service providers. The only thing done by the CEO of a virtual family office is quarterbacking or managing the other professionals who are delivering the value to the family being served. Please see Chapter 19 for more on virtual family offices.

Compliance Officer or Outsourced Compliance Firm: Depending on the complexities of your businesses and investments, you may require a chief compliance officer or outsourced compliance firm to make sure that your firm is adhering to the latest regulations and requirements. This is especially true if you are making alternative investments, taking outside capital for investments, or engaging in similarly sophisticated arrangements that may fall under a statute that you never heard of but that could ultimately lead to fines, penalties, or lawsuits if violated. In the post-Dodd-Frank era, many family offices and private investment firms have had to reevaluate their compliance situation and make sure that they qualify for exemptions to any new laws.

Legal Assistance: It is critical to have a trusted legal counsel advising you and your single family office. Many single family offices have a legal counsel on retainer or working in-house. Some families prefer to have a highly-respected law firm on retainer so that they have the very best litigators when needed. Other families find that there are major benefits to having a lawyer available at their beck and call. This role is not only to protect the family in the unfortunate event that a business partner, employee, etc. initiates legal action, but often these professionals work to pre-emptively mitigate these risks by reviewing/ preparing all contracts, overseeing operations, and guiding any negotiations that could potentially create legal exposure for the family. Proactively protecting the family when minority investing, as a JV partner, or during potential dilution events, and hiring/firing decisions is directly connected to the core mission of protecting the net worth of the family. It never hurts to have someone with legal training review documents and counsel the family on major decisions.

Public Relations: The wealthiest families employ a team of public relations and marketing professionals. Public relations is crucial, whether a family is making sizable political donations or owns a popular sports team. A poorly-worded comment to a reporter can lead to negative headlines and ruined relationships. On the other hand, a well-publicized generous action can do wonders for a prominent family's public reputation. If your single family office is making high-profile investments that would be severely affected by negative public perception, it might be worth considering hiring a public relations and communications professional.

Chief Marketing Officer: Similar to public relations, many single family offices make prominent statements, investments, or other actions that require savvy marketing to "sell" the reasoning. For example, in 2008, T. Boone

Pickens, the billionaire energy investor, debuted a significant energy policy proposal called the "Pickens Plan." The idea was not just presented in private to politicians and policy wonks; rather, Mr. Pickens and his team introduced the plan to the public via a multi-million dollar advertising campaign that utilized social media and traditional advertising channels. Mr. Pickens' project resembled a corporate advertising campaign, but with the goal of building broad support for his Plan. This Pickens Plan example highlights how an ultra-wealthy individual occasionally requires corporate infrastructure and personnel to execute his big ideas. Depending on the size and scope of a family's projects and investments, a Chief Marketing Officer, PR team, or official spokesperson might be necessary to effectively communicate the family's passions, ideas, and motives.

Critical Questions to Ask and Rules of Thumb: We help families and family offices navigate the decisions of what to outsource vs. keep in-house. We frequently look at their level of assets under management, what are their top two or three areas of competitive edge or advantage in the marketplace, and what is so secretive or proprietary that they would never trust a third party to manage it. What I have found is that families with under $500M heavily outsource large portions of their single family office. Those families with $1B-$3B outsource just a few key areas such as IT management, some areas of investment consulting, and perhaps accounting or fund administration. For those families with more than $3B, outsourcing is limited just to functions which require global expertise or very sporadic demands for niche expertise.

Conclusion

As you have just read in this chapter, there are many different vendors and service providers that you may consider hiring for your single family office. It is important to evaluate each new relationship on its own merits and determine whether the service is truly necessary or whether you would be better off managing the service internally, if at all. Any new vendor or service provider brings along new responsibilities for coordinating between parties and, of course, new costs that will ultimately show up in the bottom line. More than a few single family offices have been startled when they realize how much money is going out the door to service providers and outside vendors so be sure to reevaluate all outside relationships at least once a year to make sure each contract still makes sense for your family.

Chapter 8: Investment Committees & Advisory Boards

"When there is a crisis, that's when some are interested in getting out and that's when we are interested in getting in."

- Carlos Slim Helu

"When most investors, including the pros, all agree on something, they're usually wrong."

- Carl Icahn

In this chapter, I would like to dive into the role of investment committees and advisory boards in shaping your single family office. I believe that it is critical for the success of your family office to have in place an investment committee and an advisory board. To begin, we will tackle the investment committee and the latter half of this chapter will cover advisory boards.

What is a Single Family Office Investment Committee?

Definition: An Investment Committee is a senior staff group that oversees the investment activities of the single family office. Family offices use the committee structure as a way of transparently discussing different investment opportunities, whether ongoing or prospective, and decide how the family should invest.

Investment Committees Gather Regularly to Discuss the Portfolio, Evaluate Current Allocations, Share Insights, and Decide How Best to Protect the Family's Wealth while Generating Returns

The role of an investment committee is to help make strategic investment decisions, evaluate or select fund managers, discuss portfolio construction and risk management approaches and implementation, and to ensure the long-term preservation of capital and implementation of the investment policy they have been given. Investment committees differ greatly in size, frequency, and rigor.

Any new investment considered by a single family office typically, but not always, will pass through the Investment Committee, as one of the key stages of the investment process. Ideally, an analyst or Investment Committee member will have initially screened any potential investment so the Committee meetings aren't bogged down with a flood of deal flow.

Bret Magpiong, a 20-year single family office veteran, spoke on the lack of formal investment committees in the single family office industry:

"My experience is that single family office investment committees, in the formal sense, are rare. It has been the ad hoc committee many times. I mean, there have been committees that have been in place, in one there was definitely a committee, but it met quarterly or not that often and it was more based around a reporting of not what should we be doing, but are we still on a good path here. There was not a lot of advice in terms of strategy on a go-forward basis; it was more almost an audit function, if you will, for that particular family.

In another case, the investment committee met every week and went through the portfolio and individual positions. It was all in-house people; they did not have outside advisors associated with it at all, and it was along the lines of what you indicated, as the principal having the significant say in things. Ultimately, he wanted to hear people's opinion, but he was going to make the decision and again, that was the situation where his personality was a significant risk taker and that's just the nature of the way that that investment committee came into being."

Many single family office professionals come from private wealth management or a multi-family office background, so this Investment Committee trend is largely a function of transferring best practices from the multi-family office world to single family offices. Still, there are some family offices that have operated successfully for decades without an investment committee.

With that in mind, I asked Andrew Hector, Executive Chairman and Managing Director of Candor Financial Management, how his family office operates without a formal investment committee.

"We have a six member investment committee who meet formally once a month. Each advisor or Private Chief Financial Officer short-list investments that belong to asset classes that our clients' asset allocations are underweight in and believe are compelling. These investments are discussed at the investment committee meetings. All relevant input is considered, although each Private Chief Financial Officer remains in control of making the investment recommendations to their clients as they know the client's circumstances the best.

That said, new investments are peer reviewed and discussed with the other advisors prior to getting to the investment committee meetings. We only have four Private Chief Financial Officers in the group at the moment and they manage over a billion dollars under management. We have a very close communicational line between the advisors here in Perth and in Sydney who we speak with at least once a day."

Who Belongs to the Investment Committee?

The Committee is comprised primarily of investment professionals, but may include other staff with value-adding backgrounds in law, accounting, or management. While a multi-family office or wealth management firm might include more than a dozen people on an Investment Committee, most single family offices only include three to five permanent members. The Single Family Office's Chief Investment Officer will most often lead these meetings and coordinate between the different members. Members of the family might attend depending on their level of interest in the subject. I recommend only inviting senior members of the investment team and family office so that the committee meetings do not become a time-wasting exercise that distracts from day-to-day operations. Successful investment committees usually include only those decision makers and essential personnel that are required for a vote on an investment. The Investment Committee will ideally have an odd number of voting members. Even if the ultimate decisions are made by the CIO or the family, it is good to have an odd number to make more minor decisions effectively.

Keeping Everyone on the Same Page

Most investment teams have a professional (or several) assigned to each investment area and the heads of each investment division will report to the Investment Committee on the performance, challenges, and decisions affecting his or her area. Assigning staff to different specialties could have the effect of "siloing" your investment team, but you can maintain a collaborative, informed investment team by holding Investment Committee meetings on a weekly, monthly, or quarterly basis. I know of one very active single family office that holds an Investment Committee meeting every morning to make sure that all of the professionals are on the same page.

Below is a quote from single family office expert Chris Allen. Chris has more than ten years of experience running a single family office. I asked Chris about how successful family office investment committees operate:

The Single Family Office by Richard C. Wilson

"Well, it's all across the board. It's very family specific, but there are some very similar tracks for the families that I've talked with over my career. There is generally one person alive or dead that made the money through some successful business operation or some transaction. Most family offices are a function of a family business that was sold. The family business tended to have a smart accountant, CFO, or treasurer-type that would take care of all the personal needs of the family. The family would split the cost of their personal activity with the business activity because, quite often, they were integrally connected.

"But the best family offices that really do make good investment decisions evaluate every single aspect of the opportunity and make a decision that's generally consensus. If you don't build consensus within your investment committee, you're going to end up in a fight down the road."

Forming a Single Family Office Investment Committee

If you are looking to form an investment committee for your single family office, you should first conduct an audit of your investment activity. As you review your investments, take note of the following:

- What areas does the family invest in?
- How often does each investment area need to be evaluated or reconfigured?
- What team members are essential decision makers for each investment area?

Once you have answered these questions, you will have a better idea of your investment committee needs. By understanding what investment areas your family office is involved in, you will begin to see the outlines of your committee and what areas you will need to address in the meetings. The frequency of change in each area is important for structuring the meetings and deciding on how often your committee should meet.

For example, one single family office that I am working with has an extensive hedge fund portfolio and the managers are constantly monitored, evaluated, and, if necessary, replaced. This type of investment management requires daily meetings by the investment team and, thus, the Investment Committee essentially meets every day on hedge fund portfolio management. That same family office manages a couple real estate assets that only require quarterly assessment. For this Investment Committee, the committee must meet every day, but the group only discusses the hedge fund portfolio and a few other areas, like fixed income and operating businesses. On a quarterly basis, the Investment Committee will meet with the property manager of the real estate assets and complete a review of the investment area and examine any prospective real estate investments.

This example shows how the frequency of meetings and the subjects discussed in the meetings are ultimately dictated by the investment portfolio. The real estate portfolio manager does not need to attend the hedge fund-dominated Investment Committee meetings because it is not his area of expertise and it would distract him from his duties managing the real estate holdings. On the other side, the Investment Committee does not need to meet every day on such mundane decisions as increasing the hours of a part-time employee maintaining one of the properties. If a decision can be reasonably made without consuming too much of the Investment Committee's time, then it is ideal to leave those decisions to your capable staff. I know of a few single family offices that only have annual Investment Committee meetings and of course many less formalized single family offices have none at all. Throughout the year, the investment team manages the portfolio and only makes formal reports to the family and the rest of the office annually—or at the specific request of the Committee. Whether you decide to meet once a quarter or once a year, you should set the date far in advance so you are sure to have all voting members attend the sessions.

One of the most important decisions when composing your Investment Committee is whether or not you want to include a member of the family. To continue with the prior example, the patriarch of that family has very little interest in the day-to-day alternative investment portfolio and, thus, would prefer not to be included in each day's meeting. However, he does like to stay informed on the operating businesses and real estate holdings because those interest him. In this case, the Committee includes the patriarch on big-topic investment meetings, such as a change in course or a major allocation, and in those quarterly meetings with the real estate team. I have met a number of single family office founders who like to stay very involved in the Investment Committee, even chairing the meetings. After all, there are few more important things than ensuring that your family's wealth is properly managed and protected. So, be sure to structure your single family office Investment Committee in a way that accurately reflects the family's own interest in the investment activities.

If the family has little interest in attending these meetings, you can have an assistant record the minutes and issue reports to the family that include a CIO-authored summary of any significant changes. It is important to keep the family well-informed on their investment activities so that you don't have to shift the portfolio radically one day when a family member takes on a more active role in the investment portfolio.

Once you have decided who will attend the meetings and you have a clear understanding of the level of engagement that is needed for each investment area, you can formalize your family Investment Committee. The Chief Investment Officer, CEO, and the family should meet to decide how the Committee should be structured. One very important issue is voting power. Does the head of the family have ultimate say over any and all investment-related decisions? Does the CIO? It is critical to the success of your Investment Committee to define exactly who makes the decisions or whether investments are made by a Committee vote. Otherwise, you will open your Investment Committee up to potential infighting and indecisiveness whenever a potential investment is considered. An explicit chain of command keeps all members 100% clear on who ultimately makes the decisions.

The voting power, mission, and structure of the Investment Committee should be reflected in the Charter. The Charter can be created beforehand or outlined in the initial Committee meeting. The meetings should have a clear structure so that all important items are addressed and the meetings move along smoothly and in a timely manner. I know one family office executive who empowers his assistant to draft the meeting schedules, record minutes, and hold the Committee accountable for sticking to the itinerary. As anyone who has worked in a corporation knows, meetings can drag on endlessly if one member dominates the agenda or members bring up a lot of different issues. You should set a clear structure in place and the Committee should do its best to adhere to the agenda and structure.

Investment Committee Best Practices

To conclude this section, I thought it would be best to share my five best practices for running a successful single family office Investment Committee:

1.) Create a Charter: As discussed above, a charter helps establish the rules for the Committee and explicitly states the purpose, goals, and structure of the Investment Committee.

2.) Don't be Afraid to Debate: Many successful Investment Committees, including those of powerhouse hedge funds like Bridgewater Associates, encourage discussion and debate among colleagues. As long as you have someone in control of the meeting (usually the CIO or a senior member) then debate can be a healthy way to consider divergent opinions on an allocation or an investment strategy.

3.) Create Strategic & Tactical Investment Committees: The more sophisticated single family offices are starting to create dual investment committees, a strategic committee that decides on major buckets of assets to allocate to, and how much to allocate to each bucket and geographical region or country, and then a small tactical group that can help the investment portfolios maneuver the markets nimbly. This is important as strategic investment committees may be made up of several outside professionals, and may only be able to meet 1-2 times a month where a tactical committee could meet weekly or daily, and on-demand. In short it is just a more formalized approach of getting the top 2-3 investment team members to decide on portfolio adjustments in a more structured fashion.

4.) Invite one to three outside experts as Committee members. Having at least one voice from outside can offer a unique perspective and reduce your chances of falling into "group-think."

5.) Include at least one other trusted single family office executive or outside ultra-wealthy family member on the Committee.

The Single Family Office by Richard C. Wilson

Video: This short video from Zurich talks about investment committees for those who are new to the concept: http://SingleFamilyOffices.com/Investment-Committees

The Single Family Office Board of Advisors

The single family office Board of Advisors is a relatively new institution for family offices, although many single family offices rely on various advisors to some degree.

While interviewing Abe Tatar, the executive we interviewed earlier who operates the Hysek Group single family office in London & New York, we asked him for his #1 investment lesson as a single family office. Abe told us: "Build and maintain a strong internal investment committee along with an advisory team."

What is a Single Family Office Advisory Board?

Definition: A single family office **Advisory Board** is a consultative group comprised of executives and experts from outside the family office. These executives meet quarterly or annually to discuss strategy, management, and any important issues that the Chairman (or Chairwoman) of the Board would like outside input on. Typically, the Advisory Board represents different areas of expertise, from corporate management to entrepreneurial expertise, and each member has a connection to the family—or at least a strong connection to an executive at the single family office. In addition to the formal Advisory Board meetings, the single family office team will often seek counsel from various Board Members on various decisions or dilemmas.

The goal of the Advisory Board is to share and discuss unique perspectives and strategies on preserving capital, running a family office, or growing the portfolio businesses of the family office. In times of uncertainty or crisis, the Advisory Board may be called upon to offer guidance to the family or the executives on the management team. For example, in the financial crisis, a time of widespread fear and uncertainty, many single family offices called on advisors and confidants to advise on the situation. It makes sense to formalize those close advisors under an Advisory Board.

A competent and complementary Board of Advisors is even more critical in today's investing environment. Your Advisory Board may have a hand in reviewing investment partners, large business deals, and new advisors. Often, a Board Member will have a connection or insight into a potential hire or partner so you can lean on your Board's expertise and network to evaluate these decisions and protect your single family office from a harmful relationship or investment. Of course, your Advisory Board will not protect you against all frauds, weak performing funds, low character individuals, and other risks, but a strong Board of Advisors can help you at various levels of evaluation and review so that you make a better decision than you might on your own. In this way, your Board of Advisors can be an important element of your overall Family Governance procedures.

Diversifying Your Advisory Board

Most operating businesses, including family office organizations, have a sounding board of trusted advisors in related industries. The more emphasis a family office places on building a diversified and robust Board of Advisors, though, the more they will benefit from having such a resource in place. Many successful family office teams that I know make a point of drawing from outside the finance and investment areas in order to benefit from a range of experience and backgrounds.

If you are seeking to construct a diverse Advisory Board, it may be helpful to consider the different scenarios and areas for which you will most likely seek counsel. Perhaps you are looking to fund a new business and you would benefit from the perspective of someone who has created companies or invested in startups before. In that case, you might ask a friend who is active in venture capital or angel investing to join the Board. Or, you may be most likely to seek guidance on managing your team and maximizing operating efficiencies. If so, you will do well to turn to the best managers and executives that you know, regardless of whether they have direct experience in managing a single family office.

Single family offices tend to have less trouble diversifying their Board of

Advisors than more traditional corporate boards because many single family offices have exposure to a range of advisors, asset classes, industries, etc. through the day-to-day operations. It is critical that a single family office builds its Board of Advisors based on the family's investment goals and areas of activity. Real estate magnate Sam Zell, for example, has likely constructed his Board of Advisors with people who at least have some expertise in real estate management and investing. As I explained above, it's great to have diversity in your Board, but you want an informed Board that understands the fundamental areas of business in which the single family office is involved.

Video: Here is a video that I recorded in Liechtenstein on the topic of Family Office Advisory Board Members:

http://SingleFamilyOffices.com/Advisory-Board

Launching Your Family Office Advisory Board

Once you have selected the members of your Board of Advisors, it is critical that you set clear expectations and responsibilities for the members. I have seen a range of involvement from members of Advisory Boards. The contribution expected of each Member varies, from a loose commitment to video conference into the annual company meeting to an informal team member offering advice and resources regularly.

On one hand, the level of involvement is in your control, as you can select members who are interested in actively fulfilling the Board duties. On the other hand, members may not understand your expectations when they agree to participate and may see the arrangement as simply putting a feather in your single family office's cap, as is sometimes the case on corporate boards. You should be clear in your expectations and detail the demands of the position in writing so that all prospective Board Members understand the desired commitment. In your first Board of Advisors meeting, you can review your expectations and make sure that everyone is on the same page. It might be that you will need to modestly scale back your expectations to accommodate busy professionals.

Similar to the Investment Committee, the Advisory Board should have a charter, mission statement, meeting agendas, and a clear set of priorities. These documents will serve your Board well in guiding your meetings and making sure that you address the issues and topics for which you created the Board. Again, it is helpful to assign a junior staff member or assistant to record minutes and notes from each meeting, coordinate the meetings with members, and keep the meetings productive and prompt.

 Each meeting should have a clear objective and direction that is communicated to members beforehand, allowing members to research the issue, organize their thoughts, and be productive in the meeting. I know of a few Single Family Offices that do not use an Advisory Board because they see it as a waste of time or inefficient. Yet, many of these family offices still seek outside counsel and advice on running their family offices. So, I think the issue is more organizational than anything else.

By tasking a member of your team with managing the Advisory Board meetings, you can hold someone accountable for the success or failure of the meetings. If you are busy running your single family office, then you are just as likely as the other Board Members to neglect your duties or fail to prepare for the meetings. That leads to inefficient meetings which leave all Members frustrated and the SFO will understandably see the exercise as a waste of time. I recommend over-preparing for every Board meeting with your designated Advisory Board manager so that you have the type of Board meetings that leave everyone excited for the next one. A successful meeting leads to new ideas, better management, and greater confidence in how you are running your Single Family Office, so I encourage you to put significant time and energy into these gatherings.

As you set about building your Investment Committee and Board of Advisors, be sure to plan a time in the future to assess the performance of these groups and make any needed revisions (including replacing non-contributing members) so that these essential advisor groups do not grow stale.

Geoffroy Dedieu Interview

 Before we end this chapter on investment committees and advisory boards, we would like to present a short interview with Geoffroy Dedieu who is CEO at TY Danjuma Family Office in Esher, UK. Geoffroy speaks at some of our live conferences in the family office industry and has a lot of experience in speaking and writing in general. He also teaches a Family Office course at the University of Orleans (France) - Master of Wealth Management program. He has published various articles on Family Wealth Management: "Retirement Schemes - Singapore's success story," "China - Year of the Monkey and good fortune (2004)," "Asia - should you invest in real estate," and "India - Service Industry players are coming of age."

Richard C. Wilson: I see that you spend time in London, Singapore, and Africa; can you talk a bit about global single family offices and their differences, and where you see the industry going over the next 7-10 years in terms of growth and changes?

Geoffroy Dedieu: Whether in this job or in my previous career as a banker, I only worked for emerging market, first-generation SFOs. So that is what I can talk about. Most SFOs for first-gen emerging market billionaires are created outside the country of origin of the family. This is a basic risk-management policy. The FO industry has a strong tendency to cluster, as we need a strong eco-system around us; lawyers, bankers, auditors, etc. But favored family office destinations also boast a strong status appeal to the well-heeled. London is a case in point, with a real estate market buoyed by foreign buyers. Not only can UHNW families find the professionals they need here, but they also like to have a house, access to prime international boarding schools and world-class medical facilities. Singapore has some appeal to Asian families, but a lot less for families from other continents. I would argue that the inability to buy landed properties in the city-state has a lot to do with its lackluster performance in attracting international family offices, despite an extremely favorable tax environment and deep talent pool. In Africa, Dubai, and South Africa are the up and coming places.

Richard C. Wilson: Do you have any strategies or advice when it comes to building a powerful advisory board & investment committee for a single family office that currently doesn't have one?

Geoffroy Dedieu: The first is to insure a good balance between the Investment Committee (IC) and the Portfolio Managers (PMs). I would recommend any family office to have its own capabilities to manage portfolios. That means buying and selling securities, not simply lounging around "allocating" money to fund managers.

Portfolio Managers can be hired and retained at only a fraction of the costs paid to fund managers, once you understand the full costs of managing those funds down to each security line. Our figures show that USD 30 to 50 Million of AUM is enough to hire a portfolio manager if he can drive trading costs down.

The IC should have some family representation, but in the case of some families, the learning curve can be quite steep at first or there may be a disconnect between perceived levels of competence and real technical skills.

Training the next generation is key. I would also recommend hiring a senior independent director or IC member to provide an independent opinion, with no conflict of interest (no skin in the game).

Richard C. Wilson: Do you work with family office governance challenges often in your current or past roles? Do you have any governance best practices, strategies, or counterintuitive insights that would be helpful to those less experienced in this industry?

Geoffroy Dedieu: Governance at the family office should really be at par with other corporate entities. Have a Senior Independent Director and an Audit Committee. It is also quite useful to adopt a structure similar to the German boards with a Supervisory Board and a Management Board, to allow the creation of a higher forum (Supervisory) with representatives of the family. The Supervisory Board or Family Council can cover a spectrum of issues broader than the family office.

Richard C. Wilson: If you could provide direct advice to a family who just decided to start a single family office, what would be your #1 piece of advice when it comes to investing and portfolio management?

Geoffroy Dedieu: Map your risk-return outlook. Draw down exactly what you believe are reasonable risk-return trade-offs. Spend some time discussing reasonable return expectations for each asset class, using long data series (we use 20 years). Once you have agreed about possible returns, map the portfolios you need in order to achieve the returns you wish for. Then calculate the risks associated with these four or five model portfolios. Risk can be mapped using metrics such as VaR and scenarios such as Lehman collapse, Dot-com burst, 9/11. Deciding which risk profile is acceptable to the family will drive all other decisions.

Killing that hypnotic focus on promised performance as the sole decision-making criteria is the hardest job for any family office. The whole financial industry plays against us in that game. Products are sold to families based on hopes, not risks; we are here to break that charm, day after day.

Continued Interview with Michael Oliver Weinberg

We continue our interview with Michael Oliver Weinberg, who has served as a CIO of a single family office and helped allocate billions of dollars into alternative investments as a fund manager. In this discussion, I ask for his view on building a powerful investment committee.

Richard C. Wilson: Many single family offices aren't sure who should be on their investment committee, how large it should be, how often they should meet, etc. Do you have any guidance you could provide on this topic for our chapter on advisory boards and investment committees?

Michael Oliver Weinberg: Family office investment committees should mirror the best practices of corporate boards. For example, akin to corporate boards, family office investment committees should have an odd number of members to facilitate majorities in investment, policy, and other decisions.

Family office investment committees should be involved in setting, monitoring, and enforcing; Asset Allocation Policy, Risk Management Rules, Ethical Standards, Performance Monitoring and Policy Benchmark, Remuneration Schemes and Family Communication Policy. Family office investment committees should meet annually to discuss remuneration schemes and ethical standards, semi-annually to discuss asset allocation policy, and monthly to discuss performance monitoring and policy benchmark, risk management and to determine family communications.

Members of family office investment committees should include the Chief Investment Officer, the Chief Operating Officer, family members and independent, third-party investment professionals. Ideally included in these third-party independent investment professionals would be members from institutional asset management firms, as opposed to purely family office members. This would bring a broader and more sophisticated viewpoint to the discussion.

Conclusion

If you build a strong investment committee and advisory board, you will be able to hire better personnel, have stronger operations and governance policies, and you should be able to adjust to both management and investment crises with more confidence and success. This chapter was included because it is so critical to establish, formalize, and get right from the very beginning and it is just an after thought for many single family offices.

Part 3:
Single Family Office Investment Portfolios

RES NON VERBA

wilson

The Single Family Office by Richard C. Wilson

Chapter 9: Family Office Investment Management

This chapter is really an introduction to Part 3 of the book, which is going to cover investing the capital of family offices. As discussed later in this part of the book, family office investment portfolios differ based on the generation of the family, their risk appetite, which industry their money was made in, the priorities of the family, and their geographical location(s). While there are many variations on what is presented here and some families who only invest in real estate, or only invest in the aviation industry, etc., we believe there are many best practices and successful models that can be applied to family offices.

Family Office Investments & Portfolio Insights Video: I recently spoke in Liechtenstein on family office investing and it may be helpful to watch a recording of my conference presentation before moving on to this next section of the book:

http://SingleFamilyOffices.com/Investments

Regardless of the area of investment, we have found that most family offices typically follow this high-level very simplified due diligence process.

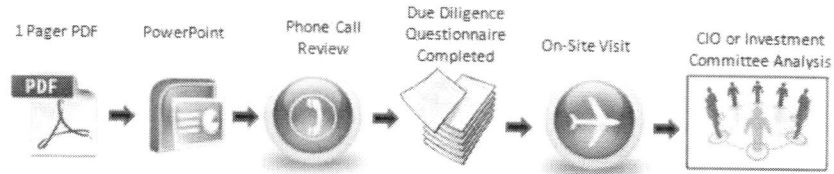

Most family offices first want to typically review a one-pager on the investment project or fund, followed by a PowerPoint, perhaps some due diligence, and then a short conference call. After that, more complete due diligence is conducted, typically including an onsite visit or invitation for the investment team to come visit with the family office. Following an in-person meeting, the family office will run compliance and background checks to help guard against fraud and illegality. For many family offices, the final due diligence phase may be completed before a decision is ever moved to the CIO or investment committee level. Other families make sure that the CIO and investment team has confidence in the deal or allocation before moving forward with even the initial due diligence process. At what stage in the process you begin your thorough due diligence work depends on your family office and how you prefer to screen opportunities.

As we move into Part 3 of this book, we begin with a chapter that explores investment fund manager selection and monitoring. This is followed by chapters on direct investments, then co-investing & club deals, and ultimately this part of the book concludes with a chapter on real estate and hard assets. There are entire books written on each topic, so we only touch on the main points here based on how our clients and association members approach each investment class.

The ensuing chapters will dig into various areas of family office investment. This was my favorite section of the book to write because investment management is what my team and I spend a lot of our day-to-day time working on with our clients and our own operating businesses. While there is a 10% content overlap we are careful here not to repeat too much of what is covered within our other publications such as The Hedge Fund Book (Wiley), The Family Office Book (Wiley), The Visual Guide to Hedge Funds (Bloomberg), and The Family Office Database Guide.

Chapter 10: Investment Fund Manager Selection & Monitoring

"Passion is the great slayer of adversity. Focus on strengths and what you enjoy."

— Charles Schwab

Actively managed investment funds almost always make up a significant part of a single family office's portfolio. For the purposes of this chapter, we will focus on alternative funds such as hedge funds, private equity, and other private fund vehicles that are only available to accredited investors of significant means. This is, of course, not to say that mutual funds, standard stock-picking funds, and fixed income managers do not deserve close scrutiny from family office investors, but this territory is well-trodden by others and "mainstream" investments are understandably familiar to most investors.

Video: I spoke on family office investment priorities in Geneva recently, and while there I recorded this video on what family offices are looking for in private equity fund managers: http://SingleFamilyOffices.com/Private-Equity

We along with everyone else representing family offices receive a lot of communications including emails, face-to-face meetings, and phone calls from fund managers looking to raise capital.

This chapter aims to help solve part of this issue with best practices and suggestions for selecting a fund manager and weeding out the risky, the fraudulent, and the underperformers. Of course, I do not guarantee that by following this chapter's advice you will be 100% protected against investing in underperforming funds—anyone who does guarantee that is either disingenuous or hasn't been in the industry long enough to know that no fund is infallible—even Warren Buffett has made many investing mistakes during his illustrious career. But this chapter *does* provide you with tools and techniques for actively monitoring your portfolio so that even if you end up awarding capital to a poor fund, you will (hopefully) identify the bad egg before it harms your portfolio to a great extent.

Video: Here is a recent update from Tokyo on the State of the Hedge Fund & Family Office Industries:

http://SingleFamilyOffices.com/Hedge-Funds

As you have learned, family offices receive an overwhelming number of requests from fund managers to review their fund and consider making an investment. My team has broken down the review process to the manageable six steps that we use to conduct our initial review. It is important to note that this is not the complete evaluation process and there are many sub-steps along the way, but this should give you a good idea of what the typical process is:

- Step 1: The initial step in the fund manager selection process is to review a one-pager (also known as a tear sheet or teaser) which is a document that provides an overview of the investment fund and its vital information. This one-pager is usually distributed as a PDF and will include most or all of the following information about the fund: investment performance and audited track record; team bios and history; investment process and philosophy; disclosures; investment structure; contact details. This teaser provides the reader with a 10,000 foot view of the fund and this document is usually sufficient for investors to decide whether or not to pursue more information about the investment or to pass on the opportunity. Our team, and most investors, can complete a review of a teaser in 5-10 minutes and know whether or not to move on with the next step of evaluation.

- Step 2: If the investor has interest in the investment after reviewing the one-pager, then the family office will request (or more likely be sent without prompting) a deck (also known as a pitch book), which is usually delivered as a PowerPoint presentation. This is a more detailed introduction to the fund and delves into the investment structure, the process by which the fund invests, why this investment is thought to be a good one, and any other information that is relevant for an investor considering an allocation to the fund. This document can range anywhere from 10 to 100 pages in length and reviews the management team, unique edge in the marketplace, investment process, risk management procedures, operations, service providers, investment examples, and future plans. This document is generally sufficient for investors to know whether there is a strong chance they will invest in the fund. By proceeding onto the third step, you are signaling that you have been satisfied with the information so far and would like to learn more with a phone call or meeting.

- Step 3: Given that family offices invest with a number of fund managers that are often based many miles from the family, a phone call is usually the most practical third step in the evaluation process. Eventually, if the phone call and evaluation goes well, almost all of the single family offices that I know will have a face-to-face meeting before making a commitment to a fund. At the early stage, however, a phone call will suffice to start the relationship. This phone call is an opportunity for the family office to ask any questions the team has about the materials or the investment and to get a feel for the fund's professionals. These calls are usually at least half an hour in length and I have participated on many calls that last hours—although active single family offices usually try to limit the phone calls as much as possible. During this call, the fund manager or investor relations professional will walk the family office through the presentation, answer any questions, and elaborate on any points that are particularly interesting to the single family office. Most pitch books and teasers are carefully prepared to present the fund in the best possible light and the phone call is an opportunity for savvy family office

CIOs and analysts to poke holes in the strategy and performance. Family offices will be able to form a better opinion of the investment after engaging in these calls and get a sense for how the fund manager operates.

- Step 4: At this stage, the family office is seriously considering an investment in the fund and now begins the full due diligence process. The primary document that is used by investors is the due diligence questionnaire, also known as the DDQ. This is an exhaustive list of questions running anywhere from 50-200 questions long and covers many different areas. This part of the due diligence process can sometimes slow down the momentum toward a deal, as it usually requires both sides working through the granularities of structure, past performance, audits, references, and other time-consuming tasks. Most large investment funds have a dedicated investor relations or compliance professional who routinely prepares these documents for investors and thus the turnaround for these funds is usually much quicker than smaller, less seasoned shops. Likewise, many investors employ a consultant or staff member who is experienced in reviewing DDQs and digging into the details of the responses. Once this DDQ has been received by the investor and reviewed, the final step in the due diligence process is to conduct an on-site visit to see how the fund operates, ensure that nothing has been misrepresented or exaggerated in the materials, and get a better feel for the potential investment partner.

- Step 5: The final step in this five-step process for fund manager review is to circle back with the family office investment team and formulate a final opinion on the investment. Many of the best-performing family offices that I have met credit their willingness to walk away from a deal, even at this late stage, as a big reason that they have been successful. The family office will usually conduct a meeting between the Investment Committee and the decision maker in the family so that the Committee and CIO can present their case for making the investment and outline the structure of the deal. The team may find that they still have some questions and then they will expand on the due diligence and evaluation. If they are satisfied with their evaluation and receive the green light to move forward, then the family office will contact the investment fund and proceed with executing the contract.

Of course, this process will have some variation from family to family, but this five-step process synthesizes the most common and important steps that leading single family offices follow when evaluating investment funds.

Measuring Performance

There are many complicated formulas and calculations that help evaluate how your investments are performing. I won't run through all of these and I know many family offices who completely disregard common tools for measuring risk and performance, while other investors almost exclusively rely on those same tools. Ultimately, the responsibility lies on your investment team and your Chief Investment Officer. It is important that the family and the Board agrees with the investment team on the various ways they measure performance because otherwise it can be very easy for an investment professional to favor one metric over another and vary from month to month how he or she measures performance. This is especially problematic if the investment team has their compensation tied to the family office's performance. There are many cases of institutional investors and family offices underperforming their peers and failing to recognize that reality because their CIO or outsourced consultant is cherry-picking the performance data to appear stronger than it is in actuality. Even when an investment team has good intentions, they may still fall prey to their own confirmation biases that hide the true risk or underperformance of the portfolio. That is why many family offices go to great lengths to establish consistent measurements of performance and require a clear explanation when the investment team deviates from traditional metrics for evaluating performance.

The following sections provide brief explanations of the common measurements used to evaluate performance of various asset classes. The usual disclaimer applies; please understand that this chapter should only serve as introductory education on different tools and metrics and should not be exclusively relied upon for evaluating investments, especially without seeking qualified investment advisory, legal, or other counsel.

Basics for Hedge Funds

Michael Weinberg, CIO of a single family office and past investment manager of over $1B for George Soros, spoke about investing in hedge funds at our recent full-day Family Office Workshop at the Harvard Club. Michael likes using hedge funds in his portfolio, because even though they are accused of having high fees, they typically lose a lot less than a market-tracking fund or long-only fund. Also, he pointed out that some funds now offer 0 and 20, or 1 and 20 fees, lowering their management fees to compete in the competitive hedge fund industry for investor attention. While investing in hedge funds, he recommended watching out for funds which provide long-term vs. short-term capital gains and how those taxation differences will affect the portfolio. He also warned against investing with hedge fund managers who have proven themselves on the long side of the portfolio, but have not proven themselves in their short book, as these are two very different skill sets.

Video: When I was traveling in Singapore, I recorded this video to provide a few ideas on what investors and family offices look for in hedge funds.

http://SingleFamilyOffices.com/Due-Diligence

Basics for Traditional Mutual Funds

A mutual fund is probably familiar to you already, as this vehicle is a hallmark of retail investing and most investors have placed money in a mutual fund at one point or another. A mutual fund is an actively managed investment fund that pools capital from investors and invests in different securities like equities and bonds. These funds are regulated by the Securities and Exchange Commission and subject to that body's regulation. Unlike an exchange-traded fund (ETF), mutual funds are run by a money manager, typically the investment adviser, who seeks to generate returns for investors by allocating to different investments.

The Single Family Office by Richard C. Wilson

You may be wondering what sets a mutual fund apart from a hedge fund. Well, a mutual fund is fairly similar to a hedge fund, but it is not necessarily restricted to only accredited and institutional investors. Mutual funds typically do not invest in as risky of assets as hedge funds do, nor do they employ the same level of leverage as hedge funds. The cost of a mutual fund is also lower than a hedge fund, although both funds collect fees for the service of investing capital. Mutual funds are restricted in what they can invest in, their ability to short stocks, and the leverage used for investments. For these reasons, mutual funds tend to be seen as a fairly safe way to invest, compared to hedge funds or other alternative funds, but more and more mutual funds are mimicking the type of investing strategies that were formerly the exclusive domain of hedge funds. Additionally, it is important to note that mutual funds have failed and investors have lost money as well, despite the various restrictions imposed on these funds. Note, there are many conservative, very consistent, excellent hedge funds which protect capital above all else, so it is important to note that a hedge fund is not necessary always a risky investment. In fact, the very name comes from the ability of a hedge fund to hedge out risk, and protect against it using a wide variety of tools.

Basics for Direct Investments

As you will learn in the direct investments chapter, family offices are rapidly expanding in-house direct investment capabilities. A direct investment, in this case, refers to a family making a capital allocation directly into a corporation or project to obtain non publicly traded equity in the entity. It is important to note that we are focused on "non publicly traded equity" because that excludes the standard investments made by families through mutual funds and traditional equities portfolios. In direct investments, family offices will typically buy a large stake in a corporation with the expectation that the equity value will appreciate over time. Other times, a family office may perform a role similar to a private equity investor by buying out an entire firm and managing it under the family's portfolio. In these cases, the family office will have an experienced deal team that is comfortable sourcing deals, evaluating the opportunities, and executing a large, often complicated buyout. Although most families making direct investments have over $1 billion in assets under management, these complete buyouts are typically financed with debt to increase the return on investment and reduce the equity at stake in any one buyout. Similar to leveraged buyouts by private equity funds, the family will contribute a sizable equity slice, but the bulk of the money for the transaction is borrowed from banks and other lenders willing to help finance the deal.

The investment generally follows a "J-Curve" model, with most of the expenses and capital investment made in the first phase of the deal and, as the company or project becomes profitable, returns are harvested in the latter part of the investment. Of course, when leverage is employed, it is important to consider the cost of debt and interest payments in the investment plan, so the investor will have a strong motivation to produce a positive return on the company quickly in order to pay down the borrowed money and avoid costly interest payments.

There are many metrics that measure the performance of a direct deal and they vary depending on whether the investment is a real estate project, a debt restructuring, a leveraged buyout, or any other direct investment. Like any investment, the important question to ask is whether the investment was worthwhile in terms of expenses incurred, return on investment, and how the investment performed relative to how you could otherwise use the invested capital. A common benchmark for equity investments is the S&P 500 Index and investors look to achieve "alpha" or an annual return greater than the benchmark. If the net return on the investment is at or below the S&P 500 or similar equity index, then it is likely that the deal was a poor use of capital because it could have been put to equivalent use through an index fund or stock portfolio, rather than the time-intensive, laborious, and expensive direct deal.

Another factor to consider in direct deals is whether an allocation should have been placed with a third-party investment manager. For example, if your family office is bullish on Chinese real estate and apartments, would it make more sense to buy and manage an apartment building in Beijing or to allocate to an experienced real estate investment fund that manages Beijing properties and subscribes to a similar investing philosophy? There are many factors to consider, such as what are the fees charged for managing your capital and are they taken from any profits on the deal? How competent is the team compared to your own? Will you have less transparency and control of your investments than you would investing directly? How concentrated will your committed capital be in the area in which you want to invest (Chinese real estate)? Will the fund expose you to greater risk than you believe you would incur on your own? What are the tax consequences and legal issues that come into play by investing in a third-party fund in a foreign country? These are all very important considerations as you weigh investing directly or allocating to an investment manager. If your team is experienced and competent, then you could conceivably achieve higher returns investing directly and have greater control over your money than you would by investing in a fund, which locks in the capital for a set time period, requires redemption requests to exit, and lessens your ability to directly manage the investment.

Basics for Private Equity investments

Private equity funds pool investor capital into a fund structure that is managed by the private equity sponsor (the GP). The investors (LPs) commit capital for about five to eight years and agree to pay a management fee annually (1.5-2% of assets under management) and a performance fee (20% of the profits generated by the fund). The fund manager will deploy that capital over the next few years into several different companies that the GP believes are undervalued, poorly managed, or can otherwise be improved under the management of the private equity fund. To buy out a company, private equity funds use leverage (borrowed money) financed by banks or other lenders. In a private equity deal, the fund may only commit a fraction of equity toward the deal value and borrow the rest, often using the acquired company as collateral for the loan. This allows the buyout fund to reap tremendous gains if the deal succeeds, distributing impressive returns to LPs. But, as is sometimes the case, the fund may fail to turn around a struggling company or otherwise fail in the deal. In this scenario, the company will sometimes protect the buyout fund and its investors from the full losses that would be incurred had the debt been taken on by the fund and not the company. Still, there are many examples of failed private equity deals that resulted in heavy losses for investors.

Investors use a number of different metrics to analyze and track private equity fund performance. The most common performance measurement is probably the Internal Rate of Return (IRR), which is the annual yield on a private equity investment. This basic metric provides investors with a better understanding of the returns generated by the fund's investments and allows an LP to compare the performance against that of other investments. There are a number of different factors that investors should consider when evaluating a private equity fund. To name a few: what is the vintage year of the fund (the year that the fund began investing capital); how did other funds perform with the same vintage year; what were the returns after fees and expenses; how did the fund perform in comparison to a public benchmark; what quartile does this fund fall into; what is the DPI (distributions to paid-in capital); and what is the typical holding period for an investment? These are all important questions that will need to be answered before investors feel comfortable making a long-term allocation to private equity.

Another important metric is Earnings Before Interest, Taxes, Depreciation and Amortization (EBITDA), which expresses what was achieved at the portfolio company during the fund's investments. For example, if a company has a $70 million EBITDA at entry and the private equity fund exits at $140 million EBITDA, then the fund has dramatically improved the company's profitability. Importantly, EBITDA is a key to valuing a company in a sale or exit and buyers often pay a multiple of EBITDA when acquiring a company. So an increase in EBITDA during the private equity ownership will usually translate into a higher valuation of the company at exit, allowing the fund to reap rewards for investors above the entry price.

For investors, the principal concern when investing in private equity is the lack of liquidity. As too many investors learned in the financial crisis and economic recession, when circumstances change and you need to rebalance the portfolio, the ability to redeem your money from an investment is incredibly important, especially when that investment is likely suffering under the same poor economic conditions. In my experience, family offices are more comfortable with the limited liquidity and long-term investing horizon given that, unlike some institutional investors, family offices can often afford to wait through a difficult cycle and not be forced by corporate policies or short-term panics to sell off investments prematurely (which can be costly, given that there are relatively few buyers for private equity stakes in the secondary market and sellers may have to discount the interest substantially to exit the position).

 **Private Equity Interviews**: To listen to several full-length private equity audio interviews please visit our web property http://PrivateEquity.com

Background Checks

Background checks are routinely used by sophisticated investors, especially in the post-Madoff era. Every year, we read stories in the news about how a con artist hoodwinked a savvy investor out of millions of dollars. It is not guaranteed that by putting a manager through a background check you can avoid fraud or bad behavior. However, a background check is a fairly standard practice that helps increase your chances of avoiding a scam or fraud and gives you a better sense as to whom you are entrusting your money. I've heard a lot of investors say that a background check on a fund manager or a new hire revealed something that otherwise never would have been found in the due diligence process. If nothing else, a background check will help you sleep better, knowing that you are not investing with a criminal. You can weed out some fraudsters simply by requiring a background check; anyone who does not submit to a background check should not receive a dime of your money. The decision to use the background check is up to you, but resisting a standard procedure like this is a big waving red flag that there is a problem.

Free Video: This video talks about the investment priorities of family offices:
http://SingleFamilyOffices.com/Investing-Priorities

 **Fund Manager Due Diligence Template:** We have created a template due diligence questionnaire that you can adopt, customize, and use while interviewing and conducting research on fund managers. Simply using this template won't be enough to guard you against all types of frauds, poor performing funds, etc., but it should help for those who don't already have a template to use.
http://SingleFamilyOffices.com/Manager-Due-Diligence-Template

Disclaimer: Use this due diligence document as a starting point but not end-all list of due diligence questions. As each investment vehicle, jurisdiction, and investor preferences may change the level and types of due diligence required, use at your own risk. No one template is complete for any investment type, we are not liable for poor investment returns, fraud, loss of capital, or loss of liquidity of capital from investment decisions made while using this template.

Continued Interview with Michael Oliver Weinberg: Once again we have reached out to Michael Weinberg for his insights on this topic. As you'll recall, he has been the CIO of the single family office MOW & AYW LLC. Since he has deep experience in fund management and also now invests on behalf of a single family office, we have asked him a few more questions here regarding fund manager selection.

Richard C. Wilson: As an experienced investment and family office professional, what do you believe are the top two most common or costly mistakes single family offices make in their investment portfolios?

Michael Oliver Weinberg: As an experienced investment and family office professional, the top two most common costly mistakes single family offices make in their investment portfolios are: 1) Chasing performance, and 2) Overestimating the value of high absolute returns whilst underestimating the value of capital preservation.

Regarding point 1, in our experience, family offices are constantly chasing performance. In defense of family offices, they do not have a monopoly on this, as we have observed it over the past two decades across the investment landscape ranging from unsophisticated retail investors to theoretically sophisticated institutional investors, such as endowments, foundations, and pension funds. All too often, we observe families committing the cardinal sin of buying funds and strategies that are up the most and selling those that are down or underperforming. In our experience, this is a recipe for underperformance.

For example, just this year, we can think of a hedge fund that a billion dollar family in New York City invested in after it was up substantially, and then redeemed roughly a year later when it was down 2/3 of what it was previously up. The worst part was if that family had a modicum of understanding of what that fund actually did, it would have been perfectly obvious why the fund was down, and the conclusion should have been to hold the position, or at the extreme to even double the position. Instead, the family locked in a loss and relinquished the incentive fee that the manager would have been working for free until it returned the investor's capital back to its high-water mark.

Family offices should learn that managers and strategies are generally mean-reverting. Investing in what is up and has out-performed is likely what will next be down and underperforming and vice versa. What we recommend to families is finding high quality managers with proven processes, risk management, and track records, where they may be having a period of underperformance or even modest losses, assuming the thesis still holds and nothing has changed, other than a weak temporary performance streak. To clarify, we are not espousing catching falling knives and investing in managers that don't have proven processes and risk management or who have had consistently poor or negative performance.

Regarding point 2, it is a derivative of point 1, which is that because family offices chase performance, they overestimate the value of high positive returns in good years, whilst underestimating the value of capital preservation in bad years. We have written articles on this subject published by Institutional Investor's Hedge Fund Intelligence, so we will only highlight the primary point here.

We believe families would be well served by re-reading something from their childhood, Aesop's fable of The Tortoise and the Hare. Families want to invest in funds that are or have been up a lot. They pay far too little attention to how much these funds lost in corrections, bear markets, or whenever they lost money. They overweigh the big-up years and underweigh the down years in their analyses. They fail to appreciate Warren Buffett's Rules Number 1 and 2. Rule Number 1, never lose money. Rule Number 2, never forget Rule Number 1. Our permutation of his rule is that the trick to making money is not losing money.

At the risk of being repetitive with respect to what we have previously published, let us look at the way compounding works for a moment. If a family looks at a fund that makes 60% in a year, it is likely to be perceived very favorably due to the strong level of returns. One starts with a net asset value of $1Mn and ends up with a NAV of $1.6Mn. Not a bad year. Now let's assume that same fund starts with $1Mn NAV and loses 60% in a year. The NAV is now of course $0.4Mn. That fund needs to earn a 150% return to break even. What families fail to appreciate is they would be far better investing in funds that have less upside in absolute terms, but substantial downside protection. These funds will compound at higher rates of return over a cycle or prolonged periods.

Richard C. Wilson: You shared your view on investing in hedge funds recently at our Family Office Workshop in New York. Do you mind summarizing those here for readers of this single family office book?

Michael Oliver Weinberg: Recently, there has been a great deal of press and family office sentiment against hedge fund investing. Family offices are less interested in hedge funds because they have underperformed the long-only indices for five years. Though this is not untrue for the indices, for starters we would not likely be inclined to invest in a hedge fund index or espousing anyone else to. One of the primary advantages of investing in hedge funds is the alpha at the manager level and the allocator level. Hedge fund indices are averages and inherently provide hedge fund beta without the alpha.

The next flaw with the viewpoint against investing in long-only versus hedge fund is the assumption that markets will go up. Though they have historically over time, they may not for very long periods. For example, the Nikkei peaked nearly 25 years ago and over that period is down roughly 60%. Another example is the S&P 500 which peaked in 2000 and did not reach that peak level again for 13 years. A buy and hold investor would have been roughly flat, other than the dividend yield, over that 13 year period.

In both of these markets over both of these time periods, we know and have been invested in top hedge funds that have earned substantial double-digit positive annual returns. Many families that are opposed to hedge funds also cite the high fees as a reason for opposition. We would pose the question to you or them, would you prefer higher fees and double-digit positive NET returns (so after fees) or passive, low-fee, long-only indices that are flat or down material amounts over long periods? We would prefer the higher fee, higher net return option. Never mind that hedge fund fees are currently under pressure and often at substantial discounts to the former 2 & 20 model.

Then the question is how hedge funds achieve these positive returns in bear, volatile, or flat markets. The answer is the short-side, risk management and the resultant downside protection and capital preservation. Sure, over a five-year bull market, long-only funds might outperform. However, at least based on history, they have dramatically underperformed over cycles, including bear markets.

For example, if one looks at the S&P 500 total return index in 2008, it was down 37%. This compares to the Credit Suisse Broad Hedge Fund Index, which was only down 19%, roughly half as much. The way the '101' compounding works is that an investor would need a roughly 60% return to break even in the S&P versus only a 25% return to break even in the CSBHFI. In addition, the hedge fund managers who are down do not collect incentive fees until they return to the high-water mark.

Similarly, when we worked at one of the top macro-funds, one of the primary risk rules was to take most if not all exposure off when down 20%, because a 25% recovery was viable in not too long a period. However, returning to break-even when down substantially more than that, such as twice as much, is much more difficult and time consuming.

Lastly, to incorporate a modicum of modern portfolio theory, if a strategy offers the same returns with less risk or higher returns with the same risk, that is akin to the proverbial 'free lunch' and should be incorporated into an optimal portfolio. Top hedge funds do exactly this, and for this reason should be incorporated into traditional portfolios. In fact, we would even go as far as to espouse minimal traditional exposure and maximum hedge fund exposure due to the aforementioned reasons.

Richard C. Wilson: What is most critical when conducting due diligence upon fund managers and can you explain a bit of your background and how you came to this opinion? (I think this particular part of your background adds high credibility and weight to your words.)

Michael Oliver Weinberg: In terms of conducting due diligence on fund managers, we believe it is relevant to explain how our dialogue with managers has evolved over the past two decades. Two decades ago, when we first began our career as a sell-side equity research analyst at Dean Witter Reynolds, subsequently acquired by Morgan Stanley, we started speaking to hedge fund clients and making investing recommendations. Fifteen years ago, at Soros, one of our responsibilities was maintaining a dialogue with hedge funds the firm had investments in; this time, the information flow was more the other way, where they shared with us what they were doing. Over the prior nine years at Financial Risk Management, FRM, an institutional fund-of-fund, we did multiple hundred meetings per year with hedge fund managers conducting investment due diligence on them and conducting operational due diligence on those that we believed warranted inclusion in our investment pool.

In our experience, having looked at multiple hundred managers per year, and winnowed those down to a couple dozen of highest conviction investments over the past 9 years, the most critical aspect when conducting due diligence on a manager is to have a holistic understanding of a manager. Holistic is defined by Farlex, Inc. online as "Emphasizing the importance of the whole and the interdependence of its parts."

When looking at a manager, the parts are its pedigree, team, remuneration schemes and incentive alignment, opportunity set, investment philosophy, strategy, process, risk management and attribution. The historic returns in terms of quantity and quality, on a risk adjusted basis, i.e. Sharpe Ratio, Sortino Ratio, Downside Deviation, etc., are a second-derivative of all of these parts. If the parts are all cohesive, the returns are likely to be attractive. If the parts are not cohesive, the returns are likely to be unattractive.

An analogy we like to use is that when we are in a meeting with our favorite managers, it is akin to listening to an extraordinary symphony or opera. There is a unity in the process, risk management, and results that can only be a function of well-engineered, interdependent parts.

Let us cite an example of a fund that we knew would not work and we were not wrong. A well-known high profile growth fund hedge fund manager brought a well-known value manager in as a co-portfolio manager. The concept was diversification away from the growth style which had been producing subpar returns. However, if one looked at the situation holistically, it was obvious that the pedigrees, philosophies, risk management, and opportunity sets were too diametrically opposed to coexist within the same fund. Sure enough, not too long thereafter, there was a divorce and the value manager was ousted and the fund restructured."

Conclusion

Many family offices that I talk to are not happy by the performance of their portfolios in recent years and express some frustration with their General Partners and investment advisors. Increasingly, family offices are looking with great interest to the investments made by institutional investors like Ontario Teachers' Pension Plan, calPERS, and Singapore's Temasek Holdings. There will always be a place for third-party funds and asset managers in the family office industry, but many large single family offices are slowly exploring direct investment programs as a way to reduce expenses and exercise greater control over investments. If investment managers can produce superior returns, however, family offices will invest where they can achieve the best return. Hopefully, the lessons in this chapter help you develop an evaluation and selection system for making these allocations and provide a sense of the different measures you can employ to gauge performance.

 I recorded an hour-long audio interview with single family office veteran Frank Casey, who was part of the team that blew the whistle on Bernie Madoff. To listen, please visit http://SingleFamilyOffices.com/Audio1

Chapter 11: Direct Investing & Operating Businesses

"I've had great fun turning quite a lot of different industries on their head and making sure those industries will never be the same again."

- *Sir Richard Branson*

Single family offices are allocating more capital toward direct investing today than ever before. The ability to directly control real tangible assets, further influence an industry they already understand, and avoid fund management fees is driving interest in this area.

Direct Investments Definition: Direct investments are those made into a corporation in minority or majority form, without using a traditional fee-based private equity, venture capital, or hedge fund vehicle.

Video: Here is a video I recently recorded while I was in Berlin, on direct investing by family offices.

http://SingleFamilyOffices.com/Family-Office-Direct-Investing

Our team is conducting a global family office benchmarking study and the following chart shows how many families prefer minority investments. In my experience, this has to be taken with a grain of salt, as many families that I know of who are doing a lot of direct investments would prefer minority investments in a perfect world, but often find they have to get their hands dirty in a majority position for most opportunities that they get involved in to protect their interests and add as much value as possible.

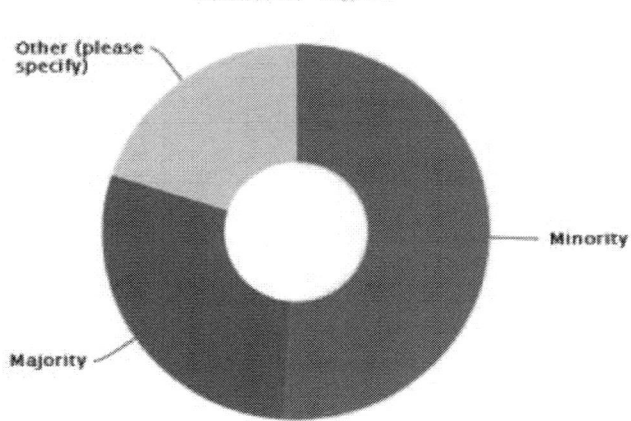

When investing in an operating business, do you prefer to be a minority investor or majority investor who takes control of the business?

Answered: 135   Skipped: 1

Other (please specify)

Minority

Majority

Recently, we had a $1B+ single family office that we are working with come speak at our Family Office Workshop at the Harvard Club. They showed case studies of businesses they had purchased, the over 1,000 patents that they now hold, and how they come up with new ideas and access deal flow. In this case, the family office is 100% vertically integrated, so they can source or come up with an idea, prototype the product, bring it to market, get mass consumer distribution for it, and keep it long-term as a revenue generator, or sell it off to a major conglomerate such as Proctor & Gamble.

A lesson to take away from this single family office is that it understands its core competencies and is careful not to stray from those strengths. If you look at the best investors in the world, they often stick to what they know. Warren Buffett, for example, has long-espoused the philosophy of maintaining a "circle of competence." The circle encompasses the areas within which you have a firm understanding and experience. Mr. Buffett was pilloried in the press and by investors for failing to join in on the tech bubble and invest in the soaring tech companies. Instead of giving in and investing in the hot stocks of the time, Mr. Buffett preferred to wait on the sidelines, knowing that he lacked the understanding of the internet businesses and believing any investment to be too far outside his circle of competence. Of course, Mr. Buffett was rewarded for his prudent patience as the bubble burst and many once-rising stocks were driven to the ground as investors realized the companies were overvalued and revenues were weak or non-existent. Mr. Buffett continues to make a killing by investing within his circle of competence and his commitment to staying inside that circle has made a compelling argument for sticking with what you know. The so-called Wizard of Omaha told University of Florida MBA students in 2007, "Everybody's got a different circle of competence. The important thing is not how big the circle is. The important thing is staying inside the circle."[1] Many family offices have had great success by staying faithful to the business areas in which they are truly great and that they really understand.

Staying within your circle of competence, to borrow the Buffettism, enables a family office to invest confidently. One family I know well for example, has committed capital to pre-revenue companies that may appear very risky to outside observers. However, for some families who operate only within their niche, the investments do not feel as risky as it might to someone who has less experience in the consumer goods space. The family office team has exceptional experience developing companies and products by prototyping, developing, and bringing to market consumer mass market products. Of course, no one is right 100% of the time, and family offices that have made many direct investments in the industry have probably suffered through a few bad investments along the way. However, what separates the strong investor from the weak is the former's commitment to investing in what he knows and understands, rather than chasing returns in a hot market or a new company outside his circle of competence. By investing in companies that they understand and can capably evaluate, some very focused family offices have been able to achieve a solid batting average of good investments, even if every single investment isn't a home run.

I've come across this insistence on staying true to what the family is familiar with time and time again at top family offices. This is something I see with commodity and mining families, real estate families, and others which specialize in one industry, or one "bring-to-market skill set" that can be used in a few parallel industries. Out of the more than fifty families I

---

[1] Buffett, Warren. 2007. MBA talk, http://www.youtube.com/watch?v=eRlQfS__u7E (accessed March 3, 2014).

know which have $1B or more in assets, only about 10% of those have successfully and consistently made good investments across more than three industries. In other words, the families with $1B+ who have kept that money almost always specialize in one, two, or three industries at most. These families are very comfortable saying "no" to investment opportunities outside these industries. To do so would be to abandon the philosophy that guided previous investments and to enter a market that is wholly unfamiliar to the family. It would take a really exceptional opportunity to move an experienced family to expand its investing to a new industry and I see families do this only rarely and under truly remarkable circumstances.

Another important aspect of the family office industry is the lack of deal flow access for most single family offices. Even well-known families who have invented many products we all use daily don't get shown as many acquisition opportunities as many investment banks. If that is true, and I know it is from working with these families and having them approach me to help them with deal origination, imagine how little deal flow an under-the-radar $100M or $500M single family office receives. You don't get much deal flow unless you have a dedicated deal origination team or partner, especially if you do not go to investment banking, industry or family office events, don't have a website, don't do press interviews, and have created niche financial, automotive, or manufacturing products in their past that are familiar to the public.

Ira J. Perlmuter, Managing Director at T5 Equity Partners, LLC, heads direct investing for the family who developed and owns the Mall of America, one of the largest shopping malls globally. Ira has acquired five companies for the family and a bank. Speaking to him about the benefits of direct investing, he talks about how control and your rolodex can be so important. When you can change management, inject capital, and consistently double the revenue of every business you buy, you create real value for your portfolio. There is also a benefit of getting many members of the family engaged again with their own investments, with the due diligence process, and how the global economy is changing on the frontlines as a business owner or owner of multiple businesses. Ira believes that everything is about people—from the CFO of a company, to a sales manager, to a production manager—the people are most important and you have to conduct excellent due diligence. Many times, Ira has uncovered information and facts that drastically change valuations by speaking to everyone at a business from a janitor to an advisory board member, and following up on fact checking. The direct investments Ira has been involved in are diverse, ranging from producing oil filters for the U.S. Navy, to a bank, and a garbage truck business. Ira also notes that buying and growing a portfolio of businesses is a lot of fun as well.

Most families get into direct investing by acquiring a few competitors within the niche industry where their wealth was made, be it textiles, technology, manufacturing, etc. After building wealth in one or two industries, many families start diversifying their investments by investing in private equity funds, hedge funds, and long-only fund managers. Depending on the timing of these investments, some ultra-wealthy families grow uncomfortable with the levels of fees, lack of transparency, and moderate returns of some of these funds. For example, in a traditional private equity fund, you may invest $30M and you know that the investment team is targeting middle market private companies, but you don't get to select or approve the individual investments being made. Pressures to allocate capital from inside the private equity team and within a time horizon of five to seven years, rather than a more long-term 10-20+ year time horizon, could directly change which types of opportunities are pursued and dissuade single family office investors from re-allocating to their next fund. Some private equity fund managers are now avoiding this "blind pool" option, to cater to those who complain about this aspect of private equity investing, but these funds are the exception.

The same issues exist on the hedge fund side: single family offices often express their dissatisfaction with hedge fund investments, especially in the years since the financial crisis. The biggest sticking point for single family offices considering a hedge fund allocation is the high fees charged by most managers. The typical fee structure is the 2 and 20 model (two percent management fee and twenty percent performance fee); however, when some hedge funds exceed $1 billion in assets under management, an interesting phenomenon tends to occur. At this high asset level, the funds can earn significant revenue just for managing the money (the two percent management fee) and the incentive to take risk in pursuit of high returns arguably diminishes. The mentality can be described as hedge fund managers not wanting to "rock the boat" and risk a big bet flopping, which could lead to redemptions and thus less management fees. On its face, a hedge fund's reluctance to take risk may sound like a good thing for investors seeking to protect capital, but managers often reach substantial AUM size because of their willingness to take risks and follow unique trading strategies. When a hedge fund is unwilling to trade at the same level simply to protect itself from potential losses, the hedge fund looks more and more like a mutual fund with exceptionally high fees charged to its investors. Single family offices face an interesting dilemma when it comes to selecting a hedge fund manager: is it better to risk feeding an overgrown hedge fund more fees for average performance or to take a risk on a less proven hedge fund with lower fees and less AUM? Of course, there are managers that have billions of dollars in assets under management and continue to justify their fees with outstanding consistent performance and inventive trading strategies, but the fear of billion dollar hedge fund "titans" growing comfortable and getting fat off of fees is a real concern that has led many single family offices to look in additional places for alpha, including by launching an in-house trading unit to replicate the hedge fund model internally without the fees.

There are many issues beyond fees that have driven single family offices away, such as a lack of transparency, poor liquidity and lockups, etc. But perhaps the most important factor leading investors away is simply mediocre or poor performance by a hedge fund. An investor will put up with a lot of inconveniences if a manager is producing top-quartile returns consistently. What investors will not put up with is consistently bad performance on top of any other issues. Whether a single family office is investing in a hedge fund, a private equity fund, or any other investment vehicle, if the returns aren't there, that single family office is going to think very seriously about finding someone else, often internally, to invest the money with (hopefully) better results and fewer headaches. One additional reaction to recent hedge fund performance and associated issues is the development of in-house trading units within single family offices. It is certainly expensive to hire top trading talent, but if a family is very active in hedge fund investing, it might make sense to open up a small proprietary trading unit to avoid fees and manage the portfolio internally. This is not as common as in-house private equity-like investment teams, but there have been a number of successful hedge

The Single Family Office by Richard C. Wilson

fund portfolio managers who have been "poached" by single family offices looking to bring their investments under the family office's own roof.

While it is important to acknowledge this trend of family offices directly investing in companies the hedge fund industry is stronger than ever with record assets under management among family offices and investors overall globally. While some more energy recently has shifted towards direct investments hedge funds will always have their place within most family office investment portfolios.

Direct Investment Types

There are many types of direct investments which involve debt financing, convertible debt financing, equity and debt funding, angel investing, venture capital-type growth capital investing, the traditional platform strategy, and build and flip private equity strategies.

Debt Financing: Many private corporations who seek debt financing from single family offices do so because banks will not lend them money, or will only do so only under outrageous terms that don't make business sense for the level of risk being taken. Family offices will typically charge a still high interest rate on the debt, but either on better terms or slightly better than what traditional lending institutions are offering. One benefit of debt investments is that you start getting interest payments back on the money invested immediately; you don't need to wait for a sale of the company to start earning your money back. The steady income component of debt is attractive to family offices. Another benefit is that debt is senior to equity, so in the unfortunate event of a bankruptcy or company failure, there are varying levels of debt seniority, but creditors are always repaid before equity stakeholders. Owners of highly collateralized debt can rest assured that they will at least receive some repayment ultimately, in addition to any prior interest payments.

Some banks are not allowed to lend money for certain types of businesses or loans backed by certain forms of collateral. A single family office, however, may be able to fill the void and offer financing. In some cases, the family office can "over-collateralize" a loan, which not only mitigates some of the risk, but it could in theory profit more if the loan defaults. For example, a bank may not lend a manufacturing business $5M in Singapore because the only collateral is $10M worth of U.S. commercial property. A single family office which has offices in both locations may be happy to do so, as they would come into $10M of commercial property potentially if the company defaults on their loan payments. A personal guarantee is typically required from the private company's founder(s), another sign of commitment by the borrower. The downside of only investing in the form of debt is that you have limited upside, while an equity investment could grow exponentially.

Convertible Debt: Convertible debt is a loan that can convert into equity in the future. In this model, financing is provided, and then upon a trigger event, part or all of the debt is converted into equity. This trigger event is often a future round of investments, a revenue threshold, taking the company public, or the sale of the business. While convertible debt allows you to receive income from the beginning, it also still tends to limit some of the upside when compared to a pure equity investment. Furthermore, investing through convertible debt instead of straight equity can lower a single family office's level of control within the company, which could be a major motivation for conducting direct investments in the first place.

Royalties: Investors commonly request that a royalty is included in any investment in a manufactured goods company that has annual revenues below $10 million. While this can be painful for a small business as it lowers their margins, this may be their only option for raising capital. The advantage for a single family office that receives a royalty is that they begin to get paid back with every sale made. For example, let's say there is a company that has been producing casing for electronics for 5 years and does $12M a year in revenue. The company usually sells 100,000 units a month for an average of $10 each, and they need $1M in capital to expand their production capabilities. If they need the capital upfront and can't wait to slowly fund the expansion from their own revenue, they may need to give away ownership plus pay a royalty. Investors often seek a royalty that lasts forever and are willing to take a lower amount of equity for that benefit, but other investors just want to get their principal money back and then the royalty stops. In this example, if the company was making $2.5M in profits on $12M of annual sales you could say that the firm may be worth $10M total. If $1M is invested just for equity, you may argue that is worth 10% of the firm, but if a royalty of 15 cents per unit is granted in perpetuity, perhaps a 7-8% equity stake would be reasonable. The terms will depend on the industry, the strategic benefits of the relationship, future financing needs of the private corporation, and leverage/options each party has in the transaction. This royalty approach is under-utilized and can often times bridge the gap between an investment being a little too early or too risky for a family as they start getting paid back on day 1.

Mezzanine (Debt & Finance): Single family offices all have substantial capital on hand and that opens up the potential to lend money and finance projects. The financial crisis created an incredible credit crunch where banks ratcheted up lending standards and put an end to the pre-crisis era of easy money and loans for individuals and corporations seeking financing. Many savvy hedge funds, private equity funds, and investment firms stepped in to fill some of the financing void left by traditional lenders (i.e. banks). A small number of single family offices have waded into this territory by offering mezzanine financing and making other debt and lending-related investments. In these cases, the single family offices resemble investment banks and the SFO team will extend credit or execute mezzanine debt financing for various parties from real estate project developers to corporations and small businesses. Without traditional lenders, a single family office can charge a healthy interest rate and secure preferred terms in exchange for lending the capital. There is certainly a high degree of risk in buying debt or lending capital, but an experienced team can earn consistent profits simply from the SFO's cash. At present, this is not a widespread direct investing activity, but I have known a number of single family offices who dabble in mezzanine loans and other financing activities opportunistically. A small number even see debt and lending as a significant part of their investing strategy and employ experienced professionals in the area of debt financing and banking.

Many single family offices don't label themselves angel investors, venture capitals, or private equity investors, but I believe it is instructional to classify some of the direct investment strategies to these categories since we have no other vocabulary to do so.

Angel Investing: Angel investing by single family offices is common;

around 40% of the single family offices that we work with have made angel-like investments in the past and plan to continue doing so. The Ewing Marion Kauffman Foundation and Angel Capital Education Foundation did a study recently and they found that the median time spent on due diligence for an angel investment was 20 hours. They found that those who spent over 20 hours on an investment had a 6x return on their capital, while those who spent less than 20 hours had a 1.1x return on their capital. They also found that those who spent more than 40 hours conducting due diligence and research had a 7x return on their capital on average. This same study showed that angel investors who invest in industries they know well are able to double their return on capital in those areas due to expertise, connections, and their own strategic value-add to those acquisitions. This same study found that investors who meet with a company they have invested in once or twice a year produce, on average, a 1.7x return, while those investors who met once a month saw, on average, a 3.7x return on their capital.[2]

Video: To watch a short video discussing this study and angel investing, please see this page of our website:

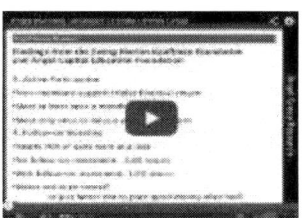

http://SingleFamilyOffices.com/Angel-Investing-Strategies

Venture Capital Investing: Many ultra-wealthy families don't just make occasional venture capital investments; they actually operate full-fledged venture capital firms. While this is an option for many families, for the purpose of this chapter we will talk about how single family offices can make venture capital investments, but we won't provide advice on forming a venture capital firm.

A venture capitalist invests in early to mid-stage companies and startups with the goal of scaling that business and producing a high return on the investment. The biggest risk for venture capital investors is that an investment will flop or even fall into bankruptcy. Many small and emerging businesses fail for various reasons and venture capitalists tend to accept

---

[2] Wiltbank, Robert and Boeker, Warren, *Returns to Angel Investors in Groups* (November 1, 2007). Available at SSRN: http://ssrn.com/abstract=1028592 or http://dx.doi.org/10.2139/ssrn.1028592

The Single Family Office by Richard C. Wilson

failure as a cost of doing business and look to notch huge returns on the few investments that do succeed. The old cliché in venture capital is that for every home run, a venture capitalist will strike out ten times. A venture capitalist hits a home run by investing early in a company's life and riding the subsequent business growth. Many entrepreneurs and small businesses look to venture capitalists to finance the company's expansion into new markets, new products, and new customers. Often times, that expansion does not go as planned and the venture capitalist takes a loss on the investment. But occasionally, a venture capitalist invests early in a company like Apple, Facebook, or Twitter and that stake in the corporation becomes incredibly valuable as the company grows. Importantly, a venture capital firm will often secure preferred terms on its investment so that a successful investment becomes even more valuable with the option to buy more shares, earn dividends, and other rewarding components of the investment deal.

Venture capital is a very attractive area of direct investing for single family offices for a number of reasons. First, the principal of a single family office often founded his own company and therefore identifies with the entrepreneurial spirit of venture capital. Second, the companies that venture capital firms invest in are exciting companies with high growth potential and an innovative business plan. For a single family office, the idea of investing in the next Facebook is extremely thrilling and potentially wildly lucrative. Lastly, single family office investors often express their preference for investing in companies that they understand, have some control in, and that they can actively improve using the SFO team's knowledge and skills. At the later stages of private equity, a single family office is often a passive investor with maybe some influence via a board seat or connection with the CEO. By investing early on in a company's life, a single family office can exercise substantially more control over the growth and direction of the company. Almost every single family office I have met is either open to or actively seeking venture capital-type deals. The biggest challenge for family offices executing venture deals is sourcing high-quality deals and performing due diligence on the companies. But more and more, through peer-to-peer networks, conferences, and active development of deal-sourcing channels, single family offices are locating better deals and developing strong venture capital platforms.

The latest strategy in the venture capital world is the spray and pray strategy, investing in 100-500 different companies within a single 2-3 year period. The most sophisticated employers of this model use quantitative models as well as their insight, the least sophisticated play follow the leader and many HNW and venture capital firms recently try to get into as many late stage pre-ipo shares traded as secondary offerings.

Private Equity / Platform Strategy Investing:

Private equity is a common area of direct investing and a natural progression for family offices who have made venture capital investments already. Private equity is the purchase of equity in a company outside of the public markets, often with the intent to take the company private (if it is already publicly traded) through a leveraged buyout transaction. The target companies are usually on the auction block or thought to be receptive to a buyout, but occasionally private equity investors launch hostile or unsolicited bids for companies. In the more common scenario of a friendly buyout, the target company may be receptive for a variety of reasons, such as: the firm could be under distress from public shareholders; underperforming; losing ground to competitors; another owner could be looking to sell; or any number of other reasons could lead a company to private equity.

Whatever the circumstances, the standard private equity model is to borrow heavily to finance the transaction with only a small fraction of the balance coming from the actual private equity buyer. In order to secure financing, the private equity buyer will often post the company as collateral (assuming the firm's Board approves the deal) and the debt payments will be made by the company, rather than the private equity investor (in this case the family office) itself.

One might wonder why, with all the billions of dollars that private equity funds and institutional investors have, wouldn't the buyer simply put up the majority of the purchase price and avoid paying down debt and incurring interest costs? The answer is explained by two factors: the profitability of leverage and the taxing of interest rate payments. Leverage (borrowed money) allows a private equity investment to produce exceptional gains. The common comparison is a home mortgage: if you purchase a house for $100,000 with $20,000 paid upfront and the rest of the purchase financed through a mortgage, then you can substantially increase your return on investment if you sell for a much higher price. Let's say, 5 years later, the housing market greatly improves and you sell the house for $500,000. You pay back the initial $80,000 loan and with your $20,000 initial investment, you have earned $400,000 in profit on the sale. Of course, this is an exaggerated example and the comparison is not perfect, but you can see how by purchasing a company with mostly borrowed money there is the potential to reap huge gains if you sell the company for a higher price later on. The other attractive element of financing these transactions through debt is that the interest expenses incurred by private equity portfolio companies can be deducted from the business' gross income for tax purposes, a major benefit.

Single family offices that are active direct investors will often look to build a *platform* of operating businesses through private equity buyout transactions, mergers, and acquisitions. As has been discussed in this book, single family offices may look to invest within a single industry or related industries in which the investment team or family has extensive experience. The family can realize synergies and cost-savings by building a platform of aligned businesses. If the family office builds this platform strategically, there can be huge benefits by sharing customers, marketing, overhead expenses, core sales staff, etc. The existing companies might dictate future investments, as the family seeks to acquire companies that will benefit current holdings. This model is similar to the conglomerates that dominated the corporate world in the 1960s or the portfolios owned and operated by today's private equity firms.

Merchant Banks & Investment Banks: It is helpful at this point to review what a merchant bank is and the role that investment banks play in the direct investing world. A merchant bank typically deals with commercial clients, assisting in foreign exchange and international financing, making long-term loans to corporations, and underwriting business loans. Investment banks perform a similar function and the lines between merchant banks and investment banks are sometimes blurry, especially in Europe where the definitions are different.

Investment banks primarily deal with corporate activities, securities, alternative investments, market making, and similar transactions. An investment bank is concerned chiefly with serving corporate clients and helping them access the capital markets and investors. Merchant banks, in the traditional definition, principally deal with trade financing, especially facilitating international trade and business activities. Family offices would rarely classify themselves as a merchant bank or investment bank, because that definition is too narrow and does not encompass all of the different activities in which large single family offices engage. Regardless of whether family offices will self-identify as a merchant or investment bank, many of these family offices have executed trade financing deals, helped raise capital for businesses, provided loans to corporations, and performed similar activities that are usually done by banks. This expansion speaks to a theme of this chapter and the family office industry: the willingness by family offices to expand their investment activities beyond the typical portfolio one might associate with a high-net-worth individual or even large institutional investors.

Deal Origination: Remember the 2007 Wiltbank study cited earlier in this chapter, that the deals which returned the most capital had at least 40 hours of research placed into them? That means that you can only look at around one deal a week, on average, assuming you have a full-time professional dedicated to this space. Most single family offices can't fully dedicate a professional to sourcing deals and conducting due diligence and that is why many rely upon merchant banks, investment banks, and other families to bring them quality deals. However, that process is reactive; often these deals have been shopped already, and may not be as powerful as sourcing a deal directly with a private company owner.

There are several ways to source direct deals with corporations, including:

1. **Call Center:** If you want to ensure a steady flow of deals, you should consider adopting a more proactive strategy of calling on business relationships to feel out potential deals. You can take that one step further and even set up a dedicated team for calling on past relationships and forming new ones in a specific sector or area of business.

2. **Niche Industry Events & Thought Leadership**: If you are looking to invest in a specific sector or type of company, say, a food

company with revenues exceeding $10 million, then you will be well served by attending the top conferences and sharing your expertise investing in the area. By establishing your family as a thought leader in this area and building relationships in the area, you'll become a known face in the industry and become more likely to hear the latest rumors and potential deals before they are shopped to every investor in town.

A number of private equity investors joined us at the Harvard Club in New York for a panel discussion on private equity investing and direct deal sourcing. Investors like these participants often agree to speak as a means for meeting quality private equity partners and sourcing deals at events.

3. **Middle Market Associations & Events:** There are a number of associations and conferences that bring together business leaders in the middle market and investors. Many of these associations are looking for family office speakers to discuss what deals they are looking for, so you may have a chance to address a whole audience of potential deal partners. By publicly presenting your ideal partnership (sector, market capitalization, terms, etc.), then you will receive relevant inquiries over time from audience members and their relationships.

4. **Top 50 Relationship Focus:** Narrowing your focus is a key to a productive deal sourcing strategy. Otherwise, you might "drown in opportunity," chasing too many deals and having a burdensome amount of conversations and inquiries every day. If you narrow your search to building relationships with 50 or so high-value targets, then you can really work those partners and make sure that you only focus on the people that you believe will lead you to a successful deal.

5. **Deal Networks:** There are a number of deal networks out there today that are designed to bring investors and companies together on deals. There is a wide spectrum in the quality of these groups, but the better deal networks can be useful for finding new deal sources and proactively advertising the deals that you are pursuing.

Video: If you would like to watch a short video on sourcing direct investments, please see this page of our website:
http://SingleFamilyOffices.com/Sourcing-Deals-For-Direct-Investments

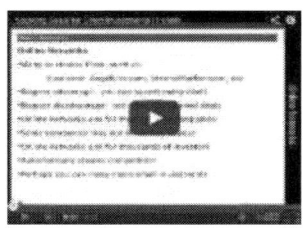

Evaluating Deals & Performing Due Diligence:
Well-known angel investor Bill Payne defines due diligence as "a process of comparing reality with a target company's business plan."

A formalized single family office should have policies and processes in place which force a certain level of due diligence that takes at least 40 hours to execute to ensure that no snap decisions are made to invest in a company without proper investigation of the offering and team behind the company.

While it is not exhaustive, has not been adapted to a specific industry, and will need to be further customized by your team, we have prepared a simple direct investment template to help you focus your due diligence and deal flow screening efforts. To download this template, please see this link:
http://SingleFamilyOffices.com/Direct-Investing.pdf

Video: Here is a short video on evaluating deals and performing due diligence on direct investment opportunities:

http://SingleFamilyOffices.com/Evaluating-Deals

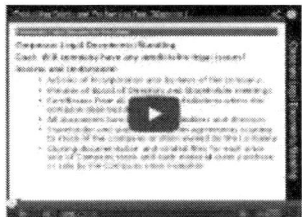

Navigating Direct Investment Contracts & Agreements: The type and length of contract you are provided in any direct investment opportunity will vary based on the age and status of the company, the experience of the entrepreneur, and also the experience level of the attorneys and investors involved as well. Many attorneys will charge $5,000 to $10,000 for early stage capital raising contracts and legal advice, while larger firms may need to pay attorneys upwards of $30,000 to put together these contracts and to receive advice. Since many companies looking for capital are low on cash by their nature as a small and growing business, you will want to ensure your lawyers make sure everything needed is in place and nothing is left to a verbal agreement.

Common legal documents often include a private placement memorandum, term sheet, and shareholders agreement. The standard starting point is the private placement memorandum or PPM. PPMs traditionally explain the offering, provide information on the company, company financials, risk factors, investor survey which confirms that you are an accredited investor, a capital table or share register which shows the current investors and their number of shares in the company, and a subscription agreement or stock purchase agreement. A PPM may include a term sheet, but some sophisticated groups will provide it later in the negotiations. A term sheet covers how many shares are being offered, the price per share, common or preferred share status details, preferences, pro-rata rights, participation rights, pre-emptive rights, conversion rights, and board rights. Typically, a subscription agreement will include agreed upon terms, confidentiality, a non-compete clause, payment terms, transfer of shares (how you will receive the shares), and any risk factors not fully disclosed in the PPM.

While the titles of other documents you may be asked to review will vary, these documents may include a shareholder's agreement or stockholder's agreement, investor's rights agreement, a restated certification of incorporation, options agreement, voting trust, or officer indemnification. With any type of contract, it is essential to have your own qualified legal counsel review the matter overall and the contract at hand.

Video: To watch a short video on direct investing contracts and agreements, please see this video:

http://SingleFamilyOffices.com/Contracts

Risks Associated with Direct Investing: Direct investing is somewhat risky, or every investor would simply allocate 100% of their capital to this area and not bother conducting thorough due diligence. One study conducted in 2011 by the Center for Venture Research at the University of New Hampshire showed that 24% of the angel investments from the 2011 market study ended in bankruptcy, 25% break even, and just over 50% of invested in companies were profitable.

Here are some of the common risks in direct investing and how to mitigate these types of risks:

1. Technology Risk: Many high-tech companies need a new technology to be user-friendly and work as expected. In these types of investments, a great deal of the company's success rides on a few programmers or the acceptance of a certain technology in the marketplace. One way to mitigate this risk is to invest in tranches or installments. For example, you could invest $1M upfront, another $1M once they have a working prototype, another $1M once they have reached $500K in revenue, and a final $1M once they reach $1M in total revenue, etc. This will help protect you further instead of investing $4M upfront without any goals for the company to meet to access the additional capital.

2. Market Risk: There is risk in many new offerings that the marketplace will not accept the products or services the company is offering. For example, Pets.com sold pet products online and too much money was spent upfront on marketing this brand in the marketplace, while the actual market was slow to adopt buying from this new company because they were so early to the online pet retailing game. To mitigate market risk, invest only in what you and your team know and understand, validate the opportunity with real competitors and customers if possible, and evaluate the management team's related experience to ensure this is not one big experiment. As Michael Masterson, a mentor of mine, says, make the company fail fast with an offering, and put the obligation on the company raising capital to prove the market is there.

3. Competitive Risk: There are risks that existing established customers will emulate your offerings and use their superior distribution or marketing reach to crowd you out of the marketplace. There is also a risk that dozens of copycat businesses will emerge and lower the margins and unique value offering that the company you are investing

in provides. To mitigate competitive risk, think about how to build barriers to enter a marketplace. These barriers can include a book, newsletter, magazine, and other thought leaderships assets. Barriers can also include trademarks, domain names, and patents, as well. You can research the market and think ahead at what potential competitors will do so that you can make it very challenging for them to succeed. If you block your competitors successfully, then they may lose interest and look for more fertile ground to compete on. Kevin Harrington, who is worth several hundred million dollars, operates the As Seen on TV brand, and he has been featured on the popular TV show *Shark Tank*, as well. During a recent interview, Kevin said that when his company launches a product now, they test it within a small niche market; then once the product is a proven winner, they buy up every domain name related to that product. Sometimes his company even creates a number of their own copycat products to make the space look more crowded than it is, and then they launch nationally with infomercials and direct marketing. Interestingly, Kevin confirms some of the studies cited in this chapter about returns on investments; after launching products and investing in companies for 20 years, he says that only one out of 10 investments will be a home run, six to seven will lose money and be quickly closed down, and two to three generate a moderate return.

4. Management Risk: This is the biggest risk for young companies, as often the person who can write code well, bake amazing bread, or write lots of books on a small topic is not also the person who is an excellent CEO. Many times, the CEO will need to grow themselves faster than the company is growing, or be replaced. To mitigate this risk, evaluate the management team to see if they are coachable or open to being on the board instead of being in a CEO position. It can also be helpful to require personal guarantees from the founding team, include performance clauses that force them to hit revenue hurdles, or retain voting rights or board seats.

At some companies with a visionary founder who does not necessarily excel at management, the investors or advisors will compromise by installing a Chief Operating Officer or similar C-Suite executive who can handle a lot of the management and day-to-day operations of the firm, even if he or she does not have the CEO title. Tim Cook served as Chief Operating Officer at Apple before rising to the CEO role following Steve Jobs' passing. As Apple grew to one of the largest corporations in the world, the challenges of management were beyond what any one person could reasonably be expected to manage, even an executive with Steve Jobs' talent, and Tim Cook provided a level of comfort to investors and customers that the company would meet the intense pressures effectively. The Apple management story highlights the importance of looking beyond only the CEO when evaluating management risk and looking for capable leaders throughout the ranks to help strengthen the top management.

5. <u>Finance Risk:</u> If a product works and sells well, the company may need additional financing to fuel the expected growth, buy inventory, enter new markets, or expand distribution channels. Sometimes clauses imposed by early investors make it difficult for future investors to participate. It is important to think forward to this point in time, and work with someone experienced in setting up such deals so that you don't block future investors, which may turn out to be critical to the company's success. Whenever possible, try to avoid abnormal deal terms, deals which require multiple rounds of investing, and think about whether you need other investors to lose in order for you to win.

Video: Here is a short video on our website discussing the risks associated with direct investments:

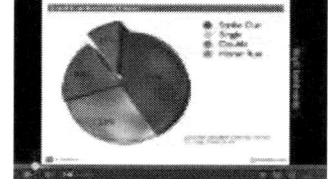

http://SingleFamilyOffices.com/Risk

Exiting and Profiting from Direct Investments: For most investors, the goal in making direct investments is exiting the investment by selling to a private company, completing a secondary sale to another investor, or taking a company public. In some markets, such as Africa where public markets are less developed, investors typically do not plan on taking portfolio companies public. Instead, investors will look for strategic buyers or to complete a deal that will allow them to receive revenue directly from the company over time as a means for getting their money back. In these (mostly emerging) markets, money is sometimes paid back as a percentage of earnings after the company hits a predetermined level of revenue or profits, or it is slowly paid back from the beginning with increased velocity as the business grows larger.

The majority of exits are mergers or acquisitions by competing companies in the marketplace, but other options include a management buyout, or secondary buyout, which means another investor such as a single family office or private equity firm buys the company or the investor's stake in the company.

Robert Wiltbank of Willamette University made several interesting discoveries while conducting the largest study of direct investments. Professor Wiltbank's study showed that 52% of exits were at a loss for investors, and only 7% of exits produced over 10x returns. On average, investments that took longer from start to finish produced superior returns than shorter term investments, signaling that patience in this space can pay off. The research showed that many times investments need at least three years to do well, and that most of the strong-performing investments were under $20M each.

There are a number of ways to increase the value of a company prior to selling it including:

- Understanding what drives the value for buyers, and what they are focused on, such as market share, technology, revenue, employees, etc.

- Positioning your company as a strategic investment and not just an additive revenue acquisition. Facebook's multi-billion dollar acquisition of WhatsApp is a great illustration of this idea. WhatsApp has meager revenues, especially considering the high price that Facebook paid for the company, but WhatsApp recognized that Facebook would have strategic benefits from the acquisition that represented value beyond revenue or traditional valuation metrics.

- Work with financial experts to improve your balance sheet and ensure your corporate structure is appropriate.

- Create an auction-like environment by ensuring that you have multiple competing interested buyers. For example, Coca-Cola may want to not only acquire your company for the business synergies or value it would add to the company, but also to block their competitors from entering a new market or growing in strength. To return to a previous example, WhatsApp's 450 million users (as of 2014) could be a huge advantage to one of Facebook's competitors and Facebook likely agreed to acquire the company at an extremely high earnings multiple partly to block its competitors from buying the company.

- Skilled negotiation and deal structuring can greatly increase the value received during a sale, and often investment bankers or a merchant bank can help with such negotiations. One of our operating assets took us 5 years to negotiate the purchase of, but it was worth it because the price came down from $400K to $138k with 50% of it financed at 0% for the asset, and it is key to growing one part of our business. Obviously when dealing with $20M or $100m transactions the importance of negotiating and using deal structures to make a lower upfront payment more appealing to the seller is the best way to have both parties comfortable that they got a good deal in the transaction. For example on the day I'm writing this I attended a 3.5 hour meeting between a buy-side single family office client I represent in New York and a $18M+ a year operating business looking to sell. The fear was that the family I work with wouldn't be able to meet the EBITDA multiple the owner desired, but after hearing about how the deal would be structured, how to make the deal tax efficient, and how incentives will be aligned with no traditional earn-out, but a 2x pre-return for the remaining piece of equity that the company owner will get to keep in the ongoing entity everyone left on a positive note that the deal is proceeding towards a close. Could it not close, sure, but for purposes of negotiating this is something to always remember to use to navigate these sensitive conversations.

Video: To watch a short video on exiting direct investments, please see this page of our website:

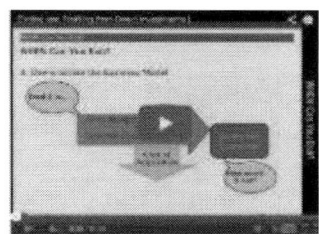

http://SingleFamilyOffices.com/Exiting

Top Mistakes in Direct Investing

There are pitfalls with any type of investing, and direct investing is no exception. Here are some of the most common mistakes made:

1. Poor Due Diligence: Many single family offices have small teams, and have limited time to investigate opportunities. This can lead to

sometimes rushed due diligence or over-reliance upon third parties who promise strengths of due diligence, but who also may be very busy and stretched thin. At the very least, most single family offices should be conducting 40 hours of due diligence, background checks, reference checks, and fact-gathering practices before making an investment.

2. <u>Not Anticipating Future Rounds</u>: Most companies will need to raise capital more than once; you should expect this and structure your deals at the outset to reflect that potential reality. If you do not structure your deal correctly, you may lose the chance to participate in future rounds, or your shares may be diluted by future capital raises.

3. <u>Not Understanding the Exit Before You Enter</u>: As a direct investor, you may experience the following performance breakdown on your investments: only 1 out of 10 investments will work out extremely well, two will make some money, and seven of the investments may on average lose money or just not grow. This is why it is important to diversify your direct investment holdings.

   As with any investment, you want to prepare a concrete strategy for exiting the investment and recouping your money (hopefully with a nice ROI). If you have a timeline in mind for holding and exiting an asset or a company, be sure to plan out when you will approach potential buyers, look for strategic mergers and acquisitions, and explore an initial public offering, if that is realistic. An IPO, for example, takes substantial effort and time investment to execute and the SEC has a set process and timeline for selling shares to the public that you will need to follow. As any wise investor can tell you, when you sell is sometimes even more important than when you buy. So it is really important to have a clear plan to exit your investments.

4. <u>Overzealous Negotiations</u>: Often negotiations can fall apart due to valuations which are not based on realized sales, or that are based on someone's past track record. CEOs tend to want the world for their company because that is their role, to be the visionary that is passionate about the opportunity. The single family office investor's job, however, is to bring the management team or owner back to reality without insulting them, wasting their time, or suggesting their hard work and business are not valuable. A difference in valuation is

a top reason for a direct investment to get derailed. There is always a tension between what the owner of the asset believes is a good, attractive price and what the seller believes is a fair, attractive price; the ability to find a balance between these is a key to completing a direct investment.

5. <u>Not Storing Dry Powder</u>: It is often valuable to invest in a company through two or three phases instead of investing all the money upfront. This is not employing the Dollar-Cost Averaging technique used in stock trading; rather, this gradual expansion of a direct stake aims to encourage the CEO and company to meet certain milestones to unlock the next level of funding, and it guards you against the company possibly going down in flames and losing your entire investment.

6. <u>Throwing Good Money in After Bad</u>: Operating businesses often ask current investors for more money to get their product to market, but statistics show that follow-on investments typically are not a good idea unless the business has been a great success already. Instead of putting another $10M into a business that is struggling, family offices should consider other opportunities where you could invest $10M into a business with great momentum and market positioning.

7. <u>Not Having an Attorney Review Everything</u>: This sounds obvious, but too often important, seemingly inconsequential clauses are not included in the contract and adjusting the contract becomes increasingly difficult as time passes since signing the agreement. You should compare an ideal or preferred contract with the one that you receive so you can see which clauses, scenarios, and terms need to be completed before signing. One rule of thumb to follow is that if the other party writes the contract and assures you that everything "looks good and ready to sign," then you are in trouble. The reverse of this mistake is also true, if you can always be the one to prepare the initial contract, and the other party either doesn't review it completely or doesn't have an experienced attorney review it you have a marked long-term advantage while forming many contracts for various partnerships and investments over time.

Video: We have recorded a short video on Direct Investing Mistakes that covers some related points, which you can watch here:

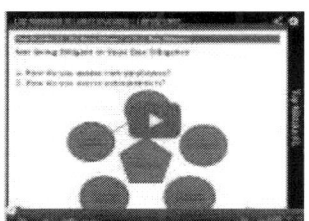

http://SingleFamilyOffices.com/Top-Mistakes

As we will discuss later in this book, there is a trend of creating buy-side deal sourcing programs for family offices or hiring investment banking or M&A firms to serve as a Chief Direct Investment Officer (CDIO) for a single family office. The trick is finding someone who understands family offices, direct investing, and can attract consistent deal flow from other families, private equity funds, and institutional investors.

Interview with Harris Fried:

To get an additional perspective on direct investing, we conducted an interview with Harris to see what lessons he has learned while completing direct investments for his single family office.

Richard C. Wilson: What advice do you have for those families who have completed due diligence on a company and would like to make a direct investment?

Harris Fried: It is increasingly important for the acquirers to establish an efficient vehicle for acquiring the company or to make an investment. This decision should reflect short and long-term changes in ownership of the investment or potential conflicts in exit timing by different generations or investment partners. Making sure that this vehicle is flexible enough to adjust to potentially multiple acquisitions or allowing international investors to participate as well are also important points. If possible, an element of liquidity should be included as well to help attract more co-investors, if that is a priority.

Richard C. Wilson: Any words of advice or warnings before a family makes their first direct investment?

Harris Fried: I would also like to add that careful consideration will be needed with regard to introducing new management and how the "new" enterprise will move forward. Many times, cost-cutting, supply chain efficiencies, market share growth, and new product development need to be re-designed from the ground up. These plans should be put together before an acquisition is made so the necessary resources and costs may be estimated upfront. Think of this as a pure private equity play where improvement in the old business will be necessary to enhance everyone's investment returns.

Richard C. Wilson: We would like to help single family offices add another layer of sophistication to their direct investment portfolios, just as fund manager selection and risk management has evolved over the last 20 years...do you have any advice on taking a more sophisticated and well-designed approach to building a direct investment portfolio?

Harris Fried: In answering this question, I am assuming that the family has aligned its own goals and financial aspirations with the concept of Direct Investing. As with all types of investments, there are issues of liquidity, risk, extent of obligations aside from simply investing money, etc. that must be taken into consideration prior to really moving into this field. Once a commitment is made, protocols must be established to allow for a businesslike approach to each and every aspect of the investment process from due diligence to closing the transaction. The investment in new businesses should at the outset be clearly delineated from the Family Office (FO) to avoid any liabilities of the business flowing over to the FO. Generally, a separate legal entity will be established for the PE activities with each new investment placed in a "silo," separate from the other investments. It is our usual practice to consider how we can exit the investment and when. While certainly this is more art than science, it is a critical exercise to engage in.

Richard C. Wilson: In your years of experience, how can families best identify high quality deal flow opportunities whether they be direct investments or co-investments?

Harris Fried: The are many ways to develop a deal flow process, but it helps to first set parameters for what kind and size deals you are looking for. Going through this thought process will help define the way in which deals will be introduced. It can be very useful to reach out to the family's advisors, such as lawyers, bankers, and accountants, to help create the platform for investing. There are now consultants, boutique investment banks, and of course business brokers that can help find deals. We early on made the decision to focus on one industry sector, which happens to be defense, so we regularly attend defense exhibits and network at all other levels to create both "domain expertise" as well as deal flow. The important thing is to get the parameters established and stick to them to make the search for promising opportunities more productive. Several of the larger wealth management firms have platforms by which WM clients will have access to the firm's investment bankers to help source deals and analyze them, as well as help with structuring an offer, presenting it and providing an avenue for financing if this is required. Management of the PE vehicle referred to above should be well versed in all aspects of corporate finance. That person (or the team) will need to be able to coordinate the acquisition process and be prepared to present it to the family for approval. We have reached the point now that Direct Investing has become a cottage industry within the Family Office space.

Richard C. Wilson: Many families would like to only invest in distressed opportunities or operating businesses which are struggling in some way, so that the potential return could be higher. What advice do you have for families in identifying these types of investment opportunities specifically?

Harris Fried: Distressed investing has never been our forte, although some groups are very adept at it. Our preference is to take over businesses with a positive cash flow, but have for whatever reason reached a point of stagnation. The one aspect of the distressed debt area that we have considered in the past is buying company debt, which ranks in terms of security near the top of the capital structure. Like so many aspects of Direct Investing, focusing on distressed debt requires a special skill set to really make it work. Without a solid understanding of what distressed debt is and capable people with a proven ability to work a company out of it, this is an area to avoid. When a company is at the distressed stage, the number of things that can go wrong multiplies dramatically.

Richard C. Wilson: Do you have any stories of a co-investment going poorly for a family (can be anonymous case study), and lessons that can be learned from that example?

Harris Fried: We don't have any actual stories of a co-investment going wrong, but we are very realistic about the challenges that are attendant here. Goals need to be aligned from very early on. A mutual understanding of how the company will be run will clearly need to be established with provisions for addressing disagreements available to all parties. Co-investing often implies a situation where there are minority shareholders, which can add another layer of possible dispute. While we will consider co-investing, as there are advantages to it especially if a family is investing alongside a family that has established domain expertise, our objective is to control the company.

Richard C. Wilson: Do you have a standard due diligence process, due diligence questionnaire, or set of tools you could share with other single family offices looking to get their direct investment division started and are investing for the first time in this space?

Harris Fried: We do have a set of policies and procedures for doing due diligence. We had our lawyers and investment bankers develop the procedures and they are considered proprietary, but just think of a 360 degree view of the company where nothing should be off-limits, so long as it does not become disruptive. Normally, we start by taking a bird's-eye view of the company and where it fits into the industry. How good is its product or service? How, when, where, and by whom can the company be leveraged to create a larger, more productive and hopefully more profitable footprint? Once the due diligence process begins, it takes on a life of its own, yielding large amounts of useful information.

Richard C. Wilson: When you look at making investments, what do you care about most? The team, the industry, or the financials (free cash flow, EBITDA, etc.)?

Harris Fried: Since we are defense-centric, we only look at opportunities in this sector. Of almost equal importance would be the quality of what they produce, the caliber of its workforce and where improvement and enhancement can be made to expand the scope of the business. Naturally, financials are critical. Audited financials, tax returns, and contracts with customers are all scrutinized. An investigation of the principals is often done. A firm belief that we can make a business better, more profitable, and efficient is what propels us forward.

Richard C. Wilson: Can you provide some advice on how to structure minority, non-controlling investments so you do retain some board control, control over executive pay, and are protected at the table as an equity holder?

Harris Fried: Protecting minority interests is generally going to be a matter of a Shareholder's Agreement. If we were to assume a minority position, we would endeavor to have included in a agreement between shareholders the right to a Board seat, right to veto major decisions, pre-emptive rights, provision against self-dealing, anti-dilution clause, tag-along rights, right of first opportunity (if a shareholder desires to sell their interests), and pro-rata dividend payments. This list could go on, but these are good examples of what should be included in the agreement if a minority shareholder wants to protect its position. How much of this you will get will depend on how much you will be investing. Obviously, the more on a percentage basis is invested, the more insistent one should be on obtaining the rights referred to above.

Richard C. Wilson: Can you speak to the fear of dilution, and to what extent should families be worried about being diluted in future rounds of capital raising?

Harris Fried: A family can protect itself to a certain extent from dilution by having an anti-dilution provision included in the Articles. Also, if an investor has pre-emptive rights, they can preserve their position so long as they are willing to invest more money. Provisions of these types are encouraged, but it should at the same time be remembered that fresh capital may be required, so a certain amount of dilution should be expected.

Podcast Interview: If you enjoyed this written interview with Harris Fried please subscribe to our Family Office Podcast on iTunes to hear him answer some different questions in audio format. To hear the latest episodes of the Family Office Podcast, go to http://FamilyOffices.com/Podcast

Interview with David Fisher

To complete this chapter, we conducted an interview with David Fisher, CEO of single family office Bentley Capital Ltd. David provides a few great insights into direct investing derived from his experience allocating capital for his family office.

Richard C. Wilson: Do you look for direct investments and co-investments in multiple industries or just one or two; and why?

David Fisher: We follow the Buffet Rule—"Never invest in anything you don't understand"—so we make sure that we have sufficient knowledge, either in-house or via co-investors we trust, before we take a serious look at an investment. We have also developed a quick screen that allows us to be more efficient in selecting which deals to pursue, since each active deal takes time, money, and effort to do properly. MOPPSCABE is an acronym that signifies the ideal elements of a good investee company. In a sentence, investors look for enterprises that demonstrate real Market Opportunities for Profitable Products or Services with Competitive Advantages and Barriers to Entry. The first two elements (MO+PPS) make a business possible. The last two elements (CA+BE) make it a good and enduring business; without these, competitors enter to drive your costs up and your prices down. This strict screen quickly eliminates most deals from consideration.

Richard C. Wilson: Many family offices invest in return for equity or provide a combination of equity and debt financing. Have you seen anyone successfully invest in return for royalties, and do you have any examples of this working well for a family office?

David Fisher: I have, but I believe it's rare as it's an off-the-top cost for the licensee who pays the royalty, whether the company is profitable or not, rather than dividends paid from profits. It does, however, simplify the accounting, control, and minority-shareholder issues that investors may face. Also, there may be tax advantages if, for example, an offshore licensor has legitimate IP and uses a Netherlands SPV to collect the royalty payments. I am open to any reasonable technique that helps protect minority shareholders. Having done a lot of minority investing in Emerging Markets, I can assure you that minority investors can lose their money in many different ways.

Richard C. Wilson: Can you talk about having a controlling vs. non-controlling or minority position in a company, what you prefer, and some nuances and lessons learned around this topic?

David Fisher: I have some strong opinions on this issue as you can surmise from my points above. Most Family Offices are now investors, rather than owners (except for the original Family Business), so they often face the "minority-position" problem. Almost jokingly, I talk about the odd concept of getting a "controlling **minority** position" before I feel comfortable making a minority investment. By this, I mean having a binding legal commitment from the majority shareholders and company management that requires the company (a) to do certain things and (b) not to do certain other things without the prior express approval of the minority shareholders. I have a long list of "Super-Majority" items, which are adapted to the deal specifics, but the main ideas are –

1. Pre-agree a Management Team, which can be changed for poor performance, with minority input
2. Pre-agree a Business Plan & Budget for each year, which cannot be changed materially without approval
3. Prohibit any related-party dealing
4. Require independent pre-agreed auditors and lawyers
5. Control capital coming into and out of the business
6. Pre-agree a fair exit process for the minority investors
7. Institute deadlock-resolution procedures for when you cannot agree
8. Establish binding and enforceable arbitration for legal disputes

 Of course, the majority shareholders will only agree to these constraints if you are an excellent value-added minority investor who can help them achieve *their* goals.

Richard C. Wilson: Do you have a case study or example of direct investments or co-investments you have made and could you take us through how they were sourced, the due diligence process, and why you selected those investments?

David Fisher: A brief example is a young company that uses the pattern of sharkskin to inhibit the growth and transfer of bacteria. It has been featured on *PBS Nova*, *CBS Sunday Morning*, *INC. Magazine* and elsewhere as an up-and-coming technology company with great potential for fighting infections.

- We often start with current macro-trends to make sure we're swimming with the tide. Then we identify businesses that we understand and comply with the MOPPSCABE screen mentioned above.

- This particular company got our attention from an internet article, coupled with the macro-trend of widespread difficulties being encountered controlling infectious bacteria, like in hospitals, cruise ships, pandemics, etc. The potential applications seem enormous for their patented (and thus protected) process.

- We cold-called company management, which was luckily in an A-Round fundraising then. We got comfort from the other investors, which included successful VC funds and other experienced investors. Since they were fundraising, many of the materials were readily available. We did all the standard due diligence—management, compensation, intellectual property, markets, technology, competition, strategy, finances, co-investors, suppliers, legal, taxes, exit, etc.

- The company was also very successful at obtaining (a) U.S. government grants (thus reducing its equity requirements and ownership dilution) and (b) corporate partners to develop specific applications of the technology, which is applying the micro-topography of sharkskin to make the surface environment hostile to bacterial growth and transfer.

- Thus far, the company has progressed well, with a new VC investor at double our A-Round valuation, about cash-flow break-even, and more well-known corporate partners developing applications for everything from medical devices to office furniture to food processing to children's toys. We also introduced Sharklet to our contacts at the Mayo Clinic and are hoping for the best. This is an investment where you really can do *well* for yourself and do *good* for society.

Richard C. Wilson: Can you talk a bit about term sheets and structuring deals?

David Fisher: A term sheet is the core of the negotiation process. It is sometimes referred to as a letter of intent, agreement in principle, or memorandum of understanding, but typically it is non-binding and indicative of what is expected of each party. Here is a small diagram showing where in the investment process term sheets come into play:

Richard C. Wilson: When it comes to structuring deals, can you lay out many of the issues that must be addressed during that part of the acquisition process?

The main points of deal structuring are (a) to assemble all the resources needed to operate the intended business (usually people and tangible/intangible property) and then (b) to finance these resources. The first part consists of securing all required legal rights to use these resources for the business and the second part concerns how the risks and rewards of the business are shared among the suppliers of the capital that finances the required people and property.

Needs of the Business - Never lose sight of the basic needs of the business; no structure is a good one unless it allows the business to operate optimally. To place things in perspective—t he market opportunity drives the business strategy, which in turn controls the financial strategy and structure of the enterprise.

Goals of the Parties - These must be consistent, or at least without any major conflict. If you can structure a deal so that your partner achieves his goals, it has a much better chance of closing and succeeding.

Preferences of the Parties - Also try to learn and accommodate the preferences of your potential partners. Often you can score points that cost you nothing (e.g., the name of the new entity).

Legal Forms - Consider the possibilities relating control, liability, formalities, cost, and tax issues. In CEE, your basic choices for investors are a contractual sharing of revenues, a limited liability company, a joint stock company, or a limited partnership.

Contracts - Standard Terms should be given out early so that the other side cannot negotiate over them later. Our contracts should be extensive and tough enough to give us the "legal high ground," since once the money's paid out, we have little leverage. Hope for the best, but prepare for the worst.

Deal Costs - We have substantial overhead and out-of-pocket expenses for doing, monitoring and nurturing deals, so we need to recover at least our direct expenses (and another 1% for overhead) at funding and 1% per year thereafter. We give real services for these fees via advice and contacts. We may also get investment banking fees for finding further financing or joint venture arrangements. Even if we give these fees to the Fund, it gets our capital back faster and makes the other equity holders share the costs for our value-added.

Taxation - Pay what you owe, but structure deals so as to minimize your tax liabilities since taxes are really just another cost of doing business. Always keep your eyes open for tax incentives.

Potential Liabilities - These must be examined in detail, since some can come with an existing business that is being contributed into the new venture, or the investor can be held liable for some in the new venture (like unpaid taxes).

Risk vs. Reward - This is the key to successful investing—structure so as to decrease the risks and increase the rewards. Look at your blended ROIC when you use several instruments and fees. Also remember that in venture capital, you must have the potential on each deal to score big since you normally also have the possibility of *losing* big. The earlier the stage of the venture, the more risk that's taken by the financiers. Therefore, we deserve bigger returns. To give more to the entrepreneur later, he/she can ratchet up based on outstanding performance by the venture.

Pricing - Basically, you price your financial instruments (i.e., debt, equity and hybrid securities) in light of (a) the competitive market for such capital and (b) your own required return. Depending on your sources of funds, the second factor may be built on a spread or constructed *ab initio* for the specific deal. Such a constructed hurdle rate or required rate of return would consider the relevant risk free rate + risk premiums + inflation effects to yield a minimum real rate of return.

Funding - Make sure that you have everything that you need before you release the funds. Also, see if you can fund in stages based upon investee needs and specific results. Sometimes, major items can be paid directly to, for example, an equipment supplier.

Constraints - Every deal has them, so consider the constraints, whatever they might be, and determine how to get around them, or live with them, in the most constructive way.

Creativity - To deal with constraints and other obstacles be creative and flexible; don't be afraid to try new approaches. Just run it by the lawyers and accountants before you sign.

Security - If we're funding debt, we deserve security. It can be in various forms and degrees—retention of title, leasing of assets, company promissory notes, assignment of accounts receivable, mortgage on real estate, pledge of shares and moveable assets, collateral bank accounts, individual and bank guarantees, and letters of credit, etc. Also remember that collateral should be maintained properly and insured with us as the loss payee to the extent of our amounts lent.

Priorities to Revenues/Assets - A business uses assets to generate a stream of revenues. A part of deal structuring is determining the **who, what, when and how** as to priority over them.

Due Diligence - Is a way of learning a lot about the business. It also uncovers potential problems which could bite you later. The contractual warranties, representations and indemnities should cover you, but often legal remedies are too little, too late. Always make your deal subject to satisfactory due diligence. If you don't like what you find you can walk or lower the price.

Monitoring & Controls - You must have adequate rights to monitor your investment; otherwise you're dead. Negative controls give you the right to veto things you **don't like** and positive controls allow you to require or encourage the things you **do like**. Examples of both include audits and inspections, business plans and budgets, signing authority on bank accounts, and super-majority votes on major business events.

Exits - Since you don't intend to stay invested forever, you must have exit provisions agreed upfront. Usually, these include a lock-up followed by a right to sell (often with a right of first negotiation to your partner) and/or a right to require a sale of the entire business. Exit provisions should be very explicit since they can be very contentious in application.

Personnel - People who run the business are key assets, so you need to tie their interests closely to the success of the business. Think about employment contracts (with provisions like exclusivity, confidentiality, non-competition), key-man life insurance, profit sharing and share ownership. You also need a mechanism to replace management that's not effective. This can be very emotional, since the entrepreneur always suspects that you're out to steal his business anyway.

Covenants - If something's important, put it in the contract as an explicit positive or negative covenant. Businessmen tend to forget their oral promises when convenient to do so.

Conflicts of Interest - Consider all the possible conflicts of interest, like self- or related-party dealing, and make sure that they must be disclosed and pre-approved by you.

Fairness - Try to look at the deal from the other side to see if you could live with the deal you're offering. A deal that's fair to both sides will have a much better chance of surviving long-term.

Dispute Resolution - Unfortunately, in complex, long-term transactions, disputes often arise. Therefore, you need a rapid, impartial and reliable forum to settle them. Usually, binding arbitration works best.

Negotiating Leverage - Think through the alternatives of the parties. Get the other side pregnant and reduce its options. Always give the impression that you can walk away from the deal. Remember that the relative leverage often shifts over time/events at several points during the negotiations. When you give something, get something in return.

Attitudes & Egos - Try to keep a positive and friendly, yet firm, attitude toward the negotiations. Let the other side save face, even if you've beaten the hell out of them. It's often hard, but try to keep off egos and on issues.

Debt vs. Equity - It's usually best to start with low leverage and then gear up to Optimal Capital Structure once the business has shown that it can service the debt. Remember, mixing high *operating* leverage with high *financial* leverage can be dangerous.

Financial vs. Non-Financial Returns - Think about the impact of each deal point on your financial returns (i.e., net cash in and out, when, and how certain?). Also consider the non-financial returns that may accrue to each side from the transaction.

Richard C. Wilson: David, you mentioned while speaking that you have a list of actions the investee company can take only with the prior consent of its minority shareholders (often the financial investors); can you list those out here?

David Fisher: Sure, please find these below:

These are extensive super-majority items that may require more than 50% of applicable votes (by classes or in the aggregate). You should select the items, voting percentages, and other limitations depending on the specifics of your deal (e.g. Are we to be majority or minority owners? How large is the Company?). Also note that a) you normally would not need all items, b) some items are more appropriate at the Board level and others at the Shareholder level, c) you need to avoid deadlocks by small shareholders, excessive voting events, and micro-management of the Company, and d) local company law may supersede these provisions in certain instances or they may need to be in different operative documents, so consult a local corporate attorney.

Approval, via the affirmative vote of not less than X% of all shares then outstanding, must be duly obtained for each of the following major business events of the Company or its subsidiaries:

1. Changing the statutes, charter, articles or bylaws.

2. Changing the share capital or other equity accounts.

3. Purchasing, selling, redeeming, transferring or issuing equity or equity-related securities by the Company.

4. Changing key personnel or their service agreements.

5. Pledging, selling, or transferring Company securities by any shareholder.

6. Borrowing, leasing, lending, guaranteeing or investing in excess of Estimated Ultimate Recoverable (EUR) or equivalent [NB: These limits can be set in % rather than in absolute amounts].

7. Changing the principal auditors.

8. Changing the basic accounting or taxation methods.

9. Changing the principal outside legal counsel.

10. Creating subsidiary or affiliated companies.

11. Establishing bank or securities accounts and their individual signatories.

12. Setting the policies for the individual Company commitment and signatory rights of officers and directors.

13. Changing Board (or Board Committee) membership, authority, or operations.

14. Settling or instigating legal claims or proceedings for greater than Estimated Ultimate Recoverable or equivalent.

15. Listing or de-listing the Company on a public securities market.

16. Making business acquisitions, consolidations, divestments, transformations, mergers, or joint ventures.

17. Taking material actions or decisions involving matters outside the normal course of business.

18. Entering into collective-bargaining or union agreements.

19. Approving the annual business plan and budget, and changes thereto greater than EUR or equivalent.

20. Declaring and paying any shareholder distributions or dividends.

21. Approving conflict of interest situations and transactions greater than EUR or equivalent. Any such transaction must be on competitive terms and the involved parties may not vote regarding such approval.

22. Pledging, charging, mortgaging, or otherwise encumbering assets for greater than EUR or equivalent.

23. Filing for voluntary dissolution, liquidation or bankruptcy.

24. Changing any above super-majority provision.

Podcast Interview: If you enjoyed this written interview with David Fisher, please subscribe to our Family Office Podcast on iTunes to hear him answer some different questions in audio format. To hear the latest episodes of the Family Office Podcast, go to http://FamilyOffices.com/Podcast

 **Direct Investing Worksheet:** Similar to other sections of the book, I would like to make sure when you finish reading this, you have something practical to take away, actionable insights, a plan for you and your family, and a talking document to work around. To that end, I have taken the one-page dossiers we create for our Billionaire Family Office clients and single family offices we work with and created a Direct Investment One-Pager Worksheet. This can be printed off or easily sent to team members in Adobe PDF format, or completed on your computer in Microsoft Word format using the links below:

 Direct Investment Worksheet (PDF):
http://SingleFamilyOffices.com/Direct-Investing.pdf

 Direct Investment Worksheet (DOC):
http://SingleFamilyOffices.com/Direct-Investing.doc

Conclusion

In conclusion, direct investing can provide transparency and potential upside rewards for taking control of your investments without a layer of fund management fees, but it comes with the risk and responsibility of conducting deep due diligence, and maintenance/monitoring on that investment portfolio. In the next few chapters, we will discuss co-investing and club investing as a follow up to this discussion to direct investing.

Chapter 12: Co-Investing & Club Deals

"In general, an asset should be sold when it has greater value to a buyer. This happens when a buyer has a complementary business or capability that would enable them to do more with that business. Many businesses we have exited were not failures, but had simply reached a point in their life cycle where they no longer provided a core capability or served as a platform for growth."

- Charles Koch

"What is dangerous is not to evolve"
- Jeff Bezos

Co-Investment Definition: When a limited partner invests directly with a general partner in a company, thereby allocating capital through the fund to the company, but also directly to the company via the co-investment.

It is wise to first answer a common question: what is co-investing? Co-investing refers to when an investor, often an institutional investor with substantial investable capital, allocates capital *alongside* an investment fund to a target investment, rather than *through* the investment fund. A common scenario that illustrates this distinction is when a private equity fund grants co-investment rights to a single family office. If that fund is investing in a company to take it private for $10 billion, then the fund may carve out a $100 million piece for the single family office to invest directly alongside the fund, rather than through the fund as a traditional LP.

The Basic Structure: Speaking generally, there are two main types of co-investments: direct and indirect. In a direct co-investment, the co-investor will make an allocation directly into the portfolio company, manage that investment from the initiation to the exit, and negotiate terms of the investment with the company itself. Indirect co-investments are more likely to be structured differently, reflecting characteristics of the investor and the company. Indirect co-investment will most often occur under a Special Purpose Vehicle (SPV) where the co-investor allocates capital to the company via the SPV and then the investment is managed under that SPV, although co-investments may be made under different structures, such as limited partnerships and LLCs, depending on the tax treatment of the vehicle. Alternately, an indirect co-investment can be made through a fund, which could aggregate multiple co-investments, rather than a singular investment through the SPV. Of course, there are many different features of both indirect and direct co-investment structures and numerous considerations for co-investors.[3]

Club Deals: Co-investments are often used interchangeably with club deals. A club deal is related to co-investing, but we will distinguish here that club deals occur between multiple investors who pool their capital and resources to tackle a large investment. A club deal can be an investment made by multiple single family offices together. Imagine that a single family office stumbles upon a business where the owner is looking to exit and sell the business to the right buyer. If the business is too big for the SFO to take down by itself, the family office may seek additional investors to put up the requisite capital.

There are a number of differences between club deals and co-investments. Co-investments differ in that club deals are often marriages of convenience between large investment funds attempting to tackle a large deal as a consortium. Co-investments, on the other hand, generally occur when a fund or lead investor on a deal grants co-investment rights to a particular LP to "double down" on its investment with an investment directly into one of the portfolio companies or indirectly through a GP-managed vehicle. While the structure often varies for co-investments based on a variety of factors, investors in a club deal generally come into the investment under the same structure. Club deals are more pre-meditated, with parties agreeing on terms and structures for the transactions in advance. A co-investment, on the other hand, is often an added feature on a deal and tends to be structured more

---

[3] Pepper Hamilton. 2013. "United States: Best Practices in Structuring Co-investments." http://www.mondaq.com/unitedstates/x/232170/M+A+Private%20equity/Best+Practices+in+Structuring+Coinvestments

opportunistically. Co-investors are typically more passive investors on the deal, which is sourced by the GP or lead investor, rather than a consortium of active, near-equal investors that team up for a club deal. This chapter deals with co-investments and how family offices can incorporate co-investments in their investing strategy.

Benefits for Investors vs. Costs to Fund Managers

General partners sometimes resist the inclusion of co-investment rights for a number of reasons: the co-investment adds a layer of complexity to the fund; the general partner sacrifices capital that would have been invested under the standard fund vehicle and instead receives that capital through the co-investment structure; other limited partners in the fund are more likely to request similar arrangements; and by allowing co-investments, the general partner encourages future co-investments and direct investments by investors.

Family offices and other investors are demanding co-investment rights for many of the same reasons that fund managers have historically opposed the model; LPs hope to use co-investments to reduce overall fees on private equity investments, manage more investments internally, gain more control through investments in companies, and gradually establish an in-house direct investment platform. Additionally, the costs and added complexity of developing co-investment structures, whether it is a Special Purpose Vehicle for a single co-investment or a co-investment fund, can be burdensome on the GP. While some of the costs specific to the co-investment may be shared with the co-investor(s), fund sponsors may be expected to forego management and performance fees on co-investments. This expectation is based on the understanding that the co-investment is benefitting from the work already done by the fund in sourcing and evaluating the company and therefore the same fees should not be charged to co-investors, and this concession is often viewed as a reward for investors. The economics of co-investments will vary depending on the GP-LP relationship, the expenses incurred by the fund sponsor, the level of involvement by the LP, the structure of the investment, and many other factors.

As we will dig into shortly, family offices are increasingly making co-investments. The benefit to the SFO making a co-investment is clear: the investor can invest directly, thus circumventing the typical fund structure and the fees that cut into its return on investment. But the investor still captures the benefit of having the private equity fund's management team to source, assess and monitor the investment and provide the majority of the capital on the investment. If the single family office were to try and invest independently without the private equity fund, it would have to find the right company to invest in, come up with sufficient capital or financing to execute the deal, persuade ownership to accept the investment, perform due diligence on the firm, manage the investment, and ultimately exit with a profit that justified the exceptional sweat equity and resources put into the deal. Thus, one can see why investors are pushing fund managers to allow these co-investments.

One topical example is the 2013 deal to take Dell, Inc. private for nearly $25 billion. The private equity-led buyout was a club deal between founder Michael Dell and the tech-focused private equity firm Silver Lake Partners. Mr. Dell helped put together the deal with Silver Lake Partners—and partly with financing help from his single family office, MSD Capital—and, after a contentious battle with shareholders (most notably activist investor Carl Icahn), the deal was finalized. The buyout was remarkable for a number of reasons: for one, a billionaire technology pioneer launched a bid to take his own troubled company private; second, the deal represents one of the largest technology buyouts in history and pitted a top private equity firm against probably the most well-known activist investor, leading to a battle lasting more than 14 months. But the most relevant aspect of this for the purposes of this book is that Michael Dell and MSD Capital, his single family office that serves as an investing arm for the billionaire, executed an exceptionally large and complicated deal that highlighted how exceptionally wealthy families are increasingly investing outside of the traditional fund structure and partnering with experienced partners (like Silver Lake) to take on bigger deals. Another interesting element to the Dell buyout is that Silver Lake investors sought and received co-investment rights to "double down" on the deal. Silver Lake disclosed in a 2013 regulatory filing that the fund had allowed its LPs to invest a total of $350 million in the deal through co-investments. This showed that investors were eager to gain additional exposure to the deal through co-investments—beyond the amount they would have through their capital commitments to the fourth Silver Lake fund. The co-investments also benefitted Silver Lake Partners by limiting the private equity fund's capital investment to about $1 billion—near the target limit that Silver Lake seeks to avoid overexposure to any one deal for the fund and its LPs. The $350 million co-investments gave investors the chance to invest more in the Dell deal and served to limit the Silver Lake fund's risk if the deal soured. These types of co-investments are becoming more and more common and investors are increasingly clamoring for the opportunity to double down on investments. The Dell deal serves as an excellent recent case study in the rise in co-investing and direct deals and how these investments are changing the investing landscape.

Scope of Co-Investing: Co-investments can start at $100K in total acquisition price and range up to $1B or more. In my experience, the families who do the most direct investing and co-investments are the $1B+ families with whom we work. These large family offices target companies in the $2M-$25M range in revenue size, but there are many exceptions to that norm. To gauge how reflective our experience was against the global family office industry, we included a question regarding the size of direct investments and co-investments that families typically target and the graph below depicts the response we got:

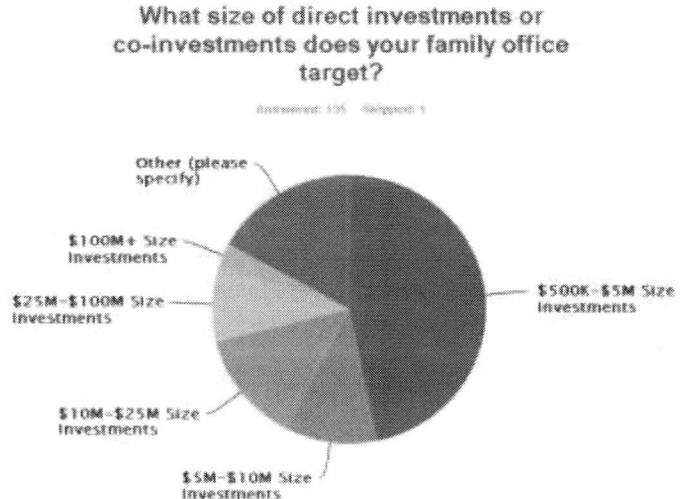

As you can see in the above breakdown, most family offices that participated in our survey favored investments in the $500,000 to $5 million range. Only a small number of participants were looking for co-investments of $100 million or greater. Only the largest family offices can handle $100 million+ co-investments and even $1B+ single family offices tell me that they are not looking to take on deals in that high range, preferring to take controlling stakes in middle market companies or ride along with a minority position in larger companies or projects. It can be very difficult for family offices to execute co-investments effectively and navigate what can often be highly complex deals with multiple parties and risks to consider. But for those family offices who have expertise in structuring and executing co-investments, the rewards can be substantial.

Growing Demand for Co-Investments

The increasing number of co-investments can be largely attributed to a recent shift in the balance of power in favor of investors and away from general partners and fund managers. As the financial crisis and recession ravaged the markets, investments funds suffered substantial capital outflows as investors fled for investments perceived to be safer, more liquid and less expensive. To make matters worse for fund managers, performance across most investment strategies and vehicles was weak at best, with many funds collapsing or recording double-digit losses. This left hedge funds, private equity funds, and other funds vulnerable and desperate to woo limited partners.

At the height of the boom in 2006-2007, many top hedge funds and private equity firms were loath to accommodate even large institutional investors, and GPs routinely dismissed LP requests for improved terms, lower fees, and greater flexibility in their investments. Now, many GPs were reconsidering their previous intransigence in light of the new reality, wherein investors possessed greater leverage in negotiating terms, fees, and structure. Co-investment rights are one of the concessions offered by fund managers to institutional investors as an inducement for committing capital to a fund.

By offering co-investment rights, a general partner can often persuade reticent investors to allocate to a fund. The investor would commit capital to the fund as a traditional limited partner investor, but also the investor would retain the right to co-invest alongside the fund directly. Thus, the investor would have two stakes in the company, one allocation to the portfolio company through the fund and the other directly to the company through the co-investment.

Not all co-investments are direct; indeed, many co-investments are indirect. Similar to a standard fund allocation, the general partner will establish a co-investment vehicle, typically a special purpose vehicle (SPV), through which the investor can invest in a single portfolio company alongside the fund. This special purpose vehicle is typically managed by the same GP that manages the broader fund and simply allows the investor to allocate more capital to a specific portfolio company, often while reducing the associated fees. This can be a great way for investors to increase their exposure to a single investment in the portfolio, rather than the standard diversification across multiple investments that tends to dilute the returns. When the investment succeeds, the co-investing party can reap far greater returns than if it invested only through the fund (which would spread its allocation and performance across multiple investments). If the investment is a flop, however, the investor will suffer proportionately worse than peers that invested through the standard pooled investment vehicle (assuming the fund's other portfolio companies fared better than the co-investment). In short, a co-investor's potential risks and rewards on a co-investment are greater than a standard diversified fund structure.

Single family offices are increasingly looking to bypass traditional fund vehicles, or at least lessen their investments through these structures. A co-investment is an attractive solution to single family offices looking to invest directly without foregoing all of the benefits of the usual investment fund structure and without committing too much capital to a single investment. If a single family office can utilize a fund's deal sourcing, due diligence, and operational capabilities while still making a sizable direct investment in the target company, then it is in some ways the best of both worlds for the SFO.

How can a single family office negotiate co-investment rights with a fund?

One common question that I have heard from family offices who want to wade into co-investing is how to broach the subject and negotiate a fair deal with deal partners. Most co-investments are done between parties that have an existing relationship, such as a family office previously committing capital to the private equity firm's past fund. This establishes at least a basic understanding of what the LP is seeking and what deals the investor might be particularly interested in for a co-investment. It is becoming more common for investors to broadcast what sectors they prefer and other desired aspects for a deal. This will often lead to unsolicited inquiries and new relationships with parties looking to partner on deals and co-investments.

Many club deals and co-investments come from formal and informal deal networks of investors, fundless sponsors, private equity firms, corporate executives, investment bankers, and other dealmakers. Investors often cultivate a network of relationships and deal sources to make sure that they are current on the latest deals and investment opportunities. For example, I know a number of single family offices that are very active in energy investments and they have made clear what types of deals they want to review. If I am working on a natural gas deal and I need additional equity partners to come in with co-investments, then I can reach out to those partners first and offer the terms. Likewise, if those family offices (or even ones with whom I do not have a prior relationship) get wind of the deal, they might approach me to see whether there is an opportunity to invest.

These types of arrangements are becoming more common, but most often co-investments come from a private equity firm raising capital for a fund or institutional investor bringing in additional investors on a deal. In these cases, the lead investor or General Partner will approach its existing investors as part of the capital raising process and it is expected that at least one investor will request co-investment rights, typically an LP with significant AUM and investment experience. Some investment firms are willing to grant co-investment rights, but will only do so if it is part of a large capital commitment or to secure a new relationship. Thus, family offices pursuing co-investments should be prepared to negotiate the terms of the deal and they may find a less receptive audience if they are a small-to-mid sized family office looking for co-investments in a large, top-quartile fund.

Investment firms, especially elite firms like TPG or Apollo, typically have an interest in limiting co-investments. For these firms, they can typically meet their fundraising targets without giving incentives to investors and the funds are often oversubscribed, requiring that they turn away investors. These funds will only allow co-investments to close a large capital commitment from a $1B+ family office, sovereign wealth fund, or other large institutional investor. On the other hand, it is much more difficult to raise capital for those firms that have had poor past performance or are relatively new or do not have strong investor support. For this latter tier, the investor relations team will often seek to lure large investors with co-investment rights, breaks on fees, and other preferred terms and they might extend these terms to smaller LPs that otherwise wouldn't be able to secure co-investment rights and similar concessions. So, we see that it is important to understand the mindset of your counterparty and assess how much they need your capital and how much they are willing to concede to obtain your commitment. In a tough capital raise, a co-investment with a large commitment can be a much-needed endorsement for the fund that will compensate for the loss of fees and the costs of structuring the co-investment and managing that investment for the LP.

Fund managers will not usually grant co-investment rights to all investors in a fund due to the complexity and unnecessary burden involved in managing such a high number of co-investments. Due to the aforementioned costs and drawbacks of co-investments for fund managers, the GP will seek to only grant these rights to only those investors that return a specific benefit such as a large capital commitment, strategic advantage, past relationship, etc. Thus, as a family office looking to co-invest, you should consider what benefit you can provide to the fund. For a small fund or one struggling to close a capital raise, the benefit might simply be an allocation to that fund instead of a similar, more established peer. If the fund manager does grant co-investment rights, this fact will be disclosed in the Limited Partnership Agreement (LPA). In my experience, I have seen a range of different co-investment agreements with specific carve-outs of a set percentage of the commitment to be structured as a co-investment with reduced fees and greater control of the investment. I've also seen co-investment rights that are largely under the discretion of the fund manager, so the GP can decide the companies that investors can co-invest in and the size of the co-investments. Other times, a family office may have a co-investment right to invest $50 million alongside the fund in a company, but the family office decides not to exercise the option because they lack confidence in the deal or otherwise prefer to limit their investment to only the initial commitment in the fund. How these deals are structured is critically important for any family office making co-investments.

Co-investments are typically structured by an attorney or investment professional with experience in putting together these agreements. The fund manager will often have a leg up on you in terms of experience structuring co-investments and negotiating the terms of the agreement, so you will have to keep an eye out for seemingly minor clauses and conditions that could have a big impact on your investment. For example, an investor may push for terms that allow the LP to thoroughly review the potential co-investment and have proper time to evaluate the due diligence documents that the fund itself is relying on to make a sound investment. Similarly, the fund may make explicit in the side letter or LPA that the investor assumes responsibility for the investment and cannot blame the GP if it turns out poorly (barring fraud or similar extraordinary failures).

In the negotiations, the LP should make clear the desired level of involvement in the company, how the investment will be structured (as a co-investment through the fund or as a direct investment in the company), and what the GP and company's expectations will be for the LP. Another important consideration is how the investment will be structured, specifically whether it will be made through a Special Purpose Vehicle (SPV) or a different vehicle.

The tax and legal consequences of the structure are very important, especially for foreign investors. The biggest sticking point usually centers on the fees of the co-investment. Investors may be willing to pay a management fee, but prefer a reduced or wholly eliminated performance fee and, as one might expect, fund managers will try to preserve a fee structure that closely resembles its standard compensation. These are only a few of the issues that you'll negotiate and it is up to the two sides to come together on an agreement that satisfies both parties and ensures a viable long-term partnership on the deal.[4]

---

[4] http://www.mondaq.com/unitedstates/x/232170/M+A+Private%20equity/Best+
Practices+in+Structuring+Coinvestments

Free Access to a Co-Investing Webinar: We recorded a 90-minute webinar with Julia Corelli, partner at Pepper Hamilton, where we discussed co-investments, how family offices are co-investing and

why, and other trends related to direct investing, co-investing, and club deals. To access this webinar for free, visit: SingleFamilyOffices.com/Co-Investing

Co-Investing Best Practices: John Jonson serves as Managing Director at Lyrical Partners, L.P. He has many years of experience managing a family office investment portfolio and along the way he has developed some best practices for making direct investments and co-investments.

An important aspect of co-investing is that you sometimes work with other parties from outside your firm. Some single family offices are used to either surrendering complete control of an investment to a fund manager or assuming complete management of the investment through direct deals done in-house. Partnering with another party in a collaborative way can be challenging but rewarding as long as you are aware of the risks and the emotional aspects of the long haul required to stay with an investment through difficult times. Before you get too far along in the process, John tells me that his team always digs deep into a deal partner's references. They keep seeking out references until they get completely comfortable. They're not just checking the person's last business partner or investor; his team reaches out to credit lenders, team members, vendors, and anyone reasonable that can give them insight into the person in question.

For those of you hoping for a set formula for executing a perfect deal, Lyrical's John Jonson says that there is no "right way" to do deals because it depends so much on the family's goals, objectives, vision, and of course the aspects of the deal. This echoes the feedback from a lot of family office executives I know who have extensive deal experience under their belt. The common refrain is that you have to consider what makes sense for your family and structure the terms around that core focus of protecting and serving the family. You don't want to commit to even a great deal for too long if it conflicts with the family's time horizon. If your family office is interested in making a co-investment or direct investment, be prepared for the long haul and the challenges you will inevitably face along the way. Jonson cautions that you will have the "stomach" for it a lot; a common refrain is that it can be like "chewing glass" at times, but with persistence and care there can be great rewards.

Jonson also warns family offices to be wary of businesses that are based on government subsidies and pending regulations or approvals. Of course, many investors have made huge returns by accurately predicting government actions and navigating complicated regulations, but most single family offices would prefer to avoid these variables if possible. There are already a number of moving parts to any substantial deal and it is wise to limit the variables that are outside your control. Furthermore, by removing obstacles like regulatory exposure and other impediments, you put the pressure on your team to succeed and eliminate any excuses. Jonson believes that once you commit to a deal, by taking away the "outlet option" that you won't succeed, and thus you will persist through the harder times. I agree and the most successful people I have met in the family office industry are those who see a problem, work to solve it, and move on with a singular focus on completing the mission at hand.

Another piece of guidance from John Jonson is to be very careful when you move from equity to debt investing. Many family office portfolios include bonds and debt instruments, but if you are making a co-investment or direct investment that involves debt, be sure that you have someone on the team that can help you navigate this area. There are many differences and quirks to the debt markets that you need to consider when shifting from equity investments to debt investments. There are plenty of stories from the financial crisis of investors entering the debt markets without a full understanding of what risks they were assuming. Make sure you have an experienced team member who can guide you and help structure the deals properly with the appropriate covenants.

Our final takeaway from John Jonson at Lyrical Partners, L.P., is that you should consider specializing in an industry and hiring experienced people in that area if you want to be active in direct deals and co-investments. As we have touched on in the direct investments chapter, it is beneficial for many family offices to focus on one niche or industry that they feel comfortable investing in—often the space in which the principal made his/her money originally. This is easier because you are not entering a new market per se, or having to learn the tricks of the trade, and have pre-existing relationships and credibility to partner with the right entities and attract co-investors. If you stick to an industry focus, then you are more likely to develop a strong network of industry players, deal flow sources, and experienced staff who can make investments confidently in the sector.

We recently invited Christian Zabbal, from the $1B+ single family office Black Coral Capital to speak at one of our family office events. Black Coral Capital is an oil & gas family with a worldview that we are running out of natural resources, so we should invest along that truth. They are not impact investors; they seek a profit in each investment they make. They are innovative in that they have formed a Cleantech investment club where they vote families and co-investors in and out of the group for the purpose of finding more co-investment opportunities. Many times Black Coral will fund individual projects, and work together with startups on project equity projects. For example, a solar company may have a new division being started installing solar panels on roofs of consumer homes. For the first two years of this project, they may provide the capital on an 18% debt note because it is more risky the first time they offer the service. Over the second phase, they may get a 12% note, on the third phase perhaps an 8% note and multiple other investors are jumping in at that point.

Christian shared many lessons they have learned along the way while investing, including that it pays to be persistent in investing, always know what you are doing, be creative and look for other ways to "skin the cat," partnerships and collaboration is key, and build real businesses—don't just build assets to flip them in a few years, as that rarely works.

Case Study

We recently spoke with a CEO of a brand-name food company that was in financial distress. The company, which I will not name for obvious reasons, was a privately-held company for many years and had changed ownership only slightly throughout its existence. Then, several years ago, the company's founders sold to a private equity investor at a valuation above $75 million. Fast forward to today and the business has been through a number of transitions, changed management, launched new products, and the company is still far from generating profits and nowhere near the level that a private equity investor would expect from such an investment. The buyout firm has grown tired of waiting and, more importantly, the fund's investors want it to exit its investment in the company and return whatever cash is realized to LPs. This has placed even more pressure on the company and we were contacted to find a family office with a more accommodating investing horizon. I know a number of single family offices who look for opportunities to invest in companies where existing investors or founders are motivated to sell, so I shared the deal with single family offices.

One family was particularly interested in the deal and thought that their investment team could create a lot of value using their operations experience. The problem was that the family office was reluctant to invest so much capital (as much as $75 million) in a single deal. The family was confident that if they had a chance to take over the company, they would be able to return it to profitability within three to five years and make a considerable return on its investment. The family needed capital, so it decided that we should approach other family offices, and a few institutional investors and private equity firms, to see if there was interest in tackling the company as a club. In this club deal, the single family office organizing the deal was the "lead" investor and the remaining investors were ostensibly passive investors contributing capital only. In a perfect world, the lead family office would have put up 100% of the capital and received 100% of the profits, without having to set up a structure that allows outside investors to pool capital and distribute profits. But the club deal enabled the single family office to digest a deal that it would otherwise not be able to swallow.

These types of deals are common and happening even more often in recent years. Family offices are often looking for deal flow, co-investment opportunities, club deals, and direct deals and I expect this trend to only strengthen in coming years. Family offices are growing more sophisticated in their investing strategies and developing internal resources that rival even some of the larger institutional investment firms. Family offices, and other LPs, will continue to look for opportunities to reduce fees and manage their investments more internally, rather than allocating strictly to third-party funds.

In the last chapter on Direct Investing, we interviewed family office executive David Fisher. Here we would like to share a list of co-investment guidelines that his team operates by in case it would be helpful to anyone else looking at helping lead or participate in club deals.

Here are some points to consider regarding investment via a club or consortium:

1. *FORMATION* – Usually done by letter agreement pre-closing and by formal documentation, which depends on the investment vehicle, upon closing.
2. *MEMBER SELECTION* – Look for a) value-added (e.g., expertise, experience, exits, connections, co-opting competition, political cover or clout) members in the investment, development and/or exit stages, b) Innova Limited Partners, and c) like-minded co-investors with similar styles, investment strategies, operating policies (e.g., leverage, guarantees, dividends, share pledging), exit concepts, tax preferences, time horizons, etc. NOTE: The more members you have, the more likely the deal will fail. AVOID: Members with a) conflicts of interest, b) different deal terms, strategies or styles, c) non-profit motives (e.g., employees, unions, and governments), or d) strong personal connections to management.
3. *ROLES & RULES* – Overall leadership, specific roles, and rules should be agreed upfront. Each member should appoint one person to be its lead officer throughout the deal.
4. *STRATEGY* – The club or syndicate should pre-agree both the basic Business Plan and the Contingencies if things don't go according to plan. This avoids many disputes and delays when problems arise.
5. *SYNDICATE EXPENSES* – The a) type, b) amounts, c) sharing, d) fronting, e) agreed advisors, and f) approvals should be covered. Most costs may be repaid by investee upon closing, and sometimes upon deal abortion. AVOID: Fronting deal expenses without written reimbursement agreements.
6. *ADVISORS* – Specific advisors (tax, legal, accounting, technical, financial) and their written terms of engagement should be pre-agreed in writing by all members. However, only the Leader should give instructions directly to advisors. NOTE: Make sure there is adequate negotiation and supervision of advisors' fees and expenses (often with

cost caps and/or discounts for aborted deals). AVOID: Each member having its own legal counsel on the deal as this increases costs, complexity, and delays dramatically.

7. *DUTIES* – Specific tasks, timelines, and deadlines should be assigned to members. The Lead should monitor, coordinate, and communicate this process on a timely basis among all members.

8. *COMMUNICATION* – If the syndicate is greater than two members, it becomes important to coordinate all communications with the investee via the Leader to avoid duplication and inconsistencies.

9. *DUE DILIGENCE* – Agree the main areas to be covered, by whom, how, and when.

10. *FEES* – What fees will be charged by or paid by the syndicate? Will the originator and/or lead member get a fee or equity bonus? How will fees and commissions be shared?

11. *GOVERNANCE* – During pre-closing, most decisions are made by unanimous consent; post-closing they are per normal company governance procedures with standard super-majority items. Question: Do you want required block-voting by members or voting freedom by each member? How are syndicate consents and approvals decided and communicated? AVOID: Blocking rights to small shareholders.

12. *BOARD* – Agree a) board membership and chair, b) non-voting member (observer) rights, c) management rights, and d) voting procedures. NOTE: U.S. VCOC rules require *direct* influence over management, not indirectly via a syndicate's board seat.

13. *INFORMATION* – Members should all have the right to ongoing financial and business information about the investee, but requests may need to be directed via the Leader to consolidate requests.

14. *SHARE TRANSFERS* – Agree whether there will be *intra*-syndicate rights of a) first refusal, b) free transfer (but subject to the investee shareholders agreement), c) co-buy, d) co-sale, or e) pre-emption. NOTE: Watch out for Affiliate and SPV transfers (or change in effective control) as they can be used to violate first-refusal rights by directly or indirectly conveying equity interests in the investee.

15. *EXITS* – Agree in principle the a) timing, b) type, c) procedures, and d) right to force an exit.

16. *CONFLICTS* – Pre-closing, any potential conflict of interest by a member should be disclosed in writing to the members upfront. Post-closing, conflicts and any related-party dealing should be disclosed to and approved by the Board. The duty is on the member to disclose any potential conflicts.

17. *NON-COMPETITION* – This must be carefully defined to prevent investments in direct competitors, but not in similar businesses or the

same business in another trading region. At a minimum, there should be a no-poaching provision covering key personnel of the investee.

18. *EXCLUSIVITY* – Members and *potential* members receiving confidential information should commit to a) exclusivity to the syndicate, b) non-circumvention, c) no competing bid and d) presenting all similar investment opportunities to the syndicate first.

19. *CONFIDENTIALITY* – All confidential and proprietary information related to the syndicate and/or investee should not be disclosed for the term of the investment + two years.

20. *PUBLIC RELATIONS* – All syndicate announcements and other PR activities should be pre-approved by all of the members, often in coordination with the investee.

21. *INVESTMENT VEHICLE* – The choices usually include a) tax-efficient holding company, b) co-investment agreement similar to a shareholders agreement, or c) none, which means syndicate members are governed by the general shareholders agreement for the investee.

22. *TAXATION* – The syndicate structure must not adversely affect the taxation of its members. NOTE: Members can often form intermediate holding vehicles to suit their specific situation.

23. *ARBITRATION* – A standard AAA or LCIA binding arbitration provision should be included to provide for speedy and confidential dispute resolution and enforcement, usually under U.S. or English law.

Deal Flow Screening Table:

There is an old saying that the hen contributed to breakfast but the pig (bacon) was committed. This is just one of the top 20 criteria we look for in a deal, 100% CEO commitment, not just contributing. There are many things to look for, before getting yourself tied up in deep due diligence, and while sometimes you have to move very quickly on a deal, conducting thorough due diligence can take weeks, months, and sometimes years. The matrix below is our Deal Investment 20, the top 20 things we look for while evaluating direct investments and co-investments. This is not a due diligence checklist, which would need to be much more comprehensive; this is for top layer screening of deals. We will not meet in person or even spend much time over the phone until we are assured that most, if not all, of these boxes look to be fulfilled.

Top 3 Industry Focus	$3x+ EBITDA (\$1M+ EBITDA)	3 Year Operating Track Record	Clear Defendable Advantage	Relationship/Trust & Transparency
Term Sheet / Offering	Liquidity via Debt, Royalties, Dividends	Third Party Entities/Payments	Distressed, Bankrupt, or Broken	Current Capital Structure & Debt
Ability to Adapt & Listen to Input	CEO 100% Committed	Team Profit Sharing Incentives	Long-Term Cognitive Bias	Re-Investing vs. Harvesting Mode?
Internal Controls & Clean Audit Reports	Team Experience & Resilience	Outside Professional vs. Family Members	Pro-active Constant Improvement	Cohesive Team & Fund Culture

This table above could be used with your team to help them screen deals for you, or just as a way to communicate your preferences to those you work with.

3 Ways Wealthy Families Can Attract Deal Flow: One common frustration for investors, from private equity fund managers to family office executives, is that it can be exceptionally difficult to source high-quality, attractive deals that haven't been shopped around to every other investor already. I wanted to share three strategies that will help you regularly gain access to better deal flow.

Plant Your Flag: In order to source great deals and investing opportunities that are in line with your objectives and criteria, you need to communicate what exactly you are seeking. It might seem counterintuitive to narrow your scope by sector, allocation size, EBITDA range, and similar filters, but doing so will tell companies, investment bankers, investment firms, and other deal sources what deals are a match for you.

You might even consider establishing yourself as an investor exclusively in a specific industry or niche like logistics, textile manufacturing, or a similarly defined segment of the market. This will enable you to focus your team on only forming relationships within this market and you will gradually establish yourself as a top player in the space.

I was recently approached by an industry friend who runs a small, regional bank and he asked if I knew of any firm that partners with banks like his. Instantly, a name popped into my head of a private equity firm that I met with that focused exclusively on independent banks and financial firms. That connection would not have been possible had that private equity firm not planted its flag firmly in the banking sector so that everyone, including myself, knows exactly what they invest in and what type of deals they are interested in.

While the very next point encourages you to stay in touch with your top 10-50 deal sources and build real relationships, if you position yourself correctly to the right groups, you should be like a bear at a waterfall catching salmon (deal flow) as they jump in your mouth instead of a bear swimming in the middle of a lake trying to hook a fish with his claws in the deep water. We take a niche focus approach to everything we do, from our Billionaire Family Office business, to our focus on finding $1M+ EBITDA co-investments in a specific industry for a buy-side client. We have found that this strategy pays off in helping us attract high-quality and relevant deal flow and is a strategy that can be used by any single family office to reduce due diligence costs and improve returns,

Proactive Relationship Management: There is a tendency, especially among investors, to wait for deals to come to them, rather than seeking out deals, building networks, forming relationships with companies and deal sources, and proactively working to develop deal flow. If you are serious about sourcing deals and developing a strong deal pipeline, then you need to get out in front of the world and attend industry events, speak publicly (with compliance/legal approval, of course), establish your brand and focus, and become a leader in whatever areas of investing you focus on. For a family office or pension fund that has always had investments presented to them in the past, this is a complete change in strategy and it can be challenging.

It is pretty difficult to bring an investor a high-quality, proprietary deal if you don't know the top executives, the firm doesn't have a website, and they do not share any of their investing priorities with outsiders. The most successful investment firms and direct investors have developed a strong foundation of deal partners, they have representatives attending and even speaking at conferences, their executives are quoted in the newspapers, and they make a strong effort to get out there and meet with companies and other investors.

Provide Value to Your Deal Partners: If you want to access better deals and ensure that you are one of the first calls when one of your deal sources comes across a new deal, then you need to take care of your network and provide value in return for their help.

For example, we maintain a number of deal partners within our database of 55 billionaire families and our Top 50 Deal Source database. We use these databases along with our Customer Relationship Management system to help our team make sure and touch base with these relationships and be certain that they are receiving value from us. Otherwise, you are expecting something for nothing if you want deal sources to simply hand you interesting or attractive deals and never receive anything in return. So we make a concerted effort to share insights, invite these parties to attend our relevant events, schedule time to meet with them at industry conferences, send them a free copy of a book we write, or provide some other piece of value that reminds them of our firm and also makes sure that they appreciate the relationship.

You might find that your network of deal sources only includes a few merchant banks, an investment banker, a couple of private equity firms, and 5-10 institutional investors. Or, if you are more active, you might need to develop a sophisticated system for tracking more than a hundred deal sources. Whatever the size of your deal source network, be sure and deliver real value consistently and treat the relationship like you would a client.

Conclusion

We dedicated an entire chapter to this topic because we strongly believe at Billionaire Family Office that co-investing and direct investing are an important trend that was previously overlooked or underestimated by investment professionals and even family office industry executives. We try to keep an eye toward the future and make sure we are current on the latest trends, changes, and evolutions. Staying up to speed on this industry is especially critical because the family office world is evolving rapidly to meet the needs of wealthy families.

Chapter 13: Real Estate Investments and Hard Assets

The rise in alternative investments, particularly private equity and hedge funds, has helped to create the impression that the ultra-wealthy and their family offices invest only in non-traditional, exclusive products. However, in my experience working with ultra-affluent families and family offices, I consistently find a desire to invest in hard assets. Family offices and HNW investors are like many investors in this respect: they want to hold a *real* asset, to invest in something with tangible value.

These hard assets range from commodity plays like investing in a copper mine to more run-of-the-mill allocations in a real estate development project. Many families did not create their wealth in finance so real world tangible assets can be more intuitive and easy to see value in owning. On top of that real estate is a major contributor to wealth globally, so naturally the creates many families capable of continuing to invest in that asset class. After the financial crisis that wiped away trillions of dollars in value for investors, it's no wonder that investors increasingly look for hard assets in their portfolios.

Real Estate Areas

It is helpful to review the main types of real estate investments before we delve into a few areas in more detail.

Residential: Residential real estate is a form of real estate that we are all familiar with because everyone has purchased a house, rented an apartment, or had some interaction with residential real estate. Tenants of residential properties pay to be able to live in the property and property owners collect rents as part of the lease agreements with tenants. Residential properties include single-family homes, multi-family homes, apartment buildings, condominiums, luxury properties, and other variations. Many affluent families hold several residential properties for personal use and for investment and diversification purposes. We have seen some families purchasing groups of 3, 10, and even 50 or more single family residences as rental properties. In other words, instead of buying a 30 unit apartment complex, they are buying 30 single family homes and using property managers and sometimes an asset manager to make money off the rent income and appreciation.

Commercial: Commercial real estate refers to those real estate properties that are used by businesses. While individuals and families are the typical tenants of residential real estate properties, businesses occupy commercial properties. These businesses range from a Bank of America branch office to a private law office and the tenant businesses abide by leases and pay for use of the property, just like any other resident. These leases are more complex than the leases one might have on a condo or apartment and the agreements can vary to include obligations for the tenant to pay for some or all of the following: property taxes, rent, insurance, required maintenance and up-keep, or other expenses that would otherwise be covered by the property owner.

Industrial: The last type of real estate to cover is industrial real estate. Industrial properties are used for manufacturing, production, assembly, storage, and related activities. Some large institutional investors own industrial properties and lease the property (usually under long-term agreements) to businesses that will use it for manufacturing and production.

Out of these three types, family offices most commonly own residential properties, from large apartment buildings to multi-million dollar houses. I know a number of family offices with commercial real estate holdings, but the complexities of operating the business, servicing clients, collecting rents, and making sure that the building maintains full occupancy can present challenges.

If these real estate holdings are primarily investments, rather than properties for use by the family or for the family office's operating businesses, then the goal is a positive return on investment. For a real estate property, this is most commonly achieved when the property's value appreciates. Although the recent bursting of the real estate bubble has made some investors question the idea that real estate investments are a sound long-term investment, traditionally real estate has been a source of steady gains that at least keep pace with inflation and hold tangible value. One simple explanation for why family offices like to hold real estate is that at the end of the day, even if inflation jumps up or the stock market crashes, your property still has some value.

If the real estate property does not appreciate or even loses value, there is still an opportunity to notch a return on investment by renting out the property to businesses or residents. In the wake of the financial crisis and real estate meltdown, for example, many investors cushioned the blow to property valuations by renting out properties. This is especially attractive if the property is purchased with a loan and thus the owner will have to make the monthly payments regardless of whether the housing market collapses or the macroeconomic picture changes. Renting out the property or otherwise monetizing the real estate can help the investor meet loan requirements and, ideally, realize returns on the investment. The income and appreciation qualities make real estate a mandatory allocation in many family office portfolios.

Real Estate Investment Structures

As you can see, there are a number of different real estate property types and there are also many different structures by which investors allocate to real estate.

Investment Models and Structures

Real Estate Investment Trusts (REITs): One way in which family offices allocate to real estate is through what is known as a Real Estate Investment Trust or a REIT. A real estate investment trust (REIT) is an investment company that invests in properties or mortgages and typically provides an income component. REITs trade on exchanges like stocks and bonds, making these securities an easily accessible and liquid avenue for investing in real estate. REITs must pass through a significant portion of their income as a dividend in order to qualify for special tax treatment. Publicly available REITs normally invest in commercial real estate, such as apartments, hotels, shopping malls, office complexes, and storage units. REITs are a way to invest in real estate without directly investing in private real estate and managing property. The tax benefits of this structure are often the most important aspect for investors considering a REIT compared to other real estate investment structures.

Real Estate Investment Firms: Similar to REITs, a real estate investment group allows a family office or other investor to invest their money with a firm that will then use that capital to make investments in real estate, manage properties, and attempt to produce gains for the investor(s).

Private Real Estate Funds: There are many different private real estate funds that are structured as a limited liability corporation or limited partnership and investors in the fund commit capital that is deployed to purchase various real estate properties and securities.

Private Equity Real Estate Funds: A variation of the private real estate fund is the private equity real estate fund, which typically refers to a fund which completes leveraged buyouts of real estate property companies or large real estate portfolios. The funds are often limited partnerships and the general partner charges a 2% management fee and 20% performance fee, like private equity funds, and invests the capital pool in a number of different portfolio companies or investments with a finite window for exiting (five to seven years typically). The use of leverage tends to "juice" returns and allows the private equity real estate fund to make larger, debt-fueled acquisitions.

Individual Purchase: Many high net worth individuals purchase real estate from outside of a pooled fund structure or sophisticated vehicle. These investments by HNW individuals and families are usually taxable, compared to more tax efficient vehicles or tax-exempt entities like government and corporate pension funds, endowments, charitable foundations, etc.

Attractive Real Estate Investments

There are dozens of types of real estate investments, but the two of the most popular in my experience with families are apartment buildings and hotels. The reason that many families prefer these investments is the income component generated by tenant rents (in the case of apartment buildings) and room rentals (in the case of hotels). The potential to earn steady, consistent income by owning and managing these properties is extremely attractive to wealthy families with a long-term investing mindset. Each family's investment mandate varies but typically these families are content to hold properties through real estate cycles and do not attempt to time the market opportunistically with quick buy-and-flip type real estate investments. Of course, single family offices try to avoid overpaying and may sell if market valuations are inflated, but hotels and apartment buildings are major, long-term commitments and families do not enter these investments looking to make a quick buck through a prompt exit.

Hotels as Operating Businesses

A hotel property is a unique real estate investment in that it is part property investment and part operating business. Hotels require a strong management team devoted to keeping expenses down and producing steady profits, while keeping in mind variables such as competing hotels, surrounding business activity, guest satisfaction, and other important components of operating a successful hotel. One cannot simply buy the hotel and assume it will succeed long-term; like any business, it is a constant improvement in management and business growth. Every year, 100's of hotels fail and fall into bankruptcy, even hotels with capable management teams and prime locations, so there is no guarantee of success and steady income—even for a stable industry like hotel and rental property management. Still, many families I meet from Los Angeles to Singapore have interest in these types of income-generating properties because a successful hotel or rental property can be exceptional investments for well-capitalized investors with long investment horizons.

We are sent hotel investment opportunities seemingly ever week and one key takeaway is that there is often a trade-off between optimal location, the resulting implied risk, and optimal pricing. Of course, this is not an earth-shattering revelation; it is fairly obvious that a great location for a hotel will command a greater price and attract rival bidders. When family offices speak about owning or investing in hotels they are often focused more on metropolitan locations and disinterested in allocating to a suburban market or even a city-center location if it isn't in a high-demand market like London, New York City, Miami, or other top destinations. This tends to frustrate fundless sponsors, real estate developers, and others looking to acquire or develop hotels with family office capital. Family offices may be willing to pay top dollar for a hotel in a prime location because they are sure that the occupancy rate will be sufficiently high to mitigate risk of bankruptcy and distress. This means they may pay more to buy the hotel and make most of their return by holding the property long term and accumulating income from the hotel business. Real estate professionals are typically more focused on buying low and making their ROI at the exit (typically a sale to a strategic buyer or investor group). This means that they are more willing to develop a hotel or buy a hotel in a growing market, even if it is not a top location at the moment. These investors, in contrast to family offices, are comfortable to putting in substantial investment in the first few years to build or remake a hotel because the ultimate payoff is expected to come from a future sale.

There is nothing right or wrong about either approach because the strategy is relative to the investor's own objectives. Family offices are typically more risk averse than a seasoned real estate professional or fund which wants to borrow and build or do a leveraged buyout of an undervalued market. Family offices tend to pay a higher price per key (one way hotels are valued) and prefer stable hotels with a strong operator (whether a brand-name chain or a veteran private manager) that will protect the long-term income stream for the family. If the family office can sell the hotel at a high multiple, they're likely to at least entertain the offer but family offices are usually less eager to sell than a limited partnership fund or a real estate group that wants to lock in the gains through a sale.

Apartment Investments

Apartment properties are similar to hotels in that they require an active property management team and frequent renovations, maintenance, and business development. Investors willing to commit to that level of involvement in a real estate investment are rewarded with the chance to earn rental income while the property's market value (hopefully) appreciates. An apartment building in a growing market can quickly see a substantial rise in market value. For example, in my hometown of Portland, Oregon, a consistently cited top 10 rental market city, rents have steadily increased as both mid-sized local businesses and large multi-national corporations, like Nike, Inc. and the Intel Corporation, decided to expand hiring and open new facilities in the area. A recent decision by Intel to open one of the largest plants in the world in Beaverton, a suburb of Portland, immediately increased local real estate prices, rental rates, and the cost of commercial property in the area. A savvy family can develop an apartment rental property in a growing area and wait for the property to appreciate and rents to rise over several years. A typical real estate fund or private equity real estate fund will often try to time the market or jump into a hot market with a quick real estate investment and a shorter investment horizon. Then, the fund will typically seek to exit by selling all or part of the property to another buyer or real estate management company, in order to distribute returns to limited partners. Single family offices and ultra-high net worth families, on the other hand, can hold properties through the entire investment cycle and continue to manage the properties and collect steady income for years. This is a big strategic advantage for affluent families and single family offices in the real estate property market and a core driver of family investment activity in the sector.

Trophy Assets and Cross-Purpose Properties

I know several wealthy families who have overpaid for various assets, particularly real estate properties, in order to secure a "trophy." By this I mean to say that a family may pay a premium for a property that has unique social or prestige benefits, such as the Empire State Building in New York or the Raffles Hotel in Singapore.

A single family office that purchases one of these trophy assets will take advantage of the branding and prestige benefits in hosting business meetings, social gatherings, and other events at their property. Most real estate developers would appreciate the trophy aspect, but they might not be willing to spend to the same degree that a single family office would in some cases. Of course, a single family office will not simply buy an overpriced asset just to show off, but the team may adopt a longer time horizon for the investment with the understanding that the short-term benefits will be largely the trophy aspect, branding, and other less tangible assets.

A panel of family office executives answers questions from the audience at one of our family office conference recently at the beautiful Raffles Hotel in Singapore. The Raffles is known around the world and is a great example of a "trophy" real estate asset that many family offices would value ownership of for many reasons, prestige being one powerful factor.

Another reason that a family may make a significant real estate purchase is to utilize the property for other purposes, beyond leasing the space or building a profitable development. A sub-$1 billion single family office that I am currently working with owns a sizeable business park just outside of the city center. The SFO uses that space primarily for its large investment operation, foundation headquarters, and a few other offices that house business partners, legal counsel, and other relevant personnel. This cross-purpose property allows the family to oversee the whole family office operation within a couple blocks' area. New partners, business divisions, and strategic relationships can take advantage of the office space and form a closer partnership with the family. I'm sure this family could rent a couple of floors in the financial district and spread their businesses around the city in different office spaces, but by purchasing this cross-purpose real estate, the family can manage its operations more easily and take advantage of unique advantages from this property.

If a family can use the property as a business asset, much like you would a private jet, or a complementary prestige asset, then it might be worth acquiring the asset, even at a premium. It is important to consider the long-term benefits, whether it is the trophy aspect or another use of the real estate, when evaluating real estate investments.

Pitfalls to Avoid

1. *Ignoring Tax Consequences*: It is very important to consider the long and short-term tax consequences of your real estate investments. You may be able to invest in a more tax efficient way by using a fund structure or alternative vehicle for your real estate investment. Foreign real estate investments can be especially hazardous in terms of tax liabilities and potential penalties, so it is important to consider your options if you decide to expand your real estate portfolio overseas. I know of many investors, particularly Asian families, that are actively buying U.S. real estate properties and they are especially sensitive to local tax regulations like the Foreign Investment in Real Property Tax Act of 1980, for example.

2. *Lack of Diversification*: The housing meltdown and financial crisis exposed a number of investors who had an extreme exposure to a particular property market or type of real estate. Investors who exclusively held Las Vegas real estate properties, for example, were particularly hurt when Nevada real estate valuation crashed. Different real estate markets recovered at different times and Nevada was one of the hardest hit and the slowest to recover. Investors with a balanced portfolio of different asset allocations and real estate holdings in different cities and markets are less likely to fall victim to the collapse of one city's overheated property market. Las Vegas suffered from extreme drops in valuations and mass foreclosures, which made it difficult for a property owner with a portfolio over-weighted toward Nevada real estate to refinance all of its properties and write off losses if the entire portfolio was sinking.

3. *Running Before You Walk*: It can be tempting to dive into the deep end of real estate, especially when financing is readily available and the opportunities seem particularly exciting. However, I would caution that single family offices should remember to walk before you run and not commit yourself to these long-term investments if you do not have the experience to manage the properties, structure the deals, and make sure that you meet the demands of real estate investing. One way to walk before you running is to invest through a

co-investment structure, club deal private investment fund, or otherwise leverage the expertise of experienced real estate investors. This might be a safer, less time-intensive way to invest in real estate, but if you still prefer to make real estate investments directly through your family office, you can hopefully learn the real estate investing game through the experience without having to go it alone on your first deal. You can partner with experienced real estate investors and other family offices with a strong real estate team to help you ease yourself into real estate, rather than biting off expensive, time-intensive, and complex real estate investments yourself.

Different Models of Real Estate Investing

Local: One of the pitfalls we covered is investing entirely in a specific area or property market. However, in almost every city, there are a few wealthy families or individuals that own a number of local buildings and real estate properties. This is a popular model because you often have a good sense of your local property market and you are more likely than non-local investors to hear about a new property on the market or to find a potential seller. This model has helped many active real estate investors steadily accumulate a large portfolio of local properties, many of which are purchased opportunistically from neighbors, business connections, and other local sellers.

The New York Real Estate Market Recovered Quickly from the Bursting of the Housing Bubble as Local Investors Swooped Up Discounted Properties and International Demand Served to Keep Prices High

The Single Family Office by Richard C. Wilson

Geographically Diversified: The counter to this model is the geographically diversified model, which, as you might expect, is a strategy of buying real estate assets in different cities and countries, rather than focusing too narrowly on one property market. This model is best executed by experienced real estate investors who can navigate new markets, comply with regulations and laws in different countries, and source deals at attractive valuations from local sellers.

Diversified Across All Types: Investing across multiple real estate structures and around the globe is certainly the least common approach for single family offices. Many family offices develop a strategy over years of real estate investing and are unlikely to stray from that model by allocating in a completely unfamiliar property market or utilizing a different structure, unless there is a particularly compelling reason to do so. There are a few family offices, though, that essentially operate as a full-fledged real estate investment firm and they employ a large team that has experience investing in a number of different structures and all over the world. For these experienced real estate-focused family offices, the team may pursue a fully-diversified model that limits exposure to any single property market or type of property and they make their investments in whatever model makes the most sense for the opportunity and accounts for tax, legal, partnerships,

Hard Assets

The rise in alternative investments, particularly private equity and hedge funds, has helped to create the impression that the ultra-wealthy and their family offices invest only in non-traditional, exclusive products. However, in my experience working with ultra-affluent families and family offices, I consistently find a desire to invest in hard assets. We've just covered real estate and one element of real estate that attracts family offices is the desire to hold a *real* asset, to invest in something with tangible value. Hard assets meet this criteria and present a wide array of different assets in which single family offices can invest.

These hard assets range from commodity plays like investing in a copper mine to more run-of-the-mill allocations to a commercial real estate development project. After the financial crisis that wiped away trillions of dollars in value for investors, it's no wonder that investors increasingly crave hard assets in their portfolios. If you look at the price of gold and silver in recent years, you can see a significant rise (followed by a large drop in line with the economic recovery). One doesn't have to be a "gold bug" to understand that investors are taking a harder look at commodities and real assets in these turbulent times.

Despite some swings on certain commodities in recent years, real estate, and investments with real asset exposure remain an attractive area for single family offices and other investors with a long-term investment horizon. Rarely do I see the CIO for a single family office or multi-family office day-trading on currencies and commodity futures. I do see, though, many wealthy families investing in various hard asset, such as buying timber in the Northwest; developing a commercial property; purchasing an apartment complex; investing in an international shipping company; and similar long-term investments.

Whereas a hedge fund trader or an average investor might not have the patience or capital to invest in hard assets and let the investment appreciate over many years, family offices and other institutional investors are often comfortable waiting through economic downturns and asset-specific cycles without selling in a panic due to liquidity concerns or general fear. Another reason that family offices like hard assets is the feeling of safety in holding something tangible which is unlikely to disappear overnight. An equity investment in a corporation could lose most or all of its value very quickly. Even some of the most well-known corporations in America, like Kodak or Lehman Brothers recently, have gone by the wayside. The Dot Com Bubble similarly revealed that public market valuations are subjective and a corporation's market capitalization can evaporate with just one bad earnings report or a single negative report. So there is a comfort in knowing that your gold holdings may fluctuate in value, but there is still universally recognized value in the asset. Similarly, even if a real estate property fails to attract occupants, there is still inherent, tangible value in the building and the property itself.

America's inflation crisis of the late 1970's and early 1980's eroded a tremendous amount of net worth for many Americans and this time was especially cruel for those who lacked any hedges against inflation in their portfolios. The Federal Reserve and Chairman Ben Bernanke shocked the markets in the fall of 2013 by deciding not to pare quantitative easing and delaying the inevitable scaling back of that stimulus program. Many economists have expressed fears about possible inflation as a result of this continued policy and other economic factors have led investors to prepare for moderate-to-high inflation (at least above the current 1.5% inflation in the U.S.) over the coming years. Of course, there is a lively debate in the financial markets, economists' classrooms, and in policy think-tanks over whether Americans should fear rampant inflation or if those fears are overblown. No matter if the U.S. continues to succeed in taming inflation, commodities and hard assets are still favored by family offices and HNW investors because they provide a comfort and diversification against inflation and other adverse circumstances that could affect a portfolio's value.

Capital preservation is still king in the family office world and hard assets are very attractive to families who primarily want to maintain their current wealth, with the second still important goal of strong returns on investments.

Conclusion

I am often asked if family offices invest in real estate or hard assets. This question always surprises me because single family offices with substantial net worth are very likely to hold multiple properties and real estate investments. With the increase of allocations to alternatives like hedge funds and private equity, it seems that real estate is becoming an overlooked asset class by investment professionals but real estate is still very much a key component of most family offices' portfolios. The crisis certainly took a toll on many real estate investments but family offices have often held real assets for decades and have seen bubbles inflate and burst in many asset classes, including real estate (although likely not as dramatic as the recent crash). The real estate downturn created buying opportunities for many investors and I know a number of single family offices who ramped up their real estate investing activities shortly after the crisis to take advantage of this buying opportunity. There continues to be a strong appetite for real estate among family offices and I do not see that changing anytime soon.

The Single Family Office by Richard C. Wilson

Part 4:

Single Family Office
Best Practices &
Models to Emulate

RES NON VERBA

wilson

The Single Family Office by Richard C. Wilson

Chapter 14: $1 Billion+ Single Family Offices

At the Family Office Club and Billionaire Family Office, we grow our relationships and reach in the family office industry by identifying client case studies, best practices, trends, operating models, and mistakes to avoid. We then actively share those trends and lessons learned with single family offices around the world through our books, webinars, podcast, newsletter, consulting clients, and events. It is in this spirit that we decided to add this chapter, $1 Billion+ Single Family Offices, focused on the most valuable, high-end, and private niche in the industry. We have based this chapter on our experience of knowing 55 families and single family offices with over $1B in assets. Typically, we are cold-called or emailed by such a family about twice a month for various reasons ranging from deal flow origination challenges or acquisition search needs, building out an advisory board, or executive search needs.

Families that are worth over $1 billion are different animals than those with $20M, or $200M; like giraffes, they cannot afford to eat small plants (operating businesses) and they typically take bigger and bigger bites and look higher up in the trees for their investment portfolio. These families are almost always global, 90% of the 55 families that I know have their own foundations, and most are very passionate about what they give to. Once families get to this level, they have complex challenges in front of them ranging from talent acquisition and compensation, deal flow sourcing and analysis, to global due diligence and asset monitoring. Every activity involves unique complexities, such as measuring legal exposure or producing seamless reports for dozens of team members, and these complexities expand exponentially at the $1 billion+ level.

There are over 1,500 billionaires in the world today and that number is growing. A 2013 BCG Wealth Report stated that there were 70 billionaires in New York, 64 in Moscow, 54 in London, 40 in Hong Kong, and 29 in

Beijing. This is not too surprising given that when I look at dozens of sources of competitiveness rankings for HNW, cities that matter to UHNW, or cities with the most residents with $100M +, the cities of New York, London, Tokyo, Paris, Hong Kong, and Singapore come up again and again. While the U.S. boasts the highest number of billionaires, growth in BRIC countries and in emerging markets has spread billionaires more globally than in years past. Countries like Brazil, Switzerland, and Singapore are making a concerted effort to attract billionaires to establish a residence in these welcoming countries, rather than more traditional wealth hubs like New York City and London. Here is some data from Knight Frank in 2012 on the number of billionaires in different countries around the world:

Country	Billionaires
United States	543
China	154
Germany	149
UK	149
India	122
Russia	102
Hong Kong	70
Switzerland	63
Brazil	55
Indonesia	31

Eduardo Saverin, one of the founders of Facebook, saw his net worth balloon to more than $2 billion in recent years as the social media company went public and the valuation of his minority stake soared. Saverin garnered a lot of attention in the media when he renounced his American citizenship and established his residence in Singapore. This decision appears to have saved Saverin millions of dollars that would have been paid in capital gains tax from the IPO, but the move speaks to a larger trend among billionaires: relocating to more tax and business-friendly countries. In this global era, it makes sense for many billionaires to open offices abroad or even relocate permanently to a different country that has particular benefits for the family. Many billionaires manage large investment portfolios and do much of their business in different countries, so the decision to move overseas is not as extreme as it might feel for someone who does not spend a great deal of time traveling or working across different countries. I expect that billionaire families and $1 billion family offices will continue to expand businesses and residences abroad and ultimately relocate to the most attractive cities for billion dollar families.

$1B+ Family Values

When you meet with a $1 billion family, you'll notice that the family prioritizes different values compared to any other investor client, even other high net worth families and individuals. Here is what I have found these billionaire families value most:

1. **Capital Preservation – A mix of risk management and opportunism:** Capital preservation through investing in outsized returns for moderate risk. This does not mean a high risk-high return strategy; it simply means they try to earn, for example, a 7% return in a way that manages risk much closer than others seeking that same return target for one area of their portfolio.

2. **Deal Flow:** High quality deal flow, profitable $1M-$50M EBITDA companies that they can write a $5M-$250M check to acquire. We have entire chapters dedicated to this topic earlier in the book.

3. **Talent & Network**: Experienced talent, insight, genuine value-add recommendations and referrals. This community works upon referrals and trusted networks. They cannot investigate completely every opportunity on its own—not thoroughly at least. As Richard Branson has said, "At my level, I cannot do anything myself, I must rely upon my team and operating business CEOs." In the same way, billionaire family offices rely on their staff, business partners, friends, and other relationships to provide referrals to valuable people and opportunities.

4. **Legacy Establishment:** Whether it is through dominating their industry, charitable contributions, continuing the growth and sustainability of their wealth, or all of the above, families of this size put an enormous amount of thought and energy into the legacy that they will leave behind.

Different families will place these values in a different order, but I find these topics and value points coming up weekly in my conversations with them. Those who can add meaningful value in a powerful way while speaking their language get invited into their inner circle.

Global Perception of $1 Billion+ Families & Reality:

I recently traveled to London to discuss co-investment opportunities with a $2B & a $5B+ family. While in town, I was invited to the *BBC World News* TV show for an interview on $1B+ families and their single family offices (pictured below).

Much of the interview focused on why these families are not spending more of their money to help the economy, the perceptions of the ultra-wealthy, and what it is like to work with them every day. Some important points came out of the show's discussion and I wanted to share these thoughts with you here.

- None of the families that I have met to-date became wealthy through sheer good fortune, such as winning the lottery, finding gold on their horse ranch, etc. Almost all of the family offices that I work with have all started and grown successful businesses and worked long hours over many years. Yet, the perception remains that many ultra-wealthy families lucked into their wealth and did not earn it through hard work and success. I'm sure many billionaires on the Forbes list have given up trying to comprehend this perception in the face of their real lives spent running between meetings with their Board, investors, clients, and employees.
- While family offices and $1B+ families are seen sometimes as secretive, hard-to-access, and under-the-radar, they are everywhere. They are behind the charities we hear about, backing the venture

capital funds, owning the sports teams we cheer for, and refining the oil going into our cars. They are omnipresent, yet somewhat secretive at the same time.

- Part of the interview with the BBC focused on what it is like to work with these families. As I explained on-air, I have found them all to be highly professional, respectful of time, and, while very busy, they do take time to identify high-quality partners and products. It is also important to note that while these families have exceptional wealth, they are always receptive to exceptional ideas and insights. If you can provide genuine insight on your area of niche expertise, then you have a knowledge-currency that they don't have. In that way, you will be seen as valuable to their team, even though you may not have $100M or $1B yourself.
- Most newspaper headlines on the ultra-wealthy focus on wasted money, crashed Ferraris, family disputes, or other negative aspects of being very wealthy. There are many family disputes, but what goes on with these families is far from what the media portrays and is not consistently negative. In fact, I believe the more that billionaires and wealthy families appear publicly, speak on TV, attend conferences, and otherwise engage the public, the more people will see the reality of affluence: the people who have built these fortunes are usually even more extraordinary than the wealth they have amassed. By and large, these individuals are successful because they have built a business, capitalized on an idea, or simply worked hard and been rewarded for their efforts.

Some may disagree—and this is as political as I ever get—but I believe that as a society we are playing the game of capitalism and, with the exception of a few corrupt politically-connected billionaires, the rest of these individuals are winners in this global game that we play. They should be studied, learned from, and respected as the leaders that they are.

$1B Single Family Office Interviews: As of the writing of this book, we have a network of 55 families and single family offices with $1B or more in capital. These families are our clients, friends in the industry, and speakers at our events. We decided to sit down with a few of them for a short interview to add some additional perspectives to this book. Below, please find interviews with two $1B+ single family office executives: Shiraz Poonevala of G.P. Group of Companies and Michael Connor of Consolidated Investment Group. We debated on keeping many interviews in this book anonymous (especially the $1B+ ones) to prevent them from receiving a flood of inquiries from readers, but, in the end, we decided transparency and authenticity was the best policy. We ask that you please respect the time of these professionals mentioned here and elsewhere in the book.

Interview with Shiraz Poonevala

 Shiraz is the CIO of G.P. Group of Companies, which owns and operates over 60 operating businesses and has well over $1B assets. Shiraz spoke at our recent event in Singapore at the Raffles Hotel and shared some great deal flow and direct investment-related insights, so I invited him back again to share more within this book. Shiraz will be a featured presenter during our $1B+ Family Office Speaker Series on Day 3 of our 500-person Family Office Super Summit.

Richard C. Wilson: What are the top three methods for $1B+ single family offices who are always "in the market" to increase their deal flow?

Shiraz Poonevala: The first way to increase deal flow clearly is to have an extensive network. In Asia, at least a lot of the deal flow comes from other Family Offices, then from Investment Banks and finally from wealth managers or bankers representing their products or knowing big business houses/families. Hence, being in the market and being known and well-connected is of paramount importance.

Second, is to have a track record and reputation of doing deals. It is quite important to have a clear strategy of what deals you can and cannot do as that quite obviously significantly improves the chances of success and also eliminates deals that are not suitable pretty early in the game, which a lot of people referring the deals really appreciate.

We pride ourselves in sending out the first response on a potential deal referred to us within 24 hours either which way. This is because we have a basic "smell test" that all deals must meet. Once the deal passes your basic criterion, working on it in a focused manner and with a finite timeframe is important. Finally closing a few deals a year gives a lot of comfort that you are a genuine investor which in turn gets you incremental deal flow. A good reputation and credibility in the market with all partners greatly helps in generating incremental deal leads.

Finally, deal flow is also a factor of market conditions and sentiment, and a lot of times we have seen that in a bear market, the deal flow slows down or dries up, but from our experience this is the best time to be looking at value and encouraging sell-side people to be showing us deals that they may otherwise think would not be of interest due to the poor market conditions.

Richard C. Wilson: Where is the highest quality deal flow for lower-middle market and mid-market deals?

Shiraz Poonevala: Normally, again from other Family Offices or Investment Banks, but this time the more niche or boutique type with some kind of specialization and not the bulge bracket banks. There are lots of focused and specialized funds or boutique houses and we have found a lot of value in dealing with these when looking for smaller mid-market deals.

Richard C. Wilson: I believe the direct investment and co-investing area within the family office world could use some additional sophistication, but often times you have to be opportunistic with such investments and the size of an investment round or terms may not line up with an ideal portfolio construction plan.

What lessons have you learned about building a portfolio of operating businesses in terms of risk, cash flow, liquidity needs, and synergies?

Shiraz Poonevala: When I first joined the Family Office, there were no real criterion for any investment decisions and it was some basic due diligence and a lot of gut feel. Over time, we managed to put some systems and processes in place with a clear focus.

One of the first things we decided to do was to stop being a financial investor and only become a strategic investor, i.e., look at businesses where we honestly believed we added value (either by domain knowledge or geographic expertise or other ways, but not just money). For new opportunities, we set up the mantra that we would look at investing in people we trust, businesses we understand, and geographies we are familiar with—any opportunity had to pass this test before we decided to go further.

Having adopted this methodology, we do believe we have greatly reduced the risk of being a passive investor (though there could be some concentration risk if there are not enough domains to invest in, but thankfully that is not the case with us).

We have also been able to unlock a lot of value with the synergies that we bring to the table, mainly by sharing good practices across similar businesses, benchmarking and a lot of cross pollination of people. Cash flow and liquidity are always a concern with any direct/co-investment and to circumvent this we like to deploy surplus funds only and not leverage too much.

An ideal portfolio construction plan is something we always work towards at the macro basis and it is one of the key functions of the Family Office to look at concentration risk, liquidity risk etc., but it is quite dynamic and something we like to keep on top of. We would not, however, pass a good opportunity only because it is not in sync with our ideal portfolio construction plan, but would look towards ways of making the investment whilst adjusting or tweaking other bits of the operating businesses or in a worst case adjusting the plan.

Most Family Offices run by a strong patriarch are very opportunistic by their very nature and would not like to see too many "policies and procedures" come in the way of a good opportunity.

Richard C. Wilson: Do you believe families are best deciding on one to two or three industries in which to complete their acquisitions or do you believe in a more generalist model when it comes to direct investing and club deals, and why?

Shiraz Poonevala: I would say a lot depends on the genesis of the family and the culture of the patriarch. If all the money has been made from a single, very successful business, like is the case in many instances in Asia, then the family is less keen to diversify into other industries (in most cases, property and property-related investments seem to be the natural progression and the first real diversification).

Also, a lot of these families prefer control over the business and are not very good at partnerships or trusting of other people, and hence diversification is generally an issue with the first gen, but not so much with the next gen who are perhaps more progressive and willing to look at acquisitions. My personal advice to any Family Office would be to look at strategic investments and initially at least look at club deals before getting into any new industries by themselves.

A lot will also depend on the nature of the opportunity available—for example, last year we acquired a construction company listed on the stock exchange of Thailand, as the largest investor was looking to sell out for some internal reasons. The company was extremely well managed with a good team in place, valuation was reasonable and the due diligence was one of the cleanest we have seen—we decided to take a controlling stake in the company for these reasons and thanks to some aggressive infrastructure development in Thailand, the construction industry in general and our company in particular has done very well. Hence, not wanting to generalize, I would also say a lot depends on each deal construct.

Richard C. Wilson: What are a few $1M pitfalls that you can help single family offices avoid when they are looking to purchase an operating business?

Shiraz Poonevala: I would say key issues to look at are:

- Understand the business and people behind it, especially if it is owned by another family
- Conduct a thorough due diligence
- Engage good lawyers
- Ensure the deal terms are good to both parties
- Check the post-acquisitions synergies thoroughly
- Pay close attention to the post-integration activities and integrate as much as you can as soon as possible.
- Retain key management for at least three to five years and motivate them to a higher extent than they were motivated before

Richard C. Wilson: Your family owns over 60 operating businesses, and has collected many best practices while doing so. Can you share some negotiation or "contract terms" related lessons learned over time?

Shiraz Poonevala: When we negotiate, we always adopt the philosophy of negotiate in good faith, document more is better than less in the contracts, and leave the legal stuff to the lawyers, but certainly not the commercial issues which we like to discuss with our counterparts directly. Key issues that we look at from experience are:

- Minority control issues and veto rights for a partner that is in such a situation
- Fund raising and dilution in case the company is in need of money and a shareholder cannot or is not keen to continue to invest
- Exit strategies when one or more shareholders want to exit
- Recourse to when a company is frustrated either because management or shareholders cannot get along and the day-to-day running is impacted
- Indemnities and warranties for acts done before the date of acquisition if we are buying into an existing business
- When we have had private equity invest in our companies, we have started naming the director we would like nominated to the Board of the investee company in the contracts because a lot of times the discussions are held by senior partners, and after the investment, a junior partner is nominated to the Board

Richard C. Wilson: At our family office conference at the Raffles Hotel in Singapore, you talked about partnerships for a while. Can you talk about the importance of partnerships here and all the ways those can help while building a portfolio of operating businesses?

Shiraz Poonevala: We really believe in partnerships and pride ourselves in partnerships, and all our businesses are effectively partnerships because where we have none—we make management our partners. I guess partnerships work really well if you have the right mindset and can find the right partners—we really do not have a large management team, but do have a lot of expertise and we therefore leverage that expertise through partnerships and their management teams.

Partnerships clearly allow you to grow faster across all verticals and geographies. They also help you to imbibe best practices that your partners may have that you may wish to embrace. From a diversification and risk perspective, they also help mitigate exposure.

I guess the downside is when it does not work out for whatever reason, but then we are very clear in our minds at least that rather than get into a protracted litigation for the right or wrong reasons, we are better off settling by having a discussion with the partners. Thus far it has worked for us and in the five years that I have been here, we have had three such discussions, all with outcomes which were considered as reasonably fair to the parties concerned.

Interview with Michael Connor

Michael Connor is Investment Director of the Consolidated Investment Group. Michael is someone that I have known for several years, work with on deal flow programs, and have had speak at my live family office events. He works for a $1B+ single family office in the U.S. and helps invest across a portfolio of direct investments, real estate, and alternative investments. You will be able to meet Michael in person at our Family Office Super Summit this November, where he will be one of the single family office speakers.

$1B+ Single Family Office Audio Interview: In this interview with Michael Connor, we discuss cash management, finding family office talent, his experience working at two different $1B+ single family offices, and a bit on due diligence, as well. This interview was conducted over the phone and recorded in MP3 format and you can listen to the full 45-minute audio interview by either streaming it through our website or downloading it as an MP3 onto your phone or computer. Simply visit this page for either option: http://SingleFamilyOffices.com/Connor

Magazine Interview

I recently completed an interview for an Asian magazine on my work and views on $1B+ families. Here are the questions that the group asked and my answers:

How are single family offices operating in Asia & Latin America compared to Europe and the United States?

Many of the $1B+ single family offices in Asia and Latin America are much more focused on operating businesses, commercial real estate, and hard assets than their U.S. and European counterparts. The last time I met with a room full of private bankers, wealth managers, and multi-family office types in Moscow, there was not a single one who had a "Westernized" diversification model in their investment portfolio, which included hedge funds, private equity, public markets, commodity/hard assets, bond investments, etc. They were all invested almost exclusively in commercial real estate and operating businesses. In both Asia and Eastern Europe, secrecy is valued as much as—if not more than—investment returns. These wealthy individuals fear being hit with additional regulation, investigations, or corruption in one form or another if anyone was to know their true net worth.

Many of the larger family offices in the East, with the exception of the most formalized in Singapore, Hong Kong, Tokyo, and Australia, are managed by family members or close friends and confidants of the family. As a family's wealth increases, their need to employ professionals underneath family members to help run operations and manage partnerships increases, but in 85%+ of my relationships with $1B+ families, there is at least one family member serving in a top position, typically as CEO or CIO. This is at odds with family offices of the West, which are typically managed by investment professionals. The biggest factors driving this divergence are secrecy concerns and loyalty.

In Latin America, I have found a middle ground; strong business ties to the U.S. and a robust Westernized banking center have led to well over 500 hedge funds and private equity funds operating in Sao Paulo alone. Furthermore, the concept of allocating to investment fund managers is becoming much more widely accepted in Latin America. Many of the most affluent families in Latin America have diversified their wealth through investment fund managers, but not to the degree of the average U.S. single family offices.

Do Asian and Latin American family offices need to formalize and become more like their U.S. counterparts?

One of my least favorite comments regarding family offices is that Eastern European and Asian family offices need to formalize themselves more to become more like U.S. families. Often this type of remark is said in a somewhat condescending tone, but the more time I spend in Asia, and Singapore specifically, the more I see that U.S. families could learn from families in other regions of the world. Some Asian families are trying to become more diversified with Western third-party investment fund management, but at the same time, U.S. families are looking for co-investments, club deals, and direct investments, almost as if it is a new solution to their troubles. A lot of U.S. families are struggling to complete due diligence, decide on a direct investment portfolio strategy, and to find talent to help them manage all of the investment due diligence and operating improvements long-term. Many Western families could learn a lot about how Eastern families have been focusing on direct investments for generations, without the distraction of public market investments.

For example, a 2nd generation family that we just started working with has over $1B and 20 operating businesses, employs 100's of team members, has brought in a seasoned CIO from Singapore to help run the single family office, and the family is now formalizing a process for acquiring assets. The family has reached an impressive level of success in a turbulent political state, and this success will likely continue due to their diversified approach, which leverages their core abilities in food production and supply chain management. Many food and agriculture families could take notes on their approach.

How do you see Single Family Offices developing in BRIC countries, and how does activity there reflect the growth of wealth globally?

Statistics and studies show that in the future, much of the new wealth and a larger percentage of new billionaires will come from Asia. BRIC countries in general will outpace most non-BRIC nations in terms of new wealth. The 2013 Wealth Report by Knight Frank suggests that only the U.S., Germany, and the UK will remain in the top seven countries, along with the four BRIC countries, in terms of most billionaires living in each country by 2022. The only reason that the U.S., Germany, and the UK are able to maintain these positions is that they attract capital, businesses, and billionaire families due to the financial marketplace and business benefits of operating in places such as Berlin, London, New York, Miami, etc.

I see the single family office industry becoming 7-10 times larger than it is now by 2035. More single family offices will emerge as families start to identify themselves as single family offices and better understand what a family office means.

When single family offices are operating on a large scale in a country known for corruption, how do families operate while staying under the radar?

Many families break up the assets across the world and across different investment managers so no one party or country knows how much money the family has. For example, one family in Singapore has $40M with a large private bank, $30M in operating businesses, and over $50M in cash. Those are the pools of capital that I know of, but I have only known the family for a few years, so the full extent of their wealth is unknown to me as well. There are some business benefits to being relatively "invisible" and under-the-radar, as sometimes state-sponsored or government-backed cell phone companies or manufacturing businesses could target a sector if they see that the industry leader of that niche has produced enormous personal wealth in the recent past.

What is the #1 frustration that you hear about while working with families that have over $1B in wealth to manage?

The top challenges we see faced by $1B+ families include access to talent, access to high-quality and well-screened deal flow, and good relationships with partners who understand their business. Where these areas connect is in coordinating a direct investment portfolio, to identify someone who understands what a single family office is and what the family's investment mandate is, but also who has managed direct investments before—or at least a portfolio of a private equity fund—at a high-level can be challenging. Many families want to get to know someone over a year or two at least, if not three to five years, before hiring someone, and this complicates everything as well. Those families with over $1B in assets have exponentially greater challenges. At $1B in wealth, every single family we work with is looking for more co-investment work, or are in the process of an acquisition or preparing for a divestiture, all of them are either looking for talent, or trying to replace someone on their team, and many can barely keep up with the due diligence demands when it comes to selecting public market and hard assets. Even one $1B+ Middle Eastern family that I have gotten to know well doesn't have the resources they claim they need to keep up with their ambitions to invest globally in hedge funds, private equity, hard assets, and operating businesses.

In short, the desire of many families to improve and diversify further often far exceeds their available resources, and this can stress already constrained resources and burn out executives at the top level.

How do families get access to direct investments while still remaining secretive, and can that even be accomplished without hiring an investment banker or third party of any type?

There are four main ways that $1B+ families can gain access to direct investments while preserving their privacy and avoiding hiring an investment banker or third party:

> 1) Deal Platforms: Right now, there is a horse race to see who can establish the largest, most-trusted deal platform in the world. These are platforms open to just investment bankers, family offices, M&A consultants, etc. and they often cost $3K-$15K/year to gain access to. This is a place where you can operate anonymously for the most part, and identify new deal opportunities. Within three to five years, a clear winner and strong #2 player should emerge and make this part of the industry more efficient and productive to use...for now the jury is out on who that will be.

2) Create a Deal-Source Team: Families can steal the operational processes of what my team helps with: crunching data and identifying original deal opportunities. Nowadays, hiring full-time professional staff to comb through private company information within industries such a healthcare, energy, commercial real estate, or hotels is relatively straightforward and inexpensive. It is the due diligence, hands-on business building, etc. that becomes very expensive...but, with organized processes and a good idea of the size of a business and industry of focus, a deal-sourcing team build out is one of the best ways to produce deal flow for a family.

3) Create a Family Investment Club: If your family has made money in the hotel business, why not form a Hotel Investment Club for you and other families who only invest in hotels? This does not require an investment banker and heavy fees; it involves a simple quarterly phone call and bi-annual meetings to discuss investment ideas, co-investment opportunities, and marketplace changes. Even having just three to four families in such a syndicate can be very helpful.

4) Hire a Direct Investment Executive: Many families don't have a full-time executive at the $200K-$500K+ level that focuses 100% of their time on generating new relationships with other $1B+ families and, in turn, co-investment opportunities. Many times, the team is so resource-constrained that everyone is doing many different things, rather than focusing on any one thing, such as managing the direct investment portfolio. There are some family offices that only stick to a few areas of investments in their portfolio, and do have full-time professionals who focus on direct investments, but they rarely are working proactively to develop new family-office-to-family-office relationships as a primary function of their role.

In addition to these four ideas above, of course, a family can hire investment bankers, a merchant bank, a direct investment consultant, or take advantage of syndicates that other families have formed, but hopefully one of the ideas above will get some wheels turning on new ideas for a few single family offices reading this. The challenge of learning more about direct investments and co-investments is that typically the best informed are trying to push a co-investment or direct investment, so they are biased towards working in this area in one very specific way and are not as open to other creative ways to meet the challenge of buying and managing operating businesses.

How can families take a more sophisticated approach to direct investing so it is not done haphazardly; what is the best model you have seen?

This is an area that my team is working to help professionalize and formalize more, and I think there is value in helping lead the way on how co-investment and direct investment portfolios should be managed. I think the most important thing is for families to develop a very specific mandate for what they are looking for and why. They should identify one to three industries (or niches within an industry ideally), a revenue range, know whether they want minority or majority positions and why, how they will be adding value to these acquisition targets, and what their ideal holding period will be. I believe it is healthy for a family to define this at the same level that a private equity is forced to while explaining to investors what their competitive edge in the marketplace will be. Even if the family may plan to hold most assets indefinitely, knowing what your edge is in the marketplace is important, yet many times can't be easily explained when I ask families about it. The more specific of a target you aim for while making acquisitions, the easier the deal-sourcing gets, because there will only be 20, 50, or 200 such companies many times in the country you are targeting for the investment. You can then develop real relationships and understand that competitive landscape on a granular level much faster than if you try to cover too much ground with a small to medium sized team.

The best model I have seen is a family which is allocating $300M towards one manufacturing niche, and they have provided two partners with exactly 15 bullet points that describe their ideal acquisition target, and know how they are going to be building a platform model with those acquisitions to produce value in that part of that manufacturing niche. They have professional staff in place to help, a few limited partners who they have known for years, and a PowerPoint presentation on exactly what their objectives, goals, and vision is for this portfolio.

So much of investing is team evaluation, you had mentioned before a model your team uses for character analysis, can you share a few comments on that?

The model our organization has been using for years now is something we call the 6 C's of Character Analysis. These include being Committed, Consistent, Can Provide References, Confident Listener, Centered, and someone who is Contributing. We have a full-hour presentation I give on this sometimes at conferences or my own events, but we use it as a cheat sheet to decide who we will do business with. The thesis here is that while everyone says the team is the most important, most decisions made about a team or individual are based on a gut feeling, on subjective emotions, first impressions, or a referral from a trusted partner or advisory board member. We need more objective ways to value the character of business partners and if you look at how committed they are, how consistent they act, the quality of their references, their ability to listen to you and others, and how helpful, insightful and contributing they are to partners and their industry at large, you can rank and evaluate teams in a more objective fashion. This is important while acquiring operating businesses, hiring talent for a family office, or working on co-investments with other families.

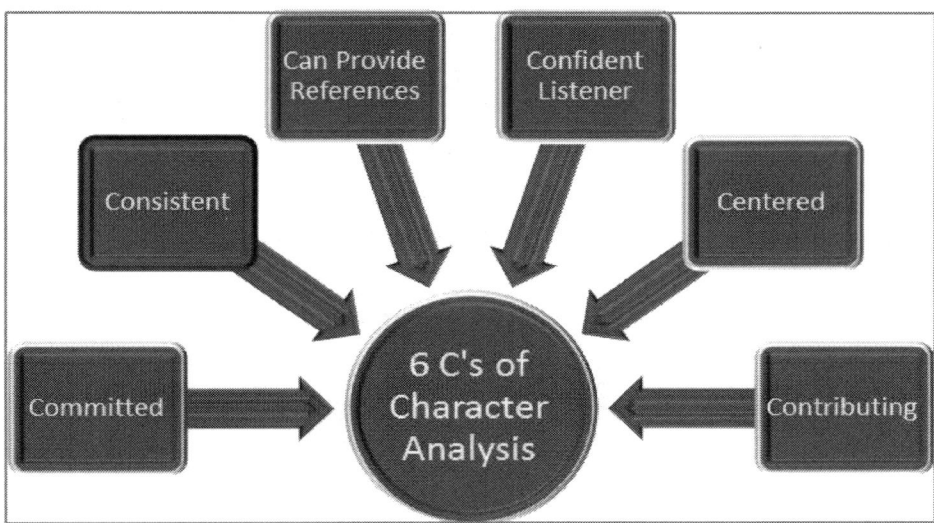

These are the 6 C's of Character Analysis we use in our business.

What is the most counterintuitive lesson you have learned from working on mandates for the largest families?

I believe the #1 lesson which surprises investment bankers or merchant banks who want access to some of our $1B+ families is that these families can be relatively thrifty and cost sensitive. If something costs $400/month or $1k/month, they want to know why they need to pay for that and why it isn't free, or why it is required to do business. One $1B+ family patriarch who we are introducing to a direct investment right now has recently "been caught" washing out a used plastic bag so it could be re-used and not discarded. The media likes to focus on waste, extravagance, tax evasion, and private jets, but many families are generous, thrifty, creative, entrepreneurial, and host a number of additional qualities not covered as often in the major news outlets.

Conclusion

$1B+ families are all around us. These families are behind the charities improving our societies, large businesses that deliver goods and services to us, sports franchises that we love (or hate), politicians, venture capital firms investing in technologies and innovations that change our lives, and the brands we see advertised on TV. They are seen as secretive, yet at the same time, their influence is omnipresent in society. If you run a single family office with close to or more than $1B in assets and would like to be introduced to other billionaire families please let us know.

Chapter 15: Intergenerational Money Management

"That some should be rich shows that others may become rich, and, hence, is just encouragement to industry and enterprise." - Abraham Lincoln

Anyone who has read their fair share of family office research and writing on the industry is probably tired of hearing the "from shirt sleeves to shirt sleeves in three generations" saying that describes how families gain and then relatively quickly lose their wealth in just two to three generations. This clichéd phrase has many different variations of the same message and is used by people from different cultures and countries—from rice paddy to rice paddy is the phrase used in Japan, for example. The reason that this message is so prevalent is that it speaks to a real truth in wealth preservation: it is difficult to maintain wealth through multiple generations and many once-wealthy families do return to more humble means in a shockingly short period of time. This happens because there are so many variables, steps, values, and a lot of focused work ethic required to retain and grow wealth.

Video: To watch a short video I recorded in the Swiss Alps recently on Multigenerational Wealth Management please visit:

http://SingleFamilyOffices.com/Wealth-Management

Planning the transfer of wealth through multiple generations is complicated and should be done using professional advisors. This chapter will focus on some insights and best practices regarding intergenerational money management, including discussions, goals, taxation, legal structures, timing, processes, and maintenance.

Discussing Money

"I am grateful for the blessings of wealth, but it hasn't changed who I am. My feet are still on the ground. I'm just wearing better shoes." - Oprah Winfrey

Talking about money can be a challenge whether you have a lot of it or a little. Many ultra-wealthy families worry that if they talk about money too much that it slants their kids to only care about money and nothing else. However, not talking about money has other ways of potentially skewing a family's understanding of money by making money seem inconsequential or easily available without instilling an appreciation for the years of hard work that went into building a fortune.

Many are afraid that even the discussion of money too often in a family could kill ambition or breed a sense of entitlement.

Struggling to Identify a Successor

I know many affluent families that are headed by a patriarch or matriarch who generated the family's wealth through exceptional effort and dedication, but these family heads are frustrated when they do not see the same qualities that drove their success in any of their descendants. It can be very difficult for these individuals to nurture a love of the family business in their children because to do so means exposing them to details on the family's wealth. A number of wealthy families have found that sharing too much about the business too early with their children can create a sense that the family has always been successful and that the company will continue to succeed for the foreseeable future. This poor understanding of the business ignores the complexities of the business, the sweat that went into creating it and that still goes into preserving the firm's position in the industry, and the risks that threaten the business.

Goals & Tax Liabilities

This book began with a discussion of industry fundamentals and then some of the family dynamics of starting a family office and making sure you have a compass to direct your actions and investments of time and money.

As the next generation of a family begins to take over management of assets, these plans need to be reviewed, refreshed, and communicated to make sure they are still relevant and that everyone feels engaged and has bought-in to the process and end goal. If these plans are never reviewed, the family will drift apart in their mission and in-fighting will almost certainly occur as miscommunication and miss-managed expectations cause family rifts.

Timing

It is often best to start planning out what your intergenerational wealth goals and intentions are as soon as you become wealthy or know that you will become wealthy (say, in the case that you run a successful company likely to be acquired or complete an IPO). To the extreme, some individuals are now setting up their family offices before they take their company public or sell their business, because the wealth-unlocking event is inevitable.

In my own case, we initially setup Wilson Holding Company because three publicly-traded companies offered to purchase our training division within a short six-month period, and during that same period, we acquired two small businesses and a piece of intellectual property and we are committed to pursuing similar acquisitions for the foreseeable future. I, like a growing number of business professionals and entrepreneurs, have decided to set up my own holding company to grow into a single family office to ensure that my business assets are properly managed and to help consolidate my advisors, from legal counsel to tax advisory.

It is important to look ahead to potential liquidity events like an inheritance, initial public offering, sale of an asset, etc., which could complicate your life and require setting up a family office. The last thing you want is to not have proper counsel when you are making important decisions and participating in negotiations that could cost you millions of dollars if a deal is poorly structured or you have inadequate guidance. You should make sure that you include any relevant family members in these discussions and the formalization of your family office, especially if they will be affected by the result of your decisions.

This leads to another important consideration that requires delicate timing: informing and explaining your wealth to children, grandchildren, and any other family members that need to be informed. As we touched on earlier in this chapter, it can be extremely challenging for any family to discuss these sensitive matters, but many heads of affluent families find that it is important and necessary to explain their wealth to the family. Here are a few tips on how to approach this conversation:

Maturity Over Age: The timing of this conversation should not be tied to a birthday or arbitrary milestone, but rather when each family member achieves a sufficient level of maturity to handle the information responsibly.

Context is Key: Some families find it helpful to gradually share the details of the family history and present an extensive explanation of how the family came to its current level of success. Providing this context is important because it ensures that the audience understands what it took to achieve its present success, how this is not the case for every family, and that they are (presumably) expected to work hard if they hope to enjoy similar fortune and preserve it for future generations.

Ease into the Explanation: It might be easier to tackle the conversation in one sitting, but this can be overwhelming and incomprehensible for some family members and it may be better to ease into your explanation by explaining different aspects of the family's wealth over multiple conversations. In this way, you can explain how the family business started and why it has been successful and make sure that the listener understands the evolution of the business. Then, in subsequent conversations, you can discuss the granularities and complexities of different areas of the family, its business, and any other relevant areas.

Processes

Developing processes by which intergenerational issues are navigated is crucial to preserving harmony and success in your family. I will share a few important processes here that you should consider implementing across all generations of your family:

- Regular family meetings
- A process for evaluating investment opportunities
- Guidelines and checks to guard against nepotism in the business and ensure a meritocratic culture

- Hiring process
- Processes for dividing and assigning responsibilities within the family

Maintenance

The work of managing intergenerational wealth never ends; not with so many changes every year that affect the family. These events vary and include changes in marital status, new family members being born, regulatory and taxation schemes expiring, and new laws coming into effect. The never-ending nature of intergenerational wealth management is bad news for most of us—except for those trust and estate planning executives who are already well-aware of this reality. Families of exceptional wealth should plan on meeting with their trust and estate advisors at least once per year. Hopefully someone on the advisory board or a core family office employee will have enough knowledge to know when to call the advisor about events that require more frequent consultation with the advisor.

The last thing anyone wants is for a family's wealth to destroy the family's unity. Nobody wants bickering siblings, bitter Thanksgiving dinners, and spoiled-rotten grandchildren.

Single Family Office Example:

One of the top-five most successful single family offices I have gotten to work with is a $1B+ family out of California. They have sustained and grown their wealth over six generations now by diversifying from what was originally a textile manufacturing family into many new areas such as hotels, asset management, and technology companies. The three principles and themes they invest by include transparency & communication, adaptability, and innovation & technology. If you look at their portfolio, it is diversified, but it relies upon these three strategies working in unison. Like our firm, this company uses the Rockefeller Habits to structure the family office just as you would a business, with monthly and quarterly goals, key performance indicators, and long-term Big Hairy Audacious Goals (BHAGs). Their family meets often, and holds investment committee meetings, and formal quarterly board meetings on-site with everyone in-person.

This single family office is a sign of what is to come for the single family office industry, as one of the family members speaks at events, they have a website, they own part of a Broker-Dealer, and they are accessing deal flow through multiple channels, where many single family offices stay very secretive and under-the-radar and as a result get no deal flow.

Compare this example above to another client I'm starting to work with who has $850M in assets under management, but has just reached out to me because now the 2nd generation is taking over the family's wealth, but only one person has been appointed to manage this large sum of money. This one person is hiring and firing fund managers, trading stocks and bonds, managing reporting, and helping coordinate real estate assets and acquisitions. They do not get great deal flow, have many formal processes in place, and they haven't allocated enough resources to protect and manage the capital they steward.

Conclusion

Whole books have been written on passing on money to your heirs, and a seasoned trust and estate attorney can cover the legal vehicles, pitfalls, etc. better than we can but this chapter was included to touch on our perspective on this important issue. Whether it is preservation or further growth of net worth for the next generation, one of the two is typically a top reason for creating a single family office in the first place, so it I core to this entire industry.

Chapter 16: Converting from a Single Family Office into a Multi-Family Office

One trend that my team is seeing consistently every month is that of single family offices converting into multi-family offices. This trend is happening for three main reasons: the first is that those wealthy enough to need their own single family office typically earned their wealth by starting a business, or helping grow a business. It is a natural progression for these individuals to eventually apply those same skills honed in their business background to operating a profitable multi-family office.

The second reason this happens is because compliance costs are rising and hiring top talent is becoming more expensive. There is a desire within many single family offices to spread the costs out among additional families. While some families spread out these costs by outsourcing and sharing a Chief Compliance Office or Chief Direct Investments Advisor across families, others welcome other families into the fold as a multi-family office.

The third reason behind the conversions from a single to multi-family office is that many single family office founders have close friends, business associates, and clients from other businesses who see what the family has built and want to benefit from the formalized family office structure, too. Eventually, many single family offices give in to repeated requests by family and friends and decide to explore the multi-family office model. The family will go through with the conversion only if it makes business sense and the family is confident that they won't be operating a money-losing venture for the benefit of everyone but their own family. This is a natural progression; a family will form a single family office with the purpose of serving their family's unique needs and preserving their wealth but, over time, other affluent families will request access to some or all of the single family office's services. It might start with a simple conversation with your neighbor about investments and financial planning and you refer him or her to your single family office wealth manager. Or, it could be that more and more members of your family join the single family office and, as so often happens with a successful business, a relative invites his cousin, his cousin brings his brother-in-law into the fold, and so on.

Most of these single family offices do not start with the intention of launching a multi-family office; it simply happens through one of the three scenarios explained above. As the general public and more of the finance community begin to understand the benefits of the family office model and why someone may like to have their wealth managed in this structure, I see the trend of new single and multi-family office startups strengthening and conversions between the types steadily increasing.

The top reason why converting into a multi-family office is resisted by some wealth creators is that, unless they made their fortune in finance or investment management, operating a multi-family office is not a core competency for the family and operating one may put some capital at risk. This violates the chief goal of capital preservation (if that is their #1 goal) and makes some families uncomfortable with an unfamiliar business in which they are not 100% confident. These families may ask, why not buy another hotel or an operating business in an industry they have great expertise in, instead of experimenting with a multi-family office venture? This is a valid question that should be carefully considered before going through with a multi-family office conversion. There are very real costs of starting a multi-family office and it can be expensive to comply with relevant laws and regulations that govern how a family office must operate if it is managing outside capital. If the family is not 100% on board with the venture and excited about the opportunity, then your chances of success as a multi-family office are greatly reduced.

The best way to mitigate this risk if you are exploring the multi-family office model is to obtain a clear understanding of all the anticipated expenses, challenges, and headaches that go with launching a multi-family office. That way, when you have to hire a new Chief Investment Officer, Business Development Head, Chief Compliance Officer, or other expensive position, the family won't have sticker shock at the compensation these senior professionals command. By explaining thoroughly how the multi-family office will be set up and all the expected difficulties, your family can make an informed decision on whether to proceed with the venture.

The Benefits of Forming a Multi-Family Office

Of course, at any point in time, a single family office can refuse to provide services to interested parties and many single family offices do just that. But if, as I've argued in this book, a single family office is a business, it makes sense for a highly successful business to take on new clients of the right type and scale and expand its operations into becoming a multi-family office. New clients can mean new fees, economies of scale, improved operational capabilities, and an expanded staff to serve the additional clients.

A good example of one of the benefits of converting to a multi-family office is wealth management infrastructure efficiencies. As a single family office, your investment returns are reduced (however indirectly) by the salaries and bonuses paid to your investment team. Many times, this model is still superior from a fee structure point of view to third-party investment funds, but the costs can still add up when you factor in the expenses of regulation, compensating a competent investment team, conducting due diligence, setting up the investment structure, purchasing analytics software and other IT products, and other associated expenses. By adding new clients, a single family office will earn fees from managing and investing other families' wealth without dramatically increasing expenses. The new revenue from the multi-family office model can then either be harvested by the family and partners or reinvested into further improving the multi-family office offering in areas such as real estate, direct investments, and/or attracting new clients.

These synergies exist in many different areas of a single family office. If your single family office keeps a counselor on retainer for all your legal needs, the costs can add up. However, you might be able to spread these costs among multiple clients and reduce the principal family's overhead. Similarly, an expert which you perhaps paid hourly in the past at a high rate could be hired full time to work exclusively for your multi-family office if you were to grow into helping manage the money of other families.

A $1B+ family that I work with has done just that—they have operated a single family office over 5 generations now, and due to their ability to retain and grow their total net worth consistently over generations, there are two other $1B+ families who are working with them consistently on co-investment deals and club deals and building a working relationship towards something that looks like a multi-family office in nature. If you will recall the chapters on co-investments and club deals, it is common for families to share deal flow to raise enough capital to close a deal—that much is common. But in this case, this is being used as a stepping-stone for a broader money management mandate.

Challenges to Forming and Operating a Multi-Family Office

One hurdle of converting a single family office into a multi-family office is the legal structure changes. You may need to create separate legal structures for different parts of the family, and for the multi-family office itself to protect a marketing or client management mishap from directly sacrificing a large amount of your family's net worth. Along these same lines, you will want to meet with an attorney who is experienced in such conversions and who can help you navigate the compliance consequences at the same time as you set up these legal structures. While trust structures and agreements produce a steady stream of clients for the legal profession, opening your single family office to help manage the wealth of others invites new legal risks and unforeseen exposures, so you may want to consider increasing or starting to retain new insurance coverage as well before accepting a new client.

Related to legal structure challenge, a single family office that converts to a multi-family office will likely face a new set of regulatory obligations. Family offices enjoy an exemption from some of the filing and disclosure requirements imposed by laws like the Dodd-Frank Act and other financial regulations. The Dodd-Frank Wall Street Reform and Consumer Protection Act specifically defined "family office" and excluded applicable family offices from registering as an investment adviser under the Investment Advisers Act of 1940. This is a tremendous relief to those family offices who are excluded from the regulations but for those who are viewed under the law as non-exempt investment advisors, the burden of compliance can be costly and tedious.

As you consider opening your family office to new family clients that are not directly related to you, be sure to have your legal advisor and compliance specialist ensure that you follow any applicable regulations. There are provisions in the Dodd-Frank Act rule on family offices that require the family office provide advice on securities only to certain family clients, that the family clients wholly own the family office, and prohibit the family office from presenting itself publicly as an investment advisor.

In an SEC letter discussing the changes to the rule, the SEC author notes her "dismay" to learn through letters submitted by family office representatives that some family offices were essentially operating as unregistered investment advisors. This suggests that many family offices did not understand how the Investment Advisers Act applied to their firm before the Dodd-Frank Act and likely these firms do not understand the recent changes either. As someone who works in the securities industry, I can certainly empathize with anyone who is seeking clarity on a ruling or law and it is really important to make sure you are complying with all applicable regulations. Be sure to check with qualified counsel before pursuing any changes to your family office or serving non-family clients. Regardless of any structural or business changes, it's a good idea to double-check that you are operating legally.[5]

Fees for Multi-Family Office Services

Most multi-family offices charge 80 to 150 basis points in fees to their clients for core services and then extra fees for additional help in the areas of real estate, investment banking, direct investments or co-investments, insurance solutions, and intensive multi-generational wealth planning. These fees are what helps pay for the changes needed to be made during an SFO to MFO conversion, but many families do not want to go through these burdens unless this second family has a significant level of wealth, so these plans are often put on hold until three to four potential clients are gathered or until at least $100M or $250M in assets, for example, are expected to quickly be

---

[5] SECURITIES AND EXCHANGE COMMISSION 17 CFR Part 275 [Release No. IA-3220; File No. S7-25-10] RIN 3235-AK66 Family Offices AGENCY: Securities and Exchange Commission.

managed.

One area that many struggle with when converting a single family office to a multi-family office is supporting the diverse investment requests and needs of multiple families when their core team was built to serve one family. In other words, some families, while operating as a single family office, only invested in real estate and the public markets (bonds and stocks), and once they bring in a new client under a multi-family office structure, they may be requested to help with co-investment transactions or buying an operating business for a family. Deciding what your multi-family office does and does not offer is important upfront and there is nothing wrong with offering a very specialized type of multi-family office. Some family offices only focus on co-investments, for example, and have a small percentage of assets outsourced to a third party, which can help manage liquid or public equity type investments for them in a hands-off fashion. While accepting outside clients can build up your resources and allow you in theory to offer a broader range of investment structures and vehicles for you and your family clients, you could alternatively just become better at the original areas in which you have historically invested. Some families who have explored converting into a multi-family office have backed away from the idea once they get a taste of the demands and expectations from some of the families they would be managing money for, while others launch, but only accept capital from those with very similar values, or from $100M+ families which make it "worth" serving in a high-quality fashion.

When you operate a single family office, many times you do not have a website, you don't need to speak at conferences, write book, or release white papers. Perhaps if you frequent social circles with dozens of $100M+ individuals, you can still operate in such a fashion, as I know several $1B+ groups do, but they are the exception to the rule. Most multi-family offices will need a website, basic marketing materials, someone to act as a director of marketing, etc. to consistently attract clients. This is where someone with an entrepreneurial background can actually move past the competition in a multi-family office model. Most multi-family offices are started by CPAs, financial advisors, or risk managers, and rarely do those professionals have any background in marketing. Many are great at client service and some are of the religion that referrals are the only way to grow a business in the family office industry, but I'm not part of that crowd. A well-crafted, focused marketing strategy could attract very well-qualified clients to you like clockwork, while most multi-family offices don't know who their ideal client is, have not focused on one type of client, and have nobody on their team working full time on marketing and public relations, even with staffs of 25 or 50+ professionals. To become a top 50 or 100 multi-family office, you will need to learn how to attract the right clients.

I recently recorded a few videos on family office marketing, business development, and something I refer to as a marketing funnel while in Switzerland and the Cayman Islands.

Video: Here is the first video (recorded in Zurich) which explores family office marketing:

http://www.SingleFamilyOffices.com/Marketing

Video: In this second video, Richard takes a few minutes to explain family office marketing and positioning:

http://www.SingleFamilyOffices.com/Marketing-Funnel

Video: The last of these family office marketing-focused videos is from Richard's most recent trip to the Cayman Islands. Richard discusses using a business development officer for your family office.

If you are considering hiring such a person, be sure to watch this video for some quick advice on what to look for in a business development officer:

http://www.SingleFamilyOffices.com/Traits

Interview with Brendan Holt Dunn

 To bring more granular detail to this process of converting a single family office into a multi-family office, we interviewed Brendan Holt Dunn, CEO of Holdun Family Office. Brendan discusses how they have converted their single family office into a multi-family office in recent years.

Richard C. Wilson: Why did you decide to convert your single-family office into a multi-family office?

Brendan Dunn: We converted to a multi-family office because we believed there was an opportunity for us to expand and offer our service to non-family members. Prior to opening up our doors, we had had a lot of friends and old business relationships asking us if we would manage their money for them. We had, and currently still have, an excellent track record of outperforming the markets, coupled with a strong brand name and reputation in Canada. Since there was a demand for our services, and we believed we could provide better service, along with better performance for our friends, we believed it was the right time to expand, and start managing money for non-family members. We currently manage money for other individuals, families, endowments and foundations, but our family still remains the largest client.

Richard C. Wilson: How long did it take you to launch the multi-family office after having your single-family office fully established? Can you talk about this process, the investment needed, and who you had to add to the team?

Brendan Dunn: To be honest, it was a fairly seamless transition for us, as we already had all the necessary licenses, policies & procedures, and staff in place to manage our existing family assets. When we became an MFO, we were already managing over 40 different portfolios for various family members, so we already had the necessary operational structure and personnel in place, which allowed us to be highly scalable. With our foundation already well-established and in place, there wasn't a significant investment required on our part to expand into an MFO, as we were already structured to provide the highest levels of service and professionalism to our numerous family members.

Richard C. Wilson: Can you talk to the reporting and IT costs associated with operating a multi-family office vs. just a single-family office?

Brendan Dunn: The major increase in reporting costs came from making sure we had all the necessary licenses across Canada to service non-family members. Since Canada does not have a National Securities Regulator, even though we already had a portfolio management license, we had to obtain licenses in other provinces where our new clients were domiciled. There was no real increase in IT costs as our back office is outsourced to one of the major Canadian banks.

The difference in costs between running an SFO and an MFO really depends on the structure of the organization. Today, it is very easy, and usually much more efficient and cost effective, to outsource your non-essential staff and compliance personnel. If this is the case, then there is no real increase or change in costs, as you don't need to hire additional staff as your client base grows. The fees you are charged by your service provider(s) would increase as your clients grow, but nothing compared to the costs of bringing in additional new employees in-house.

Richard C. Wilson: What advice and words of wisdom could you lend to other wealthy families looking to possibly say "yes" to all of those other families asking for professional help in managing their assets?

Brendan Dunn: The biggest piece of advice is to ensure you are running your SFO like it is an independent and licensed wealth management firm prior to taking on non-family clients. Make sure you have the proper Policies & Procedures, staff and investment professionals, licenses and compliance manuals in place prior to taking on any non-family clients, as you take on the professional and reputational risk if you do a poor job for your new clients.

Also, most of your non-family clients will likely be close friends, so think carefully if you want them to be clients and take on the responsibility of overseeing the management of their wealth.   Is it worth the risk of having the potential of destroying a great friendship over increasing AUMs to your firm?

Richard C. Wilson: Now that you have a multi-family office in place, do you invest your assets alongside your clients or keep them separate? If the answer is "a mix," can you explain how that works and whether you have had challenges managing conflicts of interest along these lines?

Brendan Dunn: All of our clients have segregated, customized portfolios that are designed to meet their unique needs and requirements as individuals. However, we always make sure that we always invest our own money alongside that of our clients, so we will always have money at risk as well; we simply just don't co-mingle the assets into a pool of capital.

Richard C. Wilson: I know you help clients with co-investing, club deals, direct investing into operating businesses, etc....but not all multi-family offices do. Can you explain how that works at your firm, how you help, how hands-on you get and the challenges that come with managing other's money and doing this type of investment activity?

Brendan Dunn: We have operations in over six countries, with over 100 professionals. If we decide to show a club deal to our clients, we will always act as the lead investor, and handle all the due diligence and analysis on behalf of our clients. We provide them with all the materials necessary to make a decision. When it comes to direct investments, or club deals, we always allow the clients to make the decision on whether to participate or not. Even though we have discretionary control of the assets, we don't want to create a conflict of interest by putting our clients' money into a deal that we are backing, or involved in. We always meet with the interested client, and explain the opportunity in great detail, along with how much we are investing, but we allow them to make the decision on whether to participate or not.

Conclusion:

In conclusion, it may sound exciting or profitable to move from managing a single family office to a multi-family office, but there are many important considerations for such a move. You should make sure you are aware of the impact on such critical areas as legal structure, regulatory responsibilities, insurance, investment scope, staffing, and marketing. Several of the questions asked in the interview above reflect the issues that high net worth clients and industry professionals face after converting to a multi-family office.

Chapter 17: Outsourced Chief Investment Officers

There is a growing trend right now in the family office industry to outsource the function of the Chief Investment Officer (CIO) to a third-party firm, which is effectively an investment consulting relationship. This decision is typically made with an eye toward lowering total overhead costs. Acquiring top talent dedicated only to your single family office can be expensive and difficult; so many families have decided to outsource this role to a third-party adviser. Family offices also outsource their CIO function because these outsourced CIOs are already working with multiple families and many endowments, foundations, and pension funds, as well. This breadth of portfolio management responsibilities may give the outsourced CIO greater experience, more lessons learned, tactical/strategic insights, and a diverse toolset to manage risk within a portfolio. For example, many of these consulting firms use sophisticated software and risk management reporting tools which would be expensive and time-consuming for a single family of say $10M to $300M in net worth.

Video: I recently spoke at a conference in Berlin and met with a single family office there regarding their direct investment portfolio. While there I recorded this short video on Outsourced Chief Investment Officers:

http://www.SingleFamilyOffices.com/Outsourced-CIO

For investors hiring an outsourced CIO firm, typically non-discretionary relationships are set up so that the consulting firm is advising on assets, but not holding custody of the assets or making trades and investments on behalf of the family. Still, both discretionary and non-discretionary relationships do exist. The talent resources, experience, relationship with the consultant, and time constraints of a family office's staff all play a part in the custody decision.

Most consultants have deep expertise in fund manager selection, risk management, public markets, bond and credit investments, and how to manage a diverse portfolio of traditional security-based investments. While there are exceptions, the majority of these consultants have little experience in hard assets, asset-based lending, physical real estate, physical commodities such as gold bullion, or executing direct investments into operating businesses.

As a result those families who do use an outsourced CIO service keep their real estate investments and direct investment decisions in-house. Under this arrangement, the family still makes the direct investment and hard asset decisions internally while keeping the hired consulting team updated on major changes in their holdings in case that affects their overall portfolio risk.

As in hiring any service provider or partner, it is important when selecting an outsourced CIO provider that you ensure that they are focused on the family office industry. Many investment consultants have experience at other firms in helping manage assets, and then start their own small practice with little expertise in serving the needs of ultra-wealthy families. Always ask for references, work through other families you know to find an outsourced or in-house CIO, and get to know potential partners over months or years before signing long-term contracts of engagement.

It is important to make sure that your outsourced CIO is well-versed and competent in any areas that you expect the firm to manage. For example, if you have significant Latin American investments and assets, you'll want a firm that understands your exposure to Latin economies and that can comfortably manage these existing assets.

Chief Direct Investment Officers (CDIOs): One trend that I'm just now starting to see is the offering of outsourced Chief Direct Investment Officer services to single family offices. These CDIOs supplement what a CIO provides and, as the name suggests, they bring a level of sophistication, focus, and deal flow due diligence value to single family offices. The CDIO will help a single family office with their work in the areas of co-investments, club deals, and direct investments into operating businesses.

As family offices increasingly seek to make direct investments and invest outside of the standard fund model, the need for talented professionals who can head up the direct investing activities is growing. This is one of several ways that the family office industry is maturing and developing new solutions to meet challenges that families are now facing in allocating their capital.

In some cases, a family may hire a CIO and a CDIO who work together with the family under a virtual family office or single family office setup.

Conclusion

The trend of hiring outsourced CIOs and CDIOs is growing and will continue to do so as more family offices are started every day, and existing family offices seek to expand their investing activities and formalize their portfolio management. We will continue to provide education, resources, and referrals in this area for the foreseeable future, so please let us know if you have any questions on this topic.

Chapter 18: Virtual Family Offices

A virtual family office is a lean single family office that uses an high level of outsourcing to keep the staff as low-cost and flexible as possible. A virtual family office and single family office are essentially one in the same, but the model is most typically used by families with just $20M-$200M in assets under management.

Virtual family offices first started being established for families in the 1990's in Zurich and New York as wealthy families heard about the benefits of having their own single family office and desired the direct control that can be designed into such a structure. As the family office industry has expanded over the past 20 years, this term has become more common and will likely gain traction in the future as families continue to seek out customized, affordable family office solutions.

Video: Here is a short video that I recorded in Berlin on virtual family offices, their growth and why they are being set up more often than ever before:

http://www.SingleFamilyOffices.com/Virtual

The Three Benefits of a Virtual Family Office

One might wonder why a family would set up a virtual family office rather than hiring a multi-family office or establishing a full-fledged single family office. I have outlined the three primary benefits cited by families who choose the virtual family office:

1. **Direct Control & Flexibility:** If you don't like one person on the team, you replace them; if you want to reshape your team, your portfolio, etc., you can do so swiftly at your own discretion. If instead of virtual family office you hire a multi-family office or wealth

management firm, you will highly value some members of the team, while holding others in less esteem. Many families have recently wanted to conduct more co-investments and club deals for example, and a team may be re-built around that need very quickly.

2. **Diverse Investment Perspectives:** If you hire a Chief Investment Officer (CIO) to only manage your family's wealth, they may soon lose track of what other families are investing in and techniques they are using. Inside of a virtual family office, however, you could use a multi-family office asset management service or outsourced CIO. You could negotiate the management of liquid assets or additional areas of your investment portfolio to be administered by a leading multi-family office and they would gladly accept your business. This is not common and it can be a tremendous benefit for families that use this strategy. Most virtual family offices hire an outsourced CIO who helps hire and fire investment fund managers, reviews deal flow, helps manage real estate investments, and is responsible for the overall investment portfolio design and risk management. In either case—hiring a multi-family office or outsourced CIO—you get the benefit of using the best practices collected from serving multi-family offices, but within the structure of a single family office. Yes, you can gain this perspective as a traditional single family office, but likely at a higher price point, which leads us to the next benefit.

3. **Cost**: In theory, your gross costs of running a single family office are reduced if you select highly experienced outsourcing partners. For example, a $20M family often does not require the full-time employment of a portfolio manager or trust and estate professional. By outsourcing most functions, the monthly overhead can be kept at a minimum, while still meeting the family's investment mandate.

Downside of a Virtual Family Office

Of course, if you have gotten this far in this book, you know that virtual family offices are the exception, not the rule, when it comes to family office structures. There are certainly disadvantages that you should consider when contemplating whether to set up a virtual family office compared to a multi-family office, single family office, or alternative wealth management structure for your family. Here are some of the main disadvantages and objections raised by those questioning the virtual family office model:

The Single Family Office by Richard C. Wilson

1. **Service Provider Selection Risk**: Since most of operations and the investment team are outsourced, your ability to select the right service providers at the right price is critical. This comes back to creating your Family Office Compass first, knowing where you are headed and what the mission of the family office is, and having the right experienced and well-connected advisory board constructed so that you can review the most well-qualified service providers instead of the ones who live in your city, or are family friends, etc.

2. **Speed**: Since most of your team is outsourced while operating a virtual family office, you may be disappointed in having to wait a half day or more for a reply from a provider when a critical event such a sale of an asset, end of a tax period, public offering, natural disaster, or death in the family has occurred. If someone works exclusively for your single family office, they are required to get back to you immediately during business hours, and that clear dedicated attention of someone worried only about your portfolio is an advantage sometimes worth the cost.

3. **Confidentiality**: Naturally, when everything you invest in is reviewed or managed by outside partners, there is a good chance of other families seeing your investment portfolio and benefiting from that knowledge. They may see you acquiring companies in a certain industry, or have access to potentially damaging facts about your financial situation or solvency. This is not a large worry of most families who vet their service providers thoroughly, but it is something that should be considered. The Southeast Asian families who I have worked with in Indonesia, Malaysia, and Singapore have been the most concerned with this downside of operating a virtual family office.

Let's look at three virtual family office examples to help make this idea more concrete.

Example #1: An Eastern European family has around $40M in assets and has placed the son in charge of operating the family's investment portfolio. The virtual family office consists of the son who actively manages investments, along with a series of outsourced service providers that assist with accounting, due diligence, trust & estate, and other taxation challenges. This family has office space and family in both New York and Eastern Europe, and they have no plans on building out their office further.

Example #2: A client came to me a few months ago saying that they have $100M in liquidity that they would like to invest in a hotel chain that they would like to build, and then diversify into a few other areas of investment as well. For this family, the client has done their homework and they would like to establish a two to three person virtual family office in Miami so that they can evaluate deals, meet other families, and operate out of a relatively tax-friendly environment.

Example #3: A third generation family has a strong team of advisors and family members, but a family history for frugality, and growth of wealth through low overhead maintenance over long periods of time. This family has set up a two-person virtual family office, and leveraged the skills of a second-generation family member who worked for a large auditing firm for 15 years before now working full time for the family holding company.

Virtual Family Office Checklist: The following is a list of potential service providers, partners, and consultants you may want to employ or have pre-screened and "on call" if you are launching a virtual or small single family office:

- Outsourced Chief Investment Officer and/or Risk Manager

- Investment Fund Managers

- Accounting Experts, CPA, back office administration and bookkeeping assistance

- Multi-Generational Wealth Transfer or Trust & Estate Expert

- Property Manager or Fleet Manager

- Concierge Assistance for Travel, Lifestyle Management, Fleet & House Management, etc.

- Family Office Governance Consultant

- Holistic Insurance providers who cater exclusively to HNW and UHNW

- IT assistance, software solution providers, and reporting

- Family Office Executive Search Consultant

- Diverse Advisory Board & Investment Committee Members

- Real Estate or Direct Investment Advisor if Relevant

- Analyst, Portfolio Management, or Investment Associate

The list above is not exhaustive, but should lead you in the right direction.

Interview with Tony Kypreos

 To add some color to this chapter, we decided to interview someone I have known for four years now, Tony Kypreos. Tony is the CEO of a single family office that is set up as a virtual family office, so he was able to provide some great insights into how his family office is structured and how he maintains great operating efficiency. If you attend some of our family office conferences, you may have already gotten to meet Tony in person.

Richard C. Wilson: What challenges do you face operating a global virtual family office and how have you overcome those hurdles since putting together the formal structure?

Tony Kypreos: The challenges to running a "virtual family office" are the ability to source a large scale amount of investment opportunities. While as much as you can go through as many as hundreds of potential investment opportunities in a year, for example, you know that you are never sourcing even 1% of the total global amount of investment opportunities potentially available. In some respects, the biggest challenge I would say is the ability to use your time effectively. There is constant pressure in terms of your time allocation and weighing the pros/cons of outsourcing a function vs doing it in-house (in our case, between the two co-partners of the firm). This is especially true when you are dealing with perhaps a smaller amount of wealth vs. some family offices that have $100-300 million AUM, etc.

Richard C. Wilson: Would you self-identify as a virtual family office, and whether or not you do, what functions do you complete internally vs. outsource to partners and service providers?

Tony Kypreos: I would say, considering your definition, we would be considered a "virtual family office" in terms of the framework. Most functions we complete internally—as far as due diligence, investment allocations, and operational paperwork, etc. The few things we do outsource are things related with estate planning, tax planning (we do work in-house and with outside providers) and we utilize some "investment consultants" that help bring unique opportunities to us.

Richard C. Wilson: What has been the #1 challenge in regards to multi-generational wealth transfer with your single family office? How is this problem being addressed within your single family office?

Tony Kypreos: I think multi-generational wealth transfer is always a major concern within smaller and larger family offices. We try to keep our knowledge of estate planning up to date and to work with top quality professionals in this area—to maximize our options in terms of utilizing trusts, gift allowances, etc., to effectively and efficiently transfer wealth.

Richard C. Wilson: When deciding what investment fund managers or investments to make, what are your top two priorities? For example, are you looking at track record and length of your relationship with the third party? Or are you looking for senior staff, and potential investment returns?

Tony Kypreos: When looking at fund managers and the like, there are a few key things we are looking at.

1. It is the overall investment strategy and how does that investment strategy fit with the current and projected global investment outlook going forward.
2. Another is the track record, which is important in terms of seeing how the fund manager has performed over different types of investment and market environments and if they can deliver in the types of markets and environments they say they can. While track record is important, it is by no means the only predictor of future returns.
3. Another key element we look at is the "quality of the returns." What I mean by "quality" is how repeatable are the monthly or yearly returns over time? When I look for "high quality returns," I am really looking at the amount of risk needed to be taken for each 1% of return. Along with this topic is our focus on investment fund managers and return streams that are "uncorrelated" to a majority of other asset classes. While many fund managers and the like say that they are uncorrelated

to equity and bond markets, etc., we all saw in 2008 how many of these "uncorrelated strategies" were in fact very highly correlated to each other. We have been focusing, especially over the last five to seven years or so on working with managers that are in fact able to deliver truly uncorrelated returns in all market environments. They are not typically easy to find, but can really add value to an overall portfolio.

Richard C. Wilson: Do you find as a single family office that it is relatively easy to find solutions and service providers built for your needs, or do you feel somewhat ignored by the marketplace in this respect?

Tony Kypreos: I think there are many good solutions and services built for this space and I have seen many more coming out over the past few years targeting our typical industry profile.

Richard C. Wilson: What should a single family office in the $20M-$100M size range expect to spend per year to be operational?

Tony Kypreos: This is a very difficult question to answer, I believe, as each family office is quite different in terms of in-house vs outsourcing activities, etc. I can tell you from our experience, it is extremely low. However, this may be due to the fact that we have two full-time family members working full time on our family office and RIA business.

Richard C. Wilson: What would be your #1 investment lesson learned the hard way you would like to share with other single family offices? Perhaps something you wish you knew 7 or 10 years ago.

Tony Kypreos: The one thing I think is extremely important is to construct a portfolio that is truly panoramic in its investment allocations and has many parts of the portfolio that are truly uncorrelated or negatively correlated to other parts of the portfolio.

Richard C. Wilson: Do you have an advisory board or investment committee? However formal or informal, what does that look like operationally, from a cost perspective, and how helpful is it to have in place?

Tony Kypreos: Our investment committee is comprised of two full-time family members. We also use outsiders to give insight into potential investment strategies, people whom we trust and have built relationship with over time. I think it is extremely important to develop a network of people that can help you in reviewing potential investment and then, at the top of the decision making chain, having multiple people that can make logical and disciplined decisions.

Richard C. Wilson: Assuming your family looks at deals and deal flow currently, what criteria do you use to screen for it, how do you get access to great quality deal flow, and what lessons have you learned while participating in direct investments and co-investments?

Tony Kypreos: In terms of allocating capital to fund managers, etc., we get our deal flow in three main ways:

1. First, by attending family office conferences and investment conferences
2. Second is through working with a small group of relationships with alternative investment capital raisers/investment consultants that we have built trustworthy relationships with over the years and respect their insight
3. Through our network in the industry with other family offices/fund managers/industry insiders/etc.
4. Reviewing interesting opportunities that may come to us from the "outside world" via third-party alternative investment funds, etc.

Tony Kypreos provides a great case study in how you can efficiently manage a virtual single family office.

Interview with Ingemar Hulthage

To provide an example of another virtual family office that relies upon outside expertise to operate, I have interviewed Ingemar Hulthage. I came to know Ingemar after he read my last book and attended several of our family office conferences.

Richard C. Wilson: Can you provide us a short history of your family's business activities, and why you are looking at formalizing your family's investments into something that looks more like a single family office?

Ingemar Hulthage: My grandfather grew up on a small farm. He didn't take up farming, but moved to a small town and worked as a carpenter and construction foreman. Later he started a few fruit and candy stores. This was during the First World War and there were shortages on many things. However, my grandfather and his wife, who also grew up in the countryside, knew many farmers and could secure deliveries of fruit. Just about every farmer had a few fruit trees in their backyard. This fruit became a valuable commodity due to the shortages.

After the war, they sold the stores and bought a large, high-quality apartment building. Later, my grandfather bought more real estate.

My father moved to Stockholm and was educated as an aerospace engineer. However, he got some cash after his father's death and bought an apartment building in Stockholm. Later, he bought two other buildings. When his mother passed away, he shared his parents' estate with his sister. My father retired early from the aerospace industry in order to manage his investments.

My sister and I actually got legacies after our grandmother passed away too, as a part of the estate planning setup for my grandparents' estate. With advice and some borrowed money from my father, I also bought an apartment building in Stockholm. I was educated as a physicist and pursued an academic career in the U.S. Eventually, I ended up in the financial industry, where I worked on quantitative financial models.

As our father got older, my sister started to help him to manage the apartment buildings. I retired from the financial industry in 2007, and took over much of the management responsibility.
In parallel with my involvement with the real estate business, I have taken an interest in securities investment as a complement and perhaps replacement of the real estate business. I became a Registered Investment Advisor in 2008.

Our father passed away in 2012. I formed the Hulthage Family Office in anticipation of this generation transfer. My sister and I have a total of three children and there are also four minor grandchildren. I wanted to create a framework through which my sister and I could continue to manage the apartment buildings. I also wanted to start preparing for the next generation transfer. The first step in that process is to educate our children and perhaps get them involved in the management.

Richard C. Wilson: When did you first hear about family offices and single family offices and through what source did you hear about them? A newspaper article, friends, email, or a different source?

Ingemar Hulthage: I believe I had the idea of forming a structure to continue the family business, with appropriate involvement of the different generations, before I heard about family offices. When I learned about Family Offices, probably through the internet, I decided that this was the best label for what I wanted to do. I know that your Family Office Group was one of the first resources I found.

Richard C. Wilson: What would you recommend to other single family offices trying to start a single family office when they have between $10M-$100M in assets?

Ingemar Hulthage: I'm trained as a scientist. Figuring things out is my "pride and joy." I'm trying to be generalist, as you discuss in your book. Therefore, I take a "hands-on" and "do-it-yourself" approach. I understand that this is not for everyone. However, I do think it's essential for families to understand what they invest in. I believe Warren Buffet has said that he only invests in business that he understands. I believe one, or preferably several, principals in different generations, needs to be knowledgeable about how the assets are managed. Maybe hiring or using outside money managers is the best choice for a family office, but principals in the family office still need to have a working knowledge of the wealth management, in order to select and evaluate the performance of such managers.

Richard C. Wilson: Has your family considered buying operating businesses (direct investing) or doing co-investments with other families? If not, why is that and where do you see the family's investment portfolio headed?

Ingemar Hulthage: All our apartment buildings are fully owned direct investment. Whether we will make more such investments, or even keep the ones we have, will depend on the next generation. Neither my sister nor I have enough enthusiasm to make any more such investments on our own. Whether we'll keep the apartment buildings will depend on at least one of our children developing the competence to manage them.

Richard C. Wilson: How much should families with $10M-$100M in assets prepare to spend each year on managing their wealth, between attorneys, investment managers, etc., what do you like as an estimated range?

Ingemar Hulthage: Perhaps I'm too conservative, but since one can buy good quality mutual funds with management fees below 1%, I want to see a good justification to spend more. I know hedge funds charge much more and I have no basis for denying that many of them deserve their fees. However, I also don't know how to be sure that a particular hedge fund will earn their fee. Therefore, I stay away from hedge funds.

Richard C. Wilson: Do you have an investment committee or advisory board that is formalized and in place when you need them? If so, how does that operate and if not, what informal board of advisors do you have in place and how valuable are they to you?

Ingemar Hulthage: We are getting there. I'm not making securities investment decisions all by myself anymore. I get help with the securities analysis from some family members. My sister and I have agreed to start having monthly investment conference calls. (We have such calls for the operating business, which works very well.) Since securities investment is a small part of our business, I don't see us bringing in any outside professional participation in our investment committee.

I think this is an opportunity for family offices to cooperate. Family offices could trade participation in each other's investment committees. My specialty is fundamental analysis of publicly traded companies and portfolio balancing, based on forecasts of total return and risk. Other people may have other specialties, such as hedge funds, mutual funds, bonds etc.

Richard C. Wilson: Your family has a background in real estate, so what real estate-related investment lessons have you learned that could be shared with other families?

Ingemar Hulthage: The well-known importance of location holds true. The large magnificent building my grandfather bought, in a mid-size Swedish city, stayed in the family for 60 years. I'm sure it doubled in value several times over, but the buildings my father and I bought in Stockholm have experienced a much faster appreciation. My father's philosophy, which I followed, was to buy in the inner city, which has become more and more sought after. This may not translate to the U.S., since many inner cities are run down. However, the general idea is to buy in areas that can be expected to become more and more desirable to live in.

Richard C. Wilson: Any final notes on multi-generational wealth transfer and lessons on how to handle governance issues, potential conflicts within the family, or the communication of wealth to your children and their children?

Ingemar Hulthage: It's one of life's ironies that people tend to have the least money when they need it the most. Young people typically don't earn much money, but need money for education, to create a home, start a family, bring up children, etc. I believe it's advisable to share the wealth with the younger generation, to some extent.

My father got money to buy an apartment building when he was in his early 30s. As the estate plan was set up, his mother was not obligated to give him any cash during her lifetime after his father passed away. I got a legacy after my grandmother died, which together with an equal amount borrowed from my father, allowed me to buy an apartment building when I was 24 years old. Since this was money for investments, it served to give us experience too. We didn't get a lot of spending money.

As for governance issues, I don't know anything better than to be very patient and find ways to sort things out without anybody having to give in on important issues. Complete honesty is critical to maintaining trust.

Conclusion

I hope that you enjoyed hearing a few case studies and learning about the lean single family offices and virtual family offices used by families like the Hulthage family and the Kypreos family. I feel that this chapter was important to cover because the term virtual family office is commonly used enough at this point that it is not going away, and it represents a specific segment of the single family office industry globally. As new technological solutions come online for single family office management, it will become easier to plug into platforms which make the process less burdensome.

The Single Family Office by Richard C. Wilson

Chapter 19: The Future of the Single Family Office Industry

The single family office industry is in its infancy; the term has only been widely used for about 20 years and still many people in finance (and most of the general public) have never heard of the term. A conversation during my television appearance on *The Brian Tracy Show* served to illustrate the youth of the single family office industry, and the family office industry as a whole.

My interview took place as Brian was finishing his interview with a wealth advisor guest from New Jersey. This wealth management professional lived in New Jersey, just outside New York City; he was on the show because of his success in wealth management, yet had never heard of the word family office before. Imagine how many ultra-wealthy individuals in Texas, Brazil, or Indonesia have never heard of this concept if someone who works in the industry just outside of New York has not.

I sat down with Stewart Rosman a few months ago to discuss his family's plans to start a single family office. I was curious how he had come to learn about the existence of family offices in the first place, as I see it as part of my role to help grow the industry through education. He said he had read some articles online about the topic, had read my last book The Family Office Book: Investing Capital for the Ultra-Affluent, and then he had also seen that some high-profile managers such as George Soros and Stephen Cohen had converted their funds into family offices. This is instructive, as I think that the higher level of education available today, along with family offices finally making cover pages of a *Bloomberg* magazine or front page headlines in publications like the *Wall Street Journal*, is adding fuel to the family office industry growth.

Video: Here is a short video on the future of the single family office industry:

http://SingleFamilyOffices.com/Future

As with any maturing industry, there will be segmentation and different types of single family offices will emerge. This can be seen already at the family office industry level, with the understanding of the differences between multi-family offices, single family offices, and virtual family offices. In the future, the size of the single family office industry in Asia alone will be larger than the entire family office industry is today; that is how early it is in the development of this space.

Another informed prediction that I have for the future of this industry is that there will be many more well-known single family offices who do have websites, business cards, professionalized teams, and who look to get more institutional-level access to deal flow, fund managers, and real estate opportunities. Right now, less than 5% of the single family offices in the world who operate in this way, but there are many benefits to doing so and this will become more obvious to the larger, more established groups who value high quality deal flow.

Today, finding single family office talent is very difficult. Many qualified professionals who could work in a single family office don't know how to find the opportunities. Over the next few years, there will be more sophisticated methods of identifying new career opportunities for single family office executives, and also for finding talent for single family office teams if you are a wealthy family yourself.

There are already regional hubs of family office networks globally; there are a few clubs and groups in London, at least two in Australia, and I helped launch the first family office-focused association in India earlier this year. Our Family Office Club, with over 80,000 members globally, is working with these groups and we encourage more of them to start up, regardless of whether they are partnered with us or not. We believe these groups will grow the overall industry faster and lead to more education for ultra-wealthy families. We see our role as helping grow a healthy single family office industry globally, and we look to partner with regional or national associations all over the world.

Unfortunately, more single family offices and more assets managed will mean more regulation for the industry, as well. Inevitably, there will be the .1% of the industry which gets involved with bribery, insider trading, fraud, or other troubles, and that will generate more media headlines than any other positive industry news would garner. That type of negative attention and regulatory burden seems to be a sign of any investment fund or vehicle hitting critical mass. There was already substantial attention paid to family offices during the drafting of the Dodd-Frank Act legislation in 2011. While this law created a formal exception for many family offices from the 1940 Investment Advisors Act, the proceedings also served to shine a light on the industry and could potentially expose the industry to future regulatory oversight or compliance requirements. Due to this looming prospect, those who can build experience now working as a Chief Compliance Officer for several single family offices will likely do well for themselves in the future.

Video: While I was recently in Berlin, I recorded this video on top single family office trends:

http://SingleFamilyOffices.com/Trends

Interview with Steven Goakes

The single family office industry becomes more global every day. While the U. S. dominates in terms of the number of billionaires it claims, there are more $100M+ individuals than ever before around the world. This interview with Steven Goakes—who runs Capital Access Partners in Brisbane, Australia—touches on many topics discussed in this book, including starting a single family office, operating and investing as one, and some insight on the single family office space in Australia.

Richard C. Wilson: Can you share a bit about how you created your wealth and then how you decided that you wanted it managed?

Steven Goakes: Over a period of about 15 years, my family investment company built wealth through real estate development and passive real estate investment; however, the major part of the assets came through the establishment, growth, and operation of property investment trusts, the management of those vehicles and the management and development of the underlying property assets within the trusts.

With substantial experience in hands-on management and development of property assets, my decision was to build in-house expertise in various investment categories, rather than seek the services of investment managers per se.

Richard C. Wilson: What made you set up your investment management solutions this way instead of just using a traditional wealth manager?

Steven Goakes: In most businesses and endeavors, knowledge is power is wealth, and thus I was determined to gain not only investment outcomes, but the knowledge within the family office organization of how to achieve and replicate those outcomes. I did not want my assets to be fed into the "black box" of an investment manager and just collect the returns. I also wanted to build a knowledge network, so that we always knew who to ask to:

     1. Diagnose problems

     2. Identify opportunities

     3. Measure risk and

     4. Opine on the underlying value of an investment option.

The concept of a balanced portfolio was always well down the list of aims.

Richard C. Wilson: You were at our Family Office Conference at the Harvard Club recently, do you see big differences in small single family offices or virtual family offices in Australia vs. Asia or the U.S.?

Steven Goakes: From my observations at this point, I think the biggest difference in Australia, compared with other family office markets, is that most Australian wealth is still in Generation 1 and transitioning to G2. Whilst I recognize that there are families who are further down the track, most are in this category.

Thus, in Australia, I believe that there are less defined resources for emerging wealthy families to access and learn from to set strategy. This was my experience, and I believe it continues to this day.

Richard C. Wilson: From your experience in helping a few individuals set up their own single family offices, what are their top priorities typically?

Steven Goakes:

1. Security.
2. Continuation of the family business.
3. Legacy.
4. Family unity, in the face of the challenges that emerging wealth inevitably presents.
5. Charity.

Richard C. Wilson: If someone has $50M or $100M, how much per year should they expect to spend on costs to operate their own small/lean single family office?

Steven Goakes: I would be prepared to invest up to 1% of net assets per annum on setting up and growing a small family office—with the caveat that performance is always to be measured against alternatives—not only financially, but also in terms of the other collateral benefits of running a family office. These may include benefits of family harmony from a well-managed communication regime, provision of other non-financial services to the family, etc.

Richard C. Wilson: Direct investing into operating businesses is a big trend right now. Can you explain why you and your associates are interested in this area, and perhaps why this trend is so strong right now among single family offices both small and large?

Steven Goakes: The wealth of all my wealthy family associates has come from family businesses. There are many hidden champions in the family business arena, but all family businesses eventually must face the challenge of generational change. Where family businesses seek external capital to effect this change, my experience is that no one knows family businesses as well as other family business people, and thus they make the best investors in these enterprises.

Most family businesses need a reasonable amount of management restructuring before being in the position to accept external capital; however, once this is accomplished, we can see excellent growth in the businesses involved.

Richard C. Wilson I have found most single family offices, unless they have over $500M, only want to consider buying operating businesses in their own country. Is that what you find in Australia as well?

Steven Goakes Yes, I believe so. Differences in markets, culture, time zones, etc. can all affect the ability of a foreign owner to effectively manage such a business, not to mention having a deep understanding of the environment in which it operates.

I want to thank Steven Goakes, who runs Capital Access Partners in Brisbane, Australia, for contributing his perspective here.

Conclusion

At Billionaire Family Office and the Family Office Club, we foresee the single family office industry maturing and becoming much larger in size. As that happens, we want to help lead the charge on sharing what we learn from meeting with single family offices globally and helping identify best practices, operating models, governance pitfalls, ethics standards, and we hope to create solutions to some of the most frequent problems we hear about daily from these families in regards to finding talent, high-quality deals, and other unique issues.

We have found that we naturally stay on top of the the pains and goals of single family offices because we speak with them daily, we help them form single family offices and improve them, we show them co-investment deals, work on buy-side contracts with clients, and gather their feedback on club deals, and we have relationships with dozens of $1B+ single family offices that are constantly improving their investment and operating models. These interactions allow us to easily compile material for thought leadership resources such as this book, our live conferences, and webinars. More than just making us ethically kosher, it is our work with family offices each day that gives us conviction in the thoughts we have shared with you in this book.

Video: In this video, Richard provides a brief overview of the Family Office Group association:

http://SingleFamilyOffices.com/Association

The single family office industry is still in its infancy; it is just starting to walk around and gain stability as an industry. In fact, when I started in the space 10 years ago, many said the family office space was not an industry at all. Today, new single family offices launch almost every day, yet most ultra-wealthy families, even at the $1B+ level, do not have single family offices in place yet.

Our team operates with an open collaborative mindset; if you see a way to work together, please reach out to me directly at Richard@SingleFamilyOffices.com.

Video: Single Family Office Consultant Insights:

http://www.SingleFamilyOffices.com/Insights

Video: The final video we wanted to share is one that Richard recorded in Singapore on The Future of the Single Family Office Industry:

http://www.SingleFamilyOffices.com/Future

Global Family Office Benchmark Survey

We are conducting an ongoing family office benchmark study, to date, we have 181 responses, and we expect to reach our goal of 500 responses by the end of 2015 with the help of our single family office network. If you would like to participate, please visit http://SingleFamilyOffices.com/Survey

Current Family Office Survey Results: Please find below summary data on the results of the survey to date. While some of these data points are referenced and included in a few previous sections of the book, we thought presenting them all together here in one place would be useful for some readers who want to access this data later as a reference point. I hope you find these data points as interesting and useful as we have.

What % of your investment portfolio do you have allocated to the following areas? (Totals should add up to 100%)

Answered: 179   Skipped: 2

Answer Choices		Responses	
Direct Investments (Operating Businesses)	Responses	69.83%	125
Long Only Stocks/ETFs/Mutual Funds	Responses	79.33%	142
Private Equity	Responses	64.80%	116
Hedge Funds	Responses	55.31%	99
Real Estate (& other Hard Assets)	Responses	79.33%	142
Other (Please specify as possible)	Responses	48.60%	87

Which of the following does your family office have in place?

Answered: 173   Skipped: 2

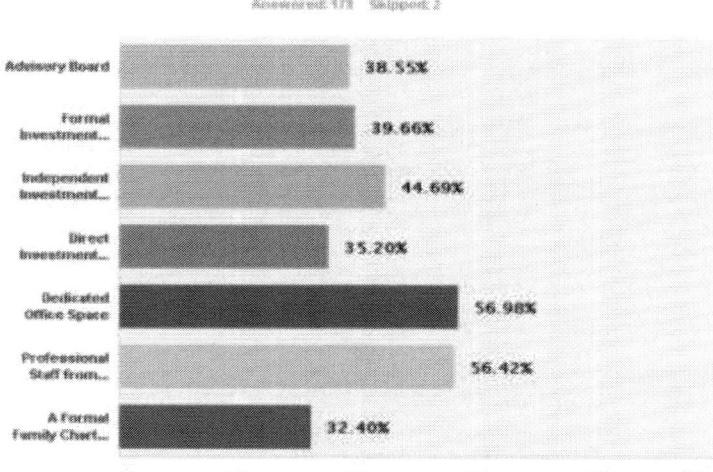

Advisory Board	38.55%
Formal Investment...	39.66%
Independent Investment...	44.69%
Direct Investment...	35.20%
Dedicated Office Space	56.98%
Professional Staff from...	56.42%
A Formal Family Chart...	32.40%

Please rank the following by most to least valuable for connecting with other ultra-wealthy families and family offices:

Answered: 173   Skipped: 2

When investing in an operating business, do you prefer to be a minority investor or majority investor who takes control of the business?

Answered: 1/3   Skipped: 2

What size of direct investments or co-investments does your family office target?

Answered: 1/3   Skipped: 2

If you would like to participate in this survey, please visit http://SingleFamilyOffices.com/Survey

Family Office Multimedia Resources
Table of Contents

If you have not had time to check out the videos and audio interviews in this book, then check out the Single Family Office Book Multimedia Table of Contents http://SingleFamilyOffices.com/Contents

With this well-organized table of contents, you can view every video and listen to every audio interview easily. Each page also has a download link so you can store each file locally and view them at your convenience.

Free Single Family Office Association Membership & Events

Family Office Club (Association): We operate the largest membership-based association in the single and multi-family office industries. We have over 1,000 single family office members globally, and over 80,000 total professionals in the community. By becoming a member you will have the opportunity to attend any of our events for free, and to meet other single family offices face-to-face each quarter

To join for free today please visit http://FamilyOffices.com

Family Office Conference Invitation: We hold family office and family business conferences each year that are focused on topics that are important to single family offices, such as the Single Family Office Summit, Direct Investment & Deal Flow Conference, Real Estate Allocator Summit, Family Office CIO Summit, or Family Office Super Summit. This year we are also hosting a private event in New York for family businesses called The Liquidity Event where we will talk about access to growth capital, financing and liquidity options for family run businesses. We hold our events at high-end locations such as the Harvard Club of NYC, the Intercontinental Hotel of Miami, and the Raffles Hotel in Singapore.

As always, registered single family offices may attend any and all of these events for free as our guests, for an updated schedule of events please see http://WilsonConferences.com

Questions? If you have questions about either of these two free resources above please call Sophia on our team at (305) 503-9077 or email us at Sophia@WilsonConferences.com

Directly-Sourced Deal Flow

Our team sources more than 2,200 deal opportunities/year through our family office relationships and exclusive intellectual property, such as PrivateEquity.com, Wilson Conferences, and the Family Office Club Association which combine to reach 1 million professionals each week.

The clients we currently advise under contract on the buy-side have an average portfolio of $1.1B, over $5.1B in aggregate AUM and well over $400M a year target allocation with this direct and co-investment focus:

- $100M+ real estate portfolios or 1,000+ unit multi-family properties
- Growth Capital for $35M+ Revenue or $5M EBITDA Private Corporations
- U.S. Based $1M to $30M+ EBITDA Companies for Sale
- Late Stage Secondary Market Pre-IPO Stock Shares

If your firm becomes a buy-side client we will document what types of co-investment and direct-investment opportunities you are seeking, and bring you vetted and directly-sourced deal flow for bolt-on or independent acquisitions

For our buy-side clients our team operates under a non-exclusive, no-retainer capacity, meaning unlike many other investment bankers we only get paid when a deal we bring you closes.

Deals we have sourced directly with founding CEOs in the last 6 months include $20M Revenue $5.7M EBITDA, $9M revenue $1.2M EBITDA, $12M revenue $3.1M EBITDA, and Fortune 100 Joint Venture backed by a leading institutional investor.

Proprietary Directly Sourced Deal Flow: If you would like access to additional qualified and due diligence vetted deals in your acquisition pipeline please call (503) 922-1811, or email me directly at Richard@BillionaireFamilyOffice.com

The Single Family Office by Richard C. Wilson

Wilson Family Crest

Background: When I was growing up, my family had an old, beaten up wooden shield in our house with the 1586 Wilson family crest painted on it (similar to what you can see to the right). It seemed only natural to focus our global family office and related finance brands on this crest. For me, the Wilson family crest symbolizes a long-term view, and the importance of family and loyalty.

In 1630 John Wilson came to the United States from England as part of the Winthrop Fleet. John came from a prominent English family helped start and was the first minister at the First Church of Boston, a well known landmark today in the city of Boston. John's father was a chaplain to the Archbishop of Cantebury and he held a high position in the Anglican Church. The Wilson family comes from western England and has several generation of capital raising, practicing medicine, and trade roots, with Thomas D. Wilson, having raised well over $1B in his career, before the current Richard C. Wilson had even started his career working with family offices, the ultra-affluent. Currently, the Wilson Holding Company acts as the over-arching umbrella organization and single family office for the family's assets and it has ongoing business operations and interests in training, data, conference, wealth advisory, and philanthropy related businesses.

The lion's head on the crest symbolizes courage and loyalty— a class symbol used in Western Europe and especially Great Britain. The ribbons seen on the sides of the crest represent experience in the battlefield, as they are a depiction of the shredded cloth that was often used to cover a shield before going into battle. The idea was that the more torn up the cloth, the more war-worn and experienced the warrior or knight must have been to survive those many battles. The three lion paws represent the three lines of the family at one point in time, three brothers who all had their own family clans within the larger overarching Wilson family.

Finally, and perhaps most importantly, the Latin phrase *Res Non Verba* appears in the banner beneath the shield. *Res Non Verba* means to take focused action instead of talking and to be resolute in your focus instead of just talking about it.

The Single Family Office by Richard C. Wilson

About the Author

Richard C. Wilson helps $100M+ net worth families create and manage their single family offices and currently manages 14 clients including mandates with three billionaire families and as the CEO of a $500M+ single family office and Head of Direct Investments for another with $200M+ in assets. Richard is also the founder of the Family Office Club, the largest membership-based family office association (FamilyOffices.com), along with  equity holdings with over $10M a year in combined revenue. The Wilson Holding Company is also the exclusive wine importer and a wine brand representative for Hofkellerei des Fursten Von Liechtenstein, the 600 year old vineyard owned by the princely family of Liechtenstein.

Richard is author of the #1 bestselling book in the family office industry, The Single Family Office: Creating, Operating, and Managing the Investments of a Single Family Office and a recently released book called How to Start a Family Office: Blueprints for Setting Up Your Single Family Office. Richard has his undergraduate degree from Oregon State University, his M.B.A. from University of Portland, and has studied master's level psychology through Harvard's ALM program. Richard currently resides 10 minutes from downtown Miami on the island of Key Biscayne, Florida with his wife and two daughters.

Learn more at http://SingleFamilyoffices.com or setup a phone call or meeting with Richard by calling (305) 333-1155 or emailing him at Clients@SingleFamilyOffices.com Richard resides on the island of Key Biscayne, Florida with his wife and two daughters.

The Single Family Office by Richard C. Wilson

Made in the USA
Middletown, DE
15 December 2017